A Primer on Augustine's Understanding of God, the Moral Order, Free Will, and Grace

A Primer on Augustine's Understanding of God, the Moral Order, Free Will, and Grace

With Contrasting Views from Other Philosophers and Theologians

MICHAEL PETRUZZELLI

WIPF & STOCK · Eugene, Oregon

A PRIMER ON AUGUSTINE'S UNDERSTANDING OF GOD, THE MORAL ORDER, FREE WILL, AND GRACE
With Contrasting Views from Other Philosophers and Theologians

Copyright © 2026 Michael Petruzzelli. All rights reserved. Except for brief quotations in critical publications or reviews, no part of this book may be reproduced in any manner without prior written permission from the publisher. Write: Permissions, Wipf and Stock Publishers, 199 W. 8th Ave., Suite 3, Eugene, OR 97401.

Wipf & Stock
An Imprint of Wipf and Stock Publishers
199 W. 8th Ave., Suite 3
Eugene, OR 97401

www.wipfandstock.com

PAPERBACK ISBN: 979-8-3852-5566-5
HARDCOVER ISBN: 979-8-3852-5567-2
EBOOK ISBN: 979-8-3852-5568-9

VERSION NUMBER 02/04/26

Quotations from Augustine's *Confessions*, 2nd ed., translated by Frank J. Sheed (Indianapolis: Hackett, 2006), reprinted by permission of Hackett Publishing Company.

Scriptures are from the The Revised Standard Version of the Bible: Catholic Edition, copyright © 1965, 1966 the Division of Christian Education of the National Council of the Churches of Christ in the United States of America. Used by permission. All rights reserved.

Contents

Introduction | vii

Chapter One: A Sketch of the Persons, Events, Beliefs, and Philosophies in Augustine's Life That Influenced His Understanding of God and Man | 1

Chapter Two: Philosophical Perspectives That Contrast with Augustine's on God, Freedom, and the Moral Order | 46

Chapter Three: An Analysis of Augustine's *On the Free Choice of the Will* with Contrasting Views of Other Philosophers and Theologians | 102

Chapter Four: An Analysis of Three of Augustine's Anti-Pelagian Works: *On Grace and Free Choice, On Reprimand and Grace*, and *On the Gift of Perseverance*, with Contrasting Views of Other Theologians | 188

Bibliography | 247
Subject Index | 251

Introduction

WRITING IN HIS EARLY forties, Augustine recalled his sixteenth year when he and a group of adolescent associates stole pears from a tree in a vineyard late one night. Augustine notes that even young thieves have no desire to be victims of theft themselves and know the moral law written on their hearts. So why did Augustine steal? He remembers that he and his cohorts barely tasted the pears before throwing them to hogs. The reason Augustine stole was really the enjoyment of doing what he knew was wrong and perhaps delighting in mimicking the Creator by freely doing what he chose to do and yet doing it seemingly without any adverse consequences. In writing about this escapade, Augustine was certain that he alone would never have stolen the fruit but stole only with the pressure of peers who collectively took delight in wrongdoing. While the adult Augustine understood his rebellious motives as a youth for his doing evil, he became focused on the cause and ultimate source of evil in himself and in the world. Augustine as a young man was drawn to a quest for wisdom that went beyond his ambitions for a career, which he was forced to pursue by necessity. He read the now non-extant book *Hortensius* by Cicero, which inspired Augustine to acquire higher knowledge of man's purpose in life and which book rejected the vices and ignorance with which mankind was so easily entrapped.

However, Augustine as a young man fell prey to the gnostic cult of Manichaeism, which claimed a liberation of the soul through the secret revelations of its founder, Mani; these revelations were believed to be only fully understood by the sect's elders, who were called the "Elect." For nine years in his twenties, Augustine became a "Hearer" or neophyte in this cult. What attracted Augustine to this cult was probably more of a natural rather than a supernatural nature. Absorbed as Augustine was in his young adulthood with self-gratification as well as being drawn to a quest for wisdom, Augustine gravitated to an occult understanding of transcendent reality that justified his own indulgent vices. Whereas Augustine has been introduced to Christian belief since childhood through his mother, his quest for God waffled and his knowledge of the Christian faith was vague. Manichaeism offered Augustine a simplistic view of the origin of good and evil by positing a dualistic notion of two gods: one a good god who was the cause of the spiritual universe including man's soul, which emanated from its divine source; and another god who was a satanic god of evil that created the material universe including man's body. From man's body came all evil inclinations and all evildoing, whereas man's soul was ordered toward a spiritual liberation from its entrapment in its evil human body. The goal of Manichaeism was to release the soul so that the soul could be reunited with its divine origin, through the enlightenment of the intellect guided by the teachings of the "Elect."

What also attracted Augustine to Manichaeism was its excusal of vice and human self-indulgence as being caused by the satanic deity that was the source of the human body. For a "Hearer" of Manichaeism, one need not be concerned with the vice and self-indulgence that one committed because one was not responsible for the evil desires of one's body. What led Augustine to reject Manichaeism was the notion that two gods could coexist so that good and evil could coexist without the evil god corrupting the goodness of the good god and with no omnipotent God capable of ensuring the ultimate triumph of goodness. For Augustine this was the denial of any real, true God and an acceptance of a disordered reality of conflict between spiritual good and material evil. Augustine came to reject Manichaeism, and he first sought a sanctuary in the intellectually agnostic Academics, whose Neoplatonism never got past the acceptance of a shadowy world where true ideal reality cannot be found and, so too, where true knowledge could not be known. Augustine would search further into the thinking of the Platonists of the first millennium, whose principal thinkers were Plotinus and Porphyry and whose rational speculations brought him closer to the transcendent, unchanging truth he sought.

Practical necessities often require a person (at times with providential direction) to seek more profitable and satisfying employment in various locations. Augustine had taught rhetoric early in his life in Carthage, somewhat later in Rome, and finally in Milan, where he learned the teachings of the Catholic faith from the preaching of the Bishop Ambrose. Augustine came to understand that the Catholic faith was more than he thought it to be and, while not yet a believing Christian, he was convinced that one could not discover truth by pure reason alone and needed the authority of divine revelation. Later, Augustine would seize on a quote from Scripture as a principle to guide his intellectual and spiritual journey: "I believe that I may understand." Augustine's intellect came to grasp God conceptually; Augustine's spirit came to grasp God personally. As a Catholic Christian, Augustine investigated the relationship between free will and grace and devoted much of his writing to countering the Christian heresy of Pelagianism that denied the real meaning of original sin and the necessity for grace in attaining salvation.

What can be said of Augustine's life is that he persisted in his great search for God and unchanging, transcendent truth. Augustine's intellectual and spiritual odyssey led him first to a vague, abstract monotheism, then to search for a personal God that led him to an acceptance of Christian revelation and the reality of three Persons in one God, and finally to the Catholic faith. Augustine's profound insight that he exhibited in his self-investigation into the nature of evil both in himself and in the world resulted in profound works of philosophy and theology that transcended cumulative, speculative knowledge accessible in the times in which he lived and provided consummate insight into man's heart and soul that was recognized by even nonbelieving and nihilistic minds of the twentieth century. Augustine's thought needs to be compared and contrasted with philosophies and theologies up to the present time. The clear and penetrating insights that Augustine provides demonstrate the need for philosophy and theology respectively not to be considered merely cumulative nor merely immersed in unresolved dialectical argument but always interactive and in need of developing and comprehending a synthesis of unchanging truth, with faith and experience supplying premises of unchanging truth and with reason providing speculative understanding. In our contemporary positivist age the very concept of unchanging truth is rejected as unverifiable or even meaningless because any statement of fact must be subject to the scientific rigors of observation and logic, quantification and controlled experimentation. What is lost in this rejection of unchangeable truth is an explanation of how order is maintained in the immensity of a universe with billions and billions of galaxies with each galaxy containing billions and billions of stars revolving around each other without an intelligent designer creating and maintaining this order. Especially with Augustine as bishop, the premises of unchanging truth would always include a harmonious reliance on divine revelation, ecclesiastical authority, and Spirit-guided experience as well as human reason.

Chapter One

A Sketch of the Persons, Events, Beliefs, and Philosophies in Augustine's Life That Influenced His Understanding of God and Man

AUGUSTINE'S YOUTH AND YOUNG ADULTHOOD

AUGUSTINE WROTE THE FIRST known autobiography in the Western world still extant, *Confessions*, providing a timeline of particular events and persons in his life from his childhood to his mid forties (*Confessions* was written ca. 397–400) that shaped his intellectual and spiritual development, including his understanding of free will. While autobiographical, *Confessions* is also an investigation into human nature, its virtuous inclinations as well as its fallenness; as such, in his *Confessions* Augustine utilizes faith as well as reason and introspective experience in articulating his observations of the complexities of human behavior and the relationship of the human person to God. *Confessions* is written as one long prayer to God, a prayer of praise as well as of sorrow for Augustine's transgressions as he recounts his moral regression and progression in his search for truth and everlasting rest in union with God.[1]

Augustine was born in Thagaste in North Africa (now western Algeria near the Tunisian border) in the year 354 when much of the Roman Empire in the West was still relatively intact. Augustine's mother,

---

1. Citations from Augustine's autobiography will be taken from the following source: Augustine, *Confessions* (trans. Sheed).

Monica, was a Christian and his pagan father, Patricius, slowly converted to Christianity through his devout wife's kindness and patient persistence. Patricius was baptized on his deathbed when Augustine was seventeen. Although nominally brought up as a Christian during his childhood, by his own admittance Augustine writes:

> With my boyhood, which was in less peril of sin than my adolescence I disliked learning and hated to be forced to it. But I was forced to it so that good was done to me though it was not my doing. Short of being driven to it, I certainly would not have learned. But no one does well against his will, even if the thing he does is a good thing to do.... But You, Lord,... used for my good... my own error, in that I had no will to learn, you used for my punishment—a punishment richly deserved by one so small a boy and so great a sinner.[2]

In the years 370–371, Augustine studied rhetoric in Carthage, where he took a mistress who bore him a son, Adeodatus. About this time Augustine read the now nonextant work of Cicero, Hortensius, which instilled in the young man a lifelong love of philosophy. Yet, by 374 Augustine, whose adherence to the Christian faith was weak, tells us:

> From my nineteenth year to my twenty-eighth, I was astray myself and led others astray, was deceived and deceived others in various forms of self-assertion... pursued the emptiness of popular glory and the applause of spectators, with competition for prize poems... and the vanity of stage shows and untempered lusts.[3]

Seeking justification for his life of vice and intemperance, Augustine became an auditor or hearer in the gnostic sect of Manichaeism, whose quasi-religious tenets and eclectic myths provided him a semi-metaphysical explanation of reality including the source and nature of good and evil and how to attain salvation for the soul from its imprisonment by the body. As a Manichaean auditor, Augustine had the duty to serve special divinely empowered fruit and "food to those who are called the elect and holy," which, when digested by these elect, turned into "angels and deities by whom I was to be set free."[4] Manichaeism was deterministic and dualistic in that all matter including the human body was evil and

2. Augustine, *Confessions* 1.12.19 (p. 13).
3. Augustine, *Confessions* 4.1.1 (p. 55).
4. Augustine, *Confessions* 4.1.1 (p. 55).

in conflict with the soul, which was of divine origin and hence good. Evil exists as an independent and substantial reality embedded in matter, which entraps the human soul within the human body. The goal of Manichaeism is to provide its followers with hidden knowledge known by the elect, as the means of enlightenment and liberation of the soul at death from further contamination with the material body so that the soul can rise to its salvation. According to Manichaeism, human persons cannot be held accountable for the evil actions they perform because it is evil forces within the body that compel the person to act as he/she does. This, no doubt, appealed to Augustine and his fellow auditor associates who, unlike the elect who lived morally rigorous lives, looked to be acquitted of wrongdoing because they believed that evil forces within themselves were beyond their control and prevented their wills from freely acting temperately.

Around 375, Augustine briefly taught in his hometown of Thagaste, where a close unnamed friend who pursued similar studies and interests suddenly became ill, was near death, and was baptized while unconscious. This friend began to recover and was able to communicate, at which time Augustine began to mock the baptism, expecting his friend to join in ridiculing the sacrament, but to his surprise his friend "warned me that if I wished to continue his friend I must cease that kind of talk."[5] However, this friend relapsed and died, which left Augustine sad and disquieted without the solace of God's presence, which real Christian faith might have provided. The following year Augustine returned to Carthage to teach, where he resumed a dissolute life still clinging to Manichaeism and the comfort it provided in excusing vice and wrongdoing on the grounds that evil forces within a person compelled the evil he/she committed. It would not be until several years later writing his *Confessions* that Augustine would personally admit his resentment toward those who committed evil against him, thus manifesting an unwillingness to ignore the responsibility that each person holds for his actions. Augustine would then experience the irony of the golden rule, when one looks for justice for oneself and sees the need for himself to manifest justice to others.

---

5. Augustine, *Confessions* 4.4.8 (p. 59).

AUGUSTINE'S PROBLEM WITH MANICHAEISM

In the year 383 Augustine moved to Rome, lured by the prospect of scholarly students who presumably took their learning seriously, unlike those in Carthage, where students lacked discipline and displayed sarcasm and even disdain for their teachers when it pleased them to do so. But even here in Rome students exhibited a marked lack of integrity. Augustine had not yet completely broken with the hold that Manichaeism had on him especially in regard to the belief that evil is physically within all persons. Concerning the vice of which Augustine was really guilty but for which he was not yet ready to admit responsibility, this religious/philosophical sect of Manichaeism provided a ready excuse for him to deny moral guilt for his freely chosen evil actions. Yet when it came to the students of Rome, Augustine felt hatred toward them instead of forbearance and understanding that acknowledged that, according to Manichaeism, the cause of the students cheating their teachers was to be found in evil forces within them and beyond their willful control. Augustine tells us:

> I was warned, "at a given moment a number of students plan together to cheat their master of his fees, and go off to some other master; for they are utterly faithless and hold justice cheap, compared with the love of money." My heart hated them, and not with righteous hatred: for pretty surely I hated them more because of what I myself had to suffer from them than for the wrong they did to teachers generally.[6]

Thus, Augustine experienced firsthand the conflict between the Manichaean belief that evil powers within one force him to do what he does and the experience of self-knowledge that when one freely chooses to commit an act he knows is evil then he bears responsibility for any evil he commits. While at Rome the problem of evil and the inadequacy of the Manichaean explanation of the problem of evil continued to plague Augustine. Still, Augustine stubbornly held to the belief that evil forces within him excused him from guilt of any wrongdoing he committed. Augustine confessed that he:

> associated with those deceived and deceiving Holy Ones not only with the Hearers, . . . but also with those whom they called the Elect. For I still held the view, that it was not we that sinned, but some other nature sinning in us; and it pleased my pride to

---

6. Augustine, *Confessions* 5.12.22 (p. 89).

be beyond fault, and when I did any evil not to confess that I had done it, that You might heal my soul because it had sinned against You.[7]

Although the personal experience of being harmed by others led Augustine to the natural reaction of resenting the wrongdoers and to his beginning to doubt the truth of the Manichaean position that the commission of evil was not a person's own fault, it would take a thorough philosophical evaluation of the sect's teachings in order for Augustine to make a break with the Manichees. While still in Carthage the Manichaean bishop named Faustus had charmed Augustine and his associates with his oratory, but by this time Augustine had also studied philosophers such as the skeptical Platonists called the Academics. Augustine recounts:

> Now I had read many works of the philosophers and retained a great deal in my memory, and I compared certain of these things with the long-winded fables of the Manichees. What the philosophers taught seemed to me the more probable, though their power was limited to making judgments of this world and they still could not pierce through to its Lord.[8]

Given that to a great extent the followers of Manichaeism had to accept in faith the basic tenets of Mani, its founder, and those of the sect's elders called the Elect, Augustine still searched in vain for rational justification for his acceptance of Manichaean teachings. Philosophers, on the other hand, appealed to reason and experience alone, for the most part, to explain the judgments they made of this world. The Academicians as skeptical philosophers exposed Augustine to an initial attitude of doubt that refused to accept the possibility of attaining real truth beyond what is directly and simply given in an immediate experience. This skepticism provided Augustine the first means of rejecting Manichaean doctrine. The Academicians in general tended to doubt specific facts of experience as establishing a basis for knowing universal truth and therefore tended to reject to an even greater extent maxims or principles of truth or scientific laws governing the real world, given their acceptance of the Platonic assumption that the world of sense is but a shadowy display of changing phenomena that does not lend itself to understanding true reality. Writing in his work *Against the Academicians* in 386, approximately a decade

---

7. Augustine, *Confessions* 10.10.18 (p. 86).
8. Augustine, *Confessions* 5.3.3 (pp. 76–77).

before his writing *Confessions*, Augustine provides a short summary of the skepticism of the Academicians:

> Not only did the Academicians say that everything is uncertain, they also reinforce their view with a rich supply of arguments. They seem to have appropriated their claim that the truth can't be apprehended from a definition given by Zeno the Stoic who said: "The truth that can be apprehended is impressed on the mind by what it comes from in such a way that it could not be from something other than what it does come from."
>
> ... The Academicians leaned heavily on this definition to prove that the truth could not be found at all. Accordingly, in defense of this contention they put great emphasis on disagreements among philosophers, errors of the senses, dreams and madnesses, fallacies and sophisms. Since they had also taken from the selfsame Zeno the view that nothing is more shameful than mere opinion, they cleverly drew the conclusion that if nothing could be perceived and mere opinion was shameful, the wise man could never give his approval to anything.[9]

WHAT IF AUGUSTINE HAD READ ARISTOTLE'S *METAPHYSICS*?

This skeptical attitude of doubt was the first step Augustine would take in beginning to dislodge the hold that Manichaeism exerted over him. It would still take Augustine several more years and a study of the more advanced Platonism of late antiquity (today referred to as Neoplatonism) of Plotinus and Porphyry to free himself from the snares of the Manichees while allowing him to find in speculative philosophy a means of pursuing human wisdom and ultimately accepting in faith the authority of Christian revelation. Skeptical philosophy, then, although unsatisfactory, did provide Augustine with certain analytical skills in evaluating discursive speculation in an effort to resolve contradictions that were inherent in Manichaean teachings. While still under the influence of Manichaeism, Augustine tells us what he believed:

> When I desired to think of my God, I could not think of Him save as a bodily magnitude, for it seemed to me that what was not such was nothing at all: this indeed was the principle and practically the sole cause of my inevitable error. Because of this I

---

9. Augustine, *Against the Academicians* 2.4.10–24 (pp. 36–37).

A SKETCH OF THE PERSONS, EVENTS, BELIEFS, AND PHILOSOPHIES   7

> thought that the substance of evil was in some sense similar and had its own hideous and formless bulk, either gross which they called earth, or thin and tenuous like the air, for they imagined it to be some malignant mind creeping over the earth. And because such poor piety as I had constrained me to hold that the good God could not have created any nature evil, I supposed that there were two opposing powers, each infinite, yet the evil one lesser and the good one greater, and from this abominable foundation other sacrilegious notions followed.[10]

The problem of God's unity and the incongruity of accepting the existence of two gods, one good and one evil (as postulated by Manichaeism) and each of them infinite in their perfections (notwithstanding the conflict of one infinite god being inferior to a second infinite god) led Augustine to doubt further the rational cohesion of Manichaean thought. The contradiction implicit in the contention of there being two infinite gods would be that the presumed infinitude of one god would be limited by the presumed infinitude of the other, thus rendering both gods finite. In contrast to the beliefs of gnostic and dualistic sects like Manichaeism, in monotheistic belief God is a unity, personal, simple, spiritual not physical, not subject to change nor part of a genus in which he shares characteristics with another of his class. Further, trying to apply to God the logical classification of things found in Aristotle's Categories, as if God were a real physical body in this world, compounded Augustine's own confusions. He writes:

> Not only, did all this not profit me, it actually did me more harm, in that I tried to understand You, my God, marvelous in Your simplicity and immutability, while imagining that whatsoever had being was to be found within these ten categories—as if you were a substance in which inhered your own greatness of beauty, as they might inhere in a body.[11]

Had Augustine read Aristotle's *Metaphysics* he would have encountered the question of what causes movement in the universe. Augustine would have been introduced to the concept of the first, unmoved mover—that eternal substance that is pure actuality, i.e., perfectly complete in itself, lacking nothing in its necessary self-existence and beyond all physical, bodily movement and change yet which being is the ultimate source

---

10. Augustine, *Confessions* 5.10.19–20 (pp. 87–88).
11. Augustine, *Confessions* 4.16.29 (p. 71).

of all movement and change in the universe. Aristotle speculates based on his observation of the heavens (i.e., observable stars and planets):

> There is something which moves while itself unmoved, existing actually, this can in no way be otherwise than as it is. For motion in space is the first kind of change, and motion in a circle the first kind of spatial motion; and this the first mover produces. The first mover, then, exists of necessity; and in so far as it exists by necessity, its mode of being is good, and it is in this sense a first principle.... On such a principle, then depend the heavens and the world of nature.[12]

This unmoved mover is a self-existing actuality, i.e., dependent on nothing for its existence, and this concept is the necessary principle upon which ultimately all movement in nature can be rationally explained. The first mover is a necessary reality because all things in movement in nature are contingent upon other things moving them, which things are in turn contingent upon still other things moving them. There must be a first cause of movement that is not moved by anything else and is essentially unmovable that would provide the necessary foundation for the entire process of things in movement and yet is not itself part of the movement process. Without an unmoved first mover, there would be no movement at all because an infinite regression of causes of movement is an impossibility. Why? An infinite regression of causes of movement fails to explain ultimately the cause of any movement. For Aristotle, this first unmoved cause of movement, i.e., the first mover, is his concept of God. Aristotle's explanation of God tends to be monotheistic (notwithstanding his embracing an unresolved dilemma of some fifty-five unmoved movers) because as an unchangeable, unmoving divine being, this "primary essence has not matter; for it is complete reality. So, the unmoved first mover is one both in definition and in number."[13]

The first mover of Aristotle produces motion not by directly moving things itself as does an efficient or propelling cause but by drawing all finite, mutable things to itself as the perfect object of desire in existence and as the final cause which is the goal or purpose toward which all finite, mutable things strive in becoming the essential being that each thing is. The God of Aristotle is an infinite, immaterial, unchanging being who is arguably a personal, rational God (though not stated explicitly as

---

12. Aristotle, *Metaphysics* 12.7.1072b.7–11, 14 (p. 880).
13. Aristotle, *Metaphysics* 12.8.1074a.36–37 (p. 884).

A SKETCH OF THE PERSONS, EVENTS, BELIEFS, AND PHILOSOPHIES 9

personal by Aristotle) who thinks only the divine thought that is worthy of himself, i.e., the thought of his own self who is pure actuality, necessary, good, and who accounts for his own existence. Says Aristotle:

> And thinking in itself deals with that which is best in itself, and that which is thinking in the fullest sense with that which is best in the fullest sense. And thought thinks on itself because it shares the nature of the object of thought; for it becomes an object of thought in coming into contact with and thinking its objects, so that thought and object of thought are the same. For that which is capable of receiving the object of thought, i.e., the essence, is thought. But it is active when it possesses this object. Therefore, the possession rather than the receptivity is the divine element which thought seems to contain, and the act of contemplation is what is most pleasant and best. If, then, God is always in that good state in which we sometimes are, this compels our wonder; and if in a better this compels it yet more. And God is in a better state. And life also belongs to God; for the actuality of thought is life, and God is that actuality; and God's self-dependent actuality is life most good and eternal. We say therefore that God is a living being, eternal, most good, so that life and duration continuous and eternal belongs to God; for this is God.[14]

Moreover, that which God thinks of is the thinking that is best in the fullest sense and it must be, says Aristotle, "most divine and precious, and it does not change. . . . Therefore it must be of itself that the divine thought thinks (since it is the most excellent of things), and its thinking is a thinking on thinking. . . . The divine thought and its object will be the same, i.e., the thinking will be one with the object of its thought."[15]

This digression on Aristotle's philosophy of God is meant to provide a complementary means of comparison between Aristotle's examination of the causality of motion in mutable things, the necessity of the first mover, and God's self-dependent actuality of thought with Augustine's dialectical approach to understanding God through the contrasting of the divine attributes of goodness and incorruptibility with the corruptibility of mutable things in nature and the corruption caused by evil rooted in the free choice of rational beings. Aristotle comes to the conception of God as the being who is most-good and eternal self-dependent actuality because he is self-existing, necessary, and unchanging first cause

---

14. Aristotle, *Metaphysics* 12.7.1072b.17–25 (p. 880).
15. Aristotle, *Metaphysics* 12.9.1074b.26, 33–34 (p. 885).

of all movement in the heavens and in nature. God draws all things to himself through his contemplation of the most excellent of things, i.e., himself. Augustine, on the other hand, approaches God dialectically by contrasting the nature of evil with that of goodness. By his thirtieth year Augustine had begun to realize that evil in man was not a force or power in opposition to the goodness of the divine (as proposed by the Manichaeans), but rather that evil in man was a corruption that came about through the deficient and perverse yet free choice of human beings. Augustine tells us: "So I set myself to examine an idea I had heard—namely that our free will is the cause of our doing evil, and Your judgment the cause of our suffering evil."[16]

AUGUSTINE'S CONCEPT OF GOD AS SUPREME AND PERFECT GOOD VS. ARISTOTLE'S CONCEPT OF GOD AS MOST EXCELLENT FINAL CAUSE

Augustine argues that if God is the perfect, good, and supreme being who accounts for his own existence he cannot be corruptible, deficient, or evil. God must be Goodness itself. Augustine establishes the rudiments of the ontological argument for God's existence and God's perfection argued more fully centuries later by St. Anselm (1033–1109), which held (stated in paraphrase) that the concept of God is that he is the most perfect being that can be conceived and must exist in reality. If God does not exist in reality but only in the mind, then God would not be the most perfect being that can be conceived because a greater being can be conceived, viz., the most perfect being which actually exists in reality. Augustine does state in a similar manner:

> For no soul ever has been able to conceive or ever will be able to conceive anything better than You, the supreme and perfect Good. Therefore since the incorruptible is unquestionably to be held greater than the corruptible—and I so held it—I could now draw the conclusion that unless You were incorruptible there was something better than my God. But seeing the superiority of the incorruptible, I should have looked for You in that truth and have learned from it where evil is—that is, learned the origin of the corruption by which your substance cannot be violated. For there is no way in which corruption can affect our God, whether by His will or by necessity or by accident: for

---

16. Augustine, *Confessions* 7.3.5 (p. 119).

He is God, and what He wills is good, and Himself is Goodness; whereas to be corrupted is not good. Nor are You against Your will constrained to anything, for Your will is not greater than Your power. It would be greater only if You were greater than Yourself: for God's will and God's power are alike, God Himself.[17]

A critical connection can be discerned between Aristotle's and Augustine's respective approaches in conceiving God's perfections. Both approaches depend in part on the observation of mutable things of nature. On the one hand, Aristotle arrives at the concept of divine perfection by his observation of nature and the movement of heavenly bodies. Movement must be caused by an unmoved first cause of all movement and change. Such an unmoved mover must be a perfectly actualized divine being who is the unchanging initiator of all movement. Aristotle speculates that God's eternal thought is a thinking on thinking the divine thought "which is most divine and precious, and it does not change." This divine thought is "the most excellent of things,"[18] and is "the final cause [which] produces motion as being loved."[19] By so doing, the final cause—God—draws all mutable beings toward himself. On the other hand, Augustine arrives at the conception of God by starting with man's own ability to conceive of God as the supreme and perfect Good who is incorruptible, which incorruptibility contrasts with man's observation of the corruptibility of things in nature. All things in nature being corruptible cannot account for their own existence or be the ultimate cause of the existence of other things. Utilizing Aristotle's argument regarding the origin of motion ascribed to the unmoved mover, there must be an incorruptible first cause of all corruptible beings or there remains an infinite regression of corruptible causes of beings in nature. In other words, without an incorruptible first cause, the origin of all corruptible causes remains unexplained and thus a mystery.

It is difficult to justify the speculation by some scholars that the God of Aristotle is somehow impersonal seeing that it is Aristotle himself who says that God is a living, self-dependent actuality who is most-good and eternal and who self-consciously thinks his own divine thought. However, the God of Aristotle is not a creator God, and neither is he a providential God who cares about the world or man. Herein

---

17. Augustine, *Confessions* 7.4.6 (p. 120).
18. See Aristotle, *Metaphysics* 12.9.1074b.26, 34 (p. 885).
19. See Aristotle, *Metaphysics* 12.7.1072b.3 (p. 879).

lies the critical difference between the God of Augustine and the God of Aristotle. Augustine comes to accept God as providential and as having created all being *ex nihilo*, i.e., from nothing preexisting, in accord with his divine plan, which means that God deliberately created man with an inclination to seek him. This inclination is not consciously chosen but is rather innate within each human person. For the person of faith, like Augustine became, who relies upon the authority of God's revelation as well as reason, this inclination indicates a special destiny for man. As we come from God, we yearn in our very being to go back to God. Augustine makes this clear at the beginning of his *Confessions*. In his prayer to God, Augustine exclaims:

> Thou dost so excite him [man] that to praise Thee is his joy. For Thou hast made us for Thyself and our hearts are restless till they rest in Thee.[20]

When Aristotle calls God "the final cause who produces motion as being loved" but leaves unexplained his reference to the nonpersonal celestial bodies, then one would have to argue in accord with Aristotle that the celestial bodies are drawn toward or yearn unconsciously for God. Augustine, not having read Aristotle's *Metaphysics*, observes the restlessness in himself and in men who yearn for union with God who is their creator. God as creator is not only the first cause of motion in the universe, then, but the providential producer of a moral order first revealed in the very nature of man by the restlessness within human persons to return to their maker with whom they seek to be united in the core of their beings. But for Augustine, man's desire to rest in God implies man's need to love God, which in turn implies personhood in man himself and personhood in the ultimate object of his love, God.

AUGUSTINE IS INFLUENCED BY THE PLATONISTS

Yet, before Augustine could accept the Christian understanding of a personal, triune God who was providential and whose divine plan included a special destiny for man, he searched to find some rational justification for such a leap of faith. By his thirty-first year, in 385, Augustine had rejected Manichaeism, moved past the skepticism of the Academics, and embraced Neoplatonism on his journey ultimately to accepting Christianity.

---

20. Augustine, *Confessions* 1.1.1 (p. 3).

In his *Confessions*, Augustine does not mention specific philosophers or works but does tell us:

> You brought in my way . . . some books of the Platonists translated from Greek into Latin. In them I found though not in the very words, yet the thing itself and proved by all sorts of reasons, that "in the beginning was the Word and the Word was with God and the Word was God: the same was in the beginning with God; all things were made by Him and without Him was made nothing that was made; in Him was life and the life was the light of men, and the light shines in darkness and the darkness did not comprehend it." . . . [T]he Word, God Himself, is "the true light which enlightens every man that comes into this world."[21]

Confessions was completed in 397 when Augustine was in his forties; it would not be until 413 that he would begin his *City of God*, a work that was not completed until 426, four years before his death. In the *City of God*, Augustine explicitly discusses Plotinus (204–270) and his philosophy concerning what that philosopher spoke of in regard to divine providence. Many religions in general and Christianity in particular place great emphasis on a caring divinity whose wise plan for man and the whole universe demonstrate an enduring love for all creation, from God's intricate design of all things from the smallest creature to the greatest galaxy, all of which reflect God's inscrutable mind, beauty, and power. Says Augustine:

> The Platonist philosopher Plotinus indeed discusses providence. He infers from the beauty of flowers and leaves that providence extends downward even to those earthly things from the supreme God, to Whom belong intelligible and ineffable beauty, and he holds that all these lowly things which fade away so quickly could not exhibit such an utter perfection of form were they not formed by Him Whose intelligible and immutable form endures in all things together.[22]

Concerning human beings, Plotinus will proceed further in reasoning that divine providence provides protection and well-being for the human race while expecting people to strive to live good lives pursuing wisdom and justice and avoiding evil. Writing in his major work *The Enneads*, edited by his student Porphyry, Plotinus tells us:

---

21. Augustine, *Confessions* 7.9.13 (p. 126). See John 1:1–5, 9.
22. Augustine, *City of God* (trans. Dyson) 10.15 (p. 413).

> Providence must certainly not exist in such a way that we are of no account . . . . And it [providence] has gone out towards what is other than it, not in order to destroy that other, but when another approaches it, a human being, for example, it stood over it protecting the human being. . . . And this is what living by the law of providence means, actually doing what its law dictates. And it dictates that those who are good will have a good life, established now and for the future, while those who are bad will have the opposite.[23]

Plotinus views providence as establishing a divine law encompassing all of creation and providing within each man a moral order of good and evil. It is incumbent upon all human persons to live according to this moral order so as to live a good life or suffer the consequence of living a bad life. However, the divine plan governing humankind will not allow man's evil to destroy the human race.

> So, although men are not the best of living things but possess and have chosen a middle rank, still the human race is not allowed by providence to be destroyed in the place in which it finds itself but is always being raised upwards to higher levels by all kinds of expedience which the divine employs to make virtue more influential; and human beings have not lost their power of being rational, but continue to have a share, even if not an elevated one, in wisdom, intellect, craft, and justice.[24]

Endowed by providence with reason and some inclination to be virtuous and to seek some degree of wisdom and justice, the human race is naturally inclined to seek to know God and to come to some knowledge of his divine plan that governs all men. But many persons are not capable of coming to advanced knowledge of God and his divine plan through the abstract speculations of philosophy; these speculations must be initially based on the observation of a mutable world and universe. Further, finding in philosophy certain foundations for faith in revealed religion is even more difficult, yet a significant means of providing motives for the belief of many, if not most, persons.

---

23. Plotinus, *Enneads* 3.2.9.1, 5–10 (p. 262).
24. Plotinus, *Enneads* 3.2.9.20–28 (p. 262).

AUGUSTINE AND CHRISTIANITY'S TRINITARIAN DOGMA VS. THE PLOTINIAN THREE HYPOSTASES

In Plotinus's and Porphyry's concepts of God's nature, there is conceived a triad of divine substances that did provide for Augustine some rational basis (albeit limited) for accepting in faith the central Christian dogma of the Trinity. Plotinus's philosophy of God is esoteric and at times highly obscure, beginning with his principle of hypostasis, which, from the Greek, has a variety of meanings, most generally meaning "to stand under" or "to stand within." The following is offered as a brief, highly simplified, and speculative indication of Plotinus's understanding of the triune nature of God. In the divinity, there are three hypostases, which in Plotinian thought are first, the One, second, Intellect, and third, Soul. These three hypostases are principles as well as substances. As divine substances, each hypostasis "stands within" the principle it actualizes for all Being. The One is the primary divine substance that provides unity to all beings, without which unity each being would cease to be the being it is. But the One is not identical with any specific being and is above and transcendent to all being while providing all being with this immanent principle of oneness. Says Plotinus:

> If someone were to claim that, because there would be no soul were it not one, soul and the One, therefore, should be viewed as identical, the reply is, first, that all things are also what they are with being one, and still the One is different from them. For body and the One are not identical; rather body partakes of the One.[25]

For Plotinus all things are what they are as distinctly unified beings by partaking of the One. So too, all things partake of the Good by partaking of the One, yet the One partakes of nothing because it is not in need of anything and is even beyond the Good while providing the Good for other things. With the exception of the One, everything that exists is in need of the Good in that the Good is that which is befitting everything and toward which everything is inclined and for which everything has a need for its own preservation or, in some sense, desires. The One, however, is not inclined toward anything because it is the self-contained, primary principle that is complete in itself and does not have a will or desire or need for anything. Again, says Plotinus:

---

25. Plotinus, *Enneads* 6.9.1.35–38 (p. 883).

> The principle of all things is in no need of all things. Anything in need, is in need because it desires the principle. If the One were in need of something, it would be seeking to be not the One, so it would be in need of what will destroy it. But everything that is said to be in need, is in need of its good, that is, what preserves it. Thus, there is no good for the One, and so it does not have a will for anything. It is beyond good, and is good not for itself but for other things, insofar as other things can participate in the Good.[26]

All things are in need of the Good that preserves each thing, and through the One each thing participates in the Good. Each thing in creation by participating in the One, and hence in the Good, is sustained as an individual unity receptive of an identifiable form or essence with a purpose or goal from Intellect, and which form or essence is actualized by Soul. Thus, the triad of divine substances—One, Intellect, and Soul—can be interpreted as providing a foundation for a transcendent moral order established at the same time immanently within the essential nature of the things of creation, including within man. This transcendent moral order implied in Plotinus's philosophy precludes the Manichaean dualism that established an infinite principle of evil rooted in matter, countering an infinite principle of good rooted in the spirit. Augustine's interpretation of Manichaeism was that "the substance of evil . . . [was] some malignant mind creeping over the earth." Further, Augustine held that:

> The good God could not have created any nature evil, I supposed that there were two opposing powers, each infinite, yet the evil one lesser and the good one greater.[27]

This notion involved a contradiction (mentioned earlier) in that two opposing powers could not both be infinite, because each power would limit the power of the other, preventing either one from being infinite. There can be only one infinite power that governs the cosmos and establishes only one moral order for all creation. Concerning evil, Augustine came to explicitly conclude that evil is not a positive substance but is, rather, an absence or a deprivation of the good found in persons and things caused by the free choice of created intelligent beings such as angels or men. Says Augustine:

---

26. Plotinus, *Enneads* 6.9.6.36–41 (p. 890).
27. Augustine, *Confessions* 5.10.20 (p. 88).

> "The true Light, which lighteth every man that cometh into the world," also enlightens every pure angel, so that he may be light not in himself, but in God. But if an angel turns away from God, he becomes impure, as are all those who are called unclean spirits, and are no longer "light in the Lord," but darkness in themselves because deprived of their participation in the eternal Light. For evil has no nature of its own. Rather, it is the absence of good which has received the name "evil."[28]

In understanding man's free choice to choose evil, there first must be an understanding by man of the good within his very being placed here by God his Creator. The question remains, however, how Christianity can philosophically explain this one God who is the creator of all things and who established a transcendent moral order for all creation as having three Persons in the unity of this one God.

A clear and precise comparison cannot be made between Plotinus's concept of the One and God the Father of Christian dogma. However, some similarity can be found between the two concepts of the divine in that, in orthodox Christianity, God the Father is the source and origin of the whole divinity, yet the Son and the Holy Spirit are both God whole and entire within the unity of the Blessed Trinity. Plotinus, on the other hand, tells us: "Generally speaking, the One is primary, while Intellect, Forms and Being are not primary for each form is a composite of many elements and is posterior to these."[29] Plotinus also tells us that "Soul is an expressed principle of Intellect."[30] While Augustine could not find in Neoplatonism a complete rational explanation of the Christian dogma of the Trinity, he could find analogous indications of this dogma in Plotinus's philosophical speculation regarding the triune nature of divinity as three distinct hypostases. The question then arises further, How do these three hypostases relate to each other in Plotinian thought, and ultimately, how do the three Plotinian hypostases specifically relate to the three Persons of the Christian Trinity?

Emanation is a primary concept in Plotinus's philosophy of God. Emanation for Plotinus means to proceed out of, or flow out of, a primary source of being that is unitary and eternal. All things flow from, and partake of, the primary divine substance of the One. Without partaking of the One, nothing is unified in itself, i.e., without the One nothing can be

---

28. Augustine, *City of God* (trans. Dyson) 11.9 (p. 461).
29. Plotinus, *Enneads* 6.9.2 (p. 884).
30. Plotinus, *Enneads* 5.1.3 (p. 536).

maintained in existence, not even the divine substances of Intellect and Soul. Does Intellect emanate from the One? In one sense, Intellect as the second hypostasis is that divine substance which, when understood as a unity, is the source of all the identifiable forms or essences of all Being, so in this sense Intellect must partake of, or emanate from, the One. Yet, Intellect is also self-sufficient in that, when analyzed by man's perspective, it is also seen as an act of intellection, i.e., thinking by the divine substance that constitutes the forms and essences of all beings. Says Plotinus:

> If, then, intellection is of that which is internal to Intellect, then the Form is that which is internal. It is the Idea itself. What, then, is this? Intellect and the intellectual Substance, with each Idea not being different from intellect, but each being Intellect. And Intellect is wholly all the Forms, and each Form is Intellect....
>
> Being and Intellect are, then, one nature.... And so, acts of intellection are the Form or shape of Being, and its actuality. They are considered by us as one before the other, since they are divided by us. For the dividing intellect is one thing, but the undivided Intellect does not divide and is Being and all things.[31]

With the Plotinian concept of Intellect, an analogous comparison might be made with the Greek concept of *logos*, which is, among other definitions, the reason for or intelligible cause of the essence of what a thing is. In Christianity the Logos can be identified with God the Son through whom all things were created. The Logos can be associated with the Word in biblical usage, which assumes the meaning of a dynamic reality as the revelation of God the Son and which divine reality is identified as the person of Jesus Christ in the beginning of the Gospel of John:

> In the beginning was the Word, and the Word was with God, and the Word was God. He was in the beginning with God; all things were made through him, and without him was not anything made that was made....
>
> And the Word became flesh and dwelt among us, full of grace and truth; we have beheld his glory, glory as of the only Son from the Father. (John 1:1–3; 14)

Plotinus's second hypostasis of Intellect provides the best rational foundation for explaining (albeit not completely) the second Person of the Christian Trinity. Plotinus's concept of Intellect is most probably to what Augustine was referring in *Confessions* in what was quoted above

---

31. Plotinus, *Enneads* 5.9.8.1–5, 17–21 (pp. 633–34).

A SKETCH OF THE PERSONS, EVENTS, BELIEFS, AND PHILOSOPHIES   19

concerning "some books of the Platonists translated from Greek into Latin" regarding "the Word was God.... All things were made by Him and without Him was made nothing that was made."[32]

The third hypostasis of Plotinian philosophy of God is Soul. In general, the soul, says Plotinus, makes "all living beings by breathing life into them."[33]

> [The divine] Soul is an expressed principle of Intellect, and its whole activity, and the life which it sends forth to make something else really exist.... Since, then, Soul is derived from Intellect, it is intellectual and its own intellect is found in its acts of calculative reasoning, and its perfection, too, comes from Intellect, like a father raising a child whom he begat as imperfect in relation to himself. Its real existence, then, comes from Intellect, and its actuality as an expressed principle derived from Intellect occurs when Intellect is seen in it. For whenever Soul looks into Intellect, what it thinks and actualizes are objects that belong to it and come from within itself. And these alone should be called activities of Soul, namely, those that are intellectual and those that belong to it.[34]

For Plotinus, then, the creative act of Soul is to actualize the essential structure of the world's individual objects based on the forms or ideas of Intellect. In this sense, it would seem that Soul assumes the work of the demiurge found in Plato's *Timaeus* as the creator or crafter of the specific things of this world in the sense of utilizing eternal, unchanging ideal forms and actualizing them within mutable matter.

THE PLATONIST PORPHYRY PROVIDES AUGUSTINE WITH SOME RATIONAL BASIS FOR ACCEPTING THE CHRISTIAN TRINITY IN FAITH

In his *City of God*, Augustine contrasts Porphyry's subtle deviation from Plotinus's three hypostases found in *The Enneads*. In so doing, Augustine provides his own comparison to the Trinity that he sees reflected in the three hypostases here referred to by the term *principia*, i.e., principles. Says Augustine:

---

32. Augustine, *Confessions* 7.9.13 (p. 126).
33. Plotinus, *Enneads* 5.1.2.1–2 (p. 534).
34. Plotinus, *Enneads* 5.1.3.9, 13–19 (p. 536).

> And we know what he [Porphyry], as a Platonist, means by the *principia*. For he here refers to God the Father and God the Son, Whom He Calls in Greek the Intellect or Mind of the Father. Of the Holy Spirit, however, he says nothing or nothing clearly, for I do not understand what he means when he speaks of some other being holding an intermediate place between these two. For if, like Plotinus, when the latter is discussing the three principal substances, Porphyry had wished us to understand the third as being the soul of nature, he surely would not have given it a place intermediate between these two: that is, between the Father and the Son. For Plotinus places the soul of nature after the intellect of the Father, whereas Porphyry, when he says that it is intermediate, does not place it after the others, but between them. No doubt he spoke as he was able or as he wished. We, however, say that the Holy Spirit is the spirit not of the Father only, nor of the Son only, but of both. For the philosophers use words in whatever way they like, and they do not bother to avoid offending the ears of religious men even in the most difficult matters. But we are obliged by religious duty to speak according to a fixed rule, lest verbal license beget impious opinions concerning the matters which our words signify.[35]

To which work of Porphyry Augustine refers is not cited in the *City of God*. Unlike Plotinus whose three hypostases as divine substances are *principia*, which may not correspond to persons, Porphyry's *principia*, according to Augustine, do apply to the divine Persons of the Father and the Son, and perhaps to the Holy Spirit. Porphyry, who wrote a multivolume treatise against Christianity, was nevertheless disposed to understand the divine substances (perhaps metaphorically) as divine Persons. In any case, the Oneness of being corresponding to the Father, and Intellect or Logos corresponding to the Son, and Soul perhaps corresponding to the Holy Spirit provided Augustine with some philosophical grounds for explaining the unity of God within the triune Personhood of the divinity.

AUGUSTINE'S UNDERSTANDING OF THE TRINITY IS BASED ON FAITH RATIONALLY EXPLAINED

While Augustine was undeniably influenced by the rational Neoplatonists in coming to an understanding of the Trinity, it would be his acceptance of Christianity especially through the influence of Ambrose

---

35. Augustine, *City of God* (trans. Dyson) 10.23 (p. 425).

and his becoming a catechumen and finally being baptized in 387 that brought Augustine to freely assent to the truth of the Trinity revealed in Scripture. Augustine's major work on the Trinity, *De Trinitate*, was begun about 400 and was not completed until about 420. But before completing this work, which ranks in importance as one of his major works along with *Confessions* and *City of God*, Augustine co-wrote a letter in 415 together with Alypius, his longtime friend who also became a fellow bishop. This letter was addressed to a physician named Maximus, a onetime Arian who converted to orthodox Christianity. In this letter many of the fundamentals of the Catholic understanding of the Trinity are found. This letter (later designated in the seventeenth century as Letter 170 by French Benedictine monks at the Abbey of St. Maur) emphasized the priority of faith over rational understanding in coming to orthodox knowledge of the Trinity as the one God revealed in Scripture. The letter states unequivocally:

> On account of their nature and inseparable life, which is one and the same, the Trinity is understood, as far as humanly possible, through faith which must come before understanding to be the one Lord our God of whom Scripture says, "you shall adore the Lord your God, and you shall serve him alone," and of whom the apostle says in his preaching, "From him and through him and in him are all things; to him be glory forever and ever" [Rom 11:36].[36]

Faith must come before understanding and reason, in that a person must ultimately adore and serve God alone and accept God's revelation without full understanding because God does not deceive. As cited above, Augustine previously argued in Book 7 of his *Confessions* that no person has been able to conceive or ever will be able to conceive anything better than God, who is the incorruptible, supreme, and perfect Good. Deception is not found in God because deception is a deficiency of which God is incapable.

Yet, faith in the Trinity requires the intellect's consent to a mystery that cannot be fully explained. At the same time, Augustine also knew that reason must be employed in the understanding of the premises of the faith found in God's revelation. Still, regarding these premises, Augustine asserts that, in order "to account for the one and only true God being a trinity, and for the rightness of saying, believing, understanding

---

36. Augustine, *Essential Letters*, letter 170.3 (p. 137).

that the Father and the Son and the Holy Spirit are of one and the same substance or essence," those who investigate this belief "must establish by the authority of the holy Scriptures whether the faith is in fact like that."[37] Relying on the beginning of John's Gospel, Augustine will assert in faith that the Son is of the same substance as the Father by first citing in Book 1 of his fifteen-book *De Trinitate* the Gospel of John 1:1–2, which states: "In the beginning was the Word, and the Word was with God, and the Word was God. This was the beginning with God; all things were made through him, and without him was made nothing." Using these first two verses of John's Gospel, Augustine makes the argument that because the Word was with God and at the same time was God, and through the Word all things were made, then obviously the Word himself was not a thing and was not made and is, therefore, not a creature. If the Word is not a creature but is the Creator, he must be of the same substance as the Father. Says Augustine:

> So, it is crystal clear that he through whom all things were made was not made himself. And if he is not made, he is not a creature, and if he is not a creature he is of the same substance as the Father. For every substance that is not God is a creature, and that [which] is not a creature is God. And if the Son is not of the same substance as the Father he is a made substance; if he is a made substance then not all things were made through him; therefore, he is of one and the same substance as the Father.[38]

Augustine does use in his work *Contra Maximinius* the Greek term *homoousios* (which is the nonbiblical term meaning "same substance" used at the First Ecumenical Council at Nicaea in 325). But here in *De Trinitate*, Augustine provides in Latin an equivalent translation that in English is rendered "of the same substance" to refer to the Son being God as the Father is God. The foundation of the Trinity is first stated at Nicaea for the believer, viz., that there is one God in which the Father and the Son are both of the same divine substance.

Regarding the third Person of the Trinity, Augustine cites John 14:17 in which Jesus refers to the Holy Spirit as he "whom this world cannot receive since it does not see him; you know him because he abides with you and is in you." Augustine also quotes Jesus six verses later: "If anyone loves me, he will keep my word; and my Father will love him, and we shall

---

37. Augustine, *De Trinitate* 1.1.4 (p. 67).
38. Augustine, *De Trinitate* 1.2.9 (p. 72).

come to him and make our abode with him" (John 14:23). Augustine will argue that in each human person in whom the Father and the Son make their abode must be the same human person in whom the Holy Spirit makes his abode as revealed in John's Gospel. Augustine argues that the Holy Spirit

> is not excluded from this abode, since it is said of him that he abides with you and is in you—unless of course there's anyone absurd enough to suppose that when Father and Son arrive to take up their abode with their admirer the Holy Spirit will withdraw, and make room as it were for his betters.[39]

Augustine further cites John 14:16 where Jesus says, "And I shall ask the Father and he will give you another advocate to be with you forever." Only a divine advocate could be given forever to the recipient and only be given by the eternal Father at the behest of the eternal Son. Augustine argues that some things said of one Person of the Trinity, in this case the Holy Spirit, must include the other two persons because the three Persons of the Trinity are one divine substance and hence one God. Says Augustine:

> It is to make us aware of the Trinity that some things are even said about the persons singly by name; however, they must not be understood in the sense of excluding the other persons, because this same three is also one, and there is one substance and Godhead of the Father and Son and Holy Spirit.[40]

Augustine proceeds in Book 1 to emphasize how the one God includes all three Persons; the mediator, Jesus Christ, will bring believers "to the direct contemplation of God, in which all good actions have their end, and there is everlasting rest in joy that shall not be taken away."[41] Here Augustine is making a sharp contrast between the personal Trinity of Christianity who is one God of love and who cares about mankind, so that each human person is made in God's image; whereas the impersonal trinity of Plotinus (and to some extent of Porphyry) consists of the One which is the ordering principle of unity in all things (vaguely analogous to God the Father). For Plotinus from this impersonal, rational principle of unity, the One, emanates divine Intellect (analogous to God the Son), whose acts of divine intellection or thought constitute the forms or

39. Augustine, *De Trinitate* 1.3.19 (p. 83).
40. Augustine, *De Trinitate* 1.3.19 (p. 83).
41. Augustine, *De Trinitate* 1.3.20 (p. 83).

essences of all beings in creation. And from divine Intellect there arises Soul (analogous to God the Holy Spirit), who breathes life into all living things and crafts mutable matter into an actualization of the unchanging ideal forms of Intellect. But nowhere in these rational, neo-Platonist speculations of the divine is found an explanation of God as being the loving Creator (as well as being divinely rational) who ordains man for eternal life with him according to his providential plan.

Augustine concludes the rest of Book 1 with an attempt to clarify the ambiguities associated with speaking of one God in three divine persons without resorting to any theory of subordination where the Son in particular is held to be inferior to the Father or even to the Holy Spirit. Subordinationist theories might also hold the Holy Spirit to be of a lower rank than that of the Father or of the Son. While subordinationist heresies do uphold a recognition of three distinct Persons in the Trinity, they reject the concept of each Person being of this same divine substance, and so reject that each Person is truly God. Even more confusing is the difficulty posed by God the Son becoming incarnate so that the same divine Person of the Son is truly God and equal to the Father and the Holy Spirit, and at the same time is truly man and thus less than the Father and the Holy Spirit.

Augustine proposes the following "rule for understanding the Scriptures about God's Son," which acknowledges the two forms of being of the second Person of the Trinity. On the one hand, the Son is in "the form of God in which he is, and is equal to the Father" while, on the other hand, the other form of being of the Son is "in the form of a servant which he took and is less than the Father." Augustine also acknowledges that the Son "is less than himself" because "he emptied himself" (Phil 2:7) and is "less than the Holy Spirit because he himself said 'Whoever utters a blasphemy against the Son of man, it will be forgiven him; but whoever utters one against the Holy Spirit, it will not be forgiven him'" (Matt 12:32).[42]

Augustine's rule then includes the following citations from the Gospel of John substantiating that the Son is in the form of God: "All things were made by him" (John 1:3); "The Father and I are one" (John 10:30); "Everything that the Father has is mine" (John 16:15). In the form of God Augustine tells us that the Son is the Word of God and that "the Word of God is the Son of God, and the Son of God is true God and eternal life

---

42. Augustine, *De Trinitate* 1.4.22 (p. 86).

as John says in his letter (1 Jn 5:20)."[43] But the Son of God assumed the nature of a creature in the womb of Mary and thereby became the Son of man. First Corinthians 15:25–27 tells us that Christ will reign until he subjects all enemies under his feet including death. First Corinthians 15:28 states: "When all things are subjected to him, then the Son himself will also be subjected to him who put all things under him, that God may be everything to everyone." This revelation from Paul's letter to the Corinthians can cause great consternation and confusion for those who accept an orthodox understanding of the Trinity when this passage is wrongly interpreted to mean that the Son of God is subjected to the Father and thus becomes his inferior. But Augustine tells us that "every creature is made subject to God, including even the creature in which the Son of God became the Son of man, for in this created form the Son shall also be made subject to the one who subjected all things to him, that God may be all in all (1 Cor 15:28)."[44] So it is that, as Son of man, Christ is subjected to the Father, even as Christ as Son of God subjects all things to himself because he is God. Augustine's painstaking clarifications of the two natures, the divine nature that is eternally God the Son and the created human nature that the second divine Person assumed in time in the womb of Mary, can resolve many of the apparent contradictions found in Scripture.

NO SUBORDINATE RELATIONSHIP OF THE SON OR THE HOLY SPIRIT TO THE FATHER

However, clarifications of Christ's two natures do not clearly resolve all questions of subordinationism that still arise regarding the mission of the second Person of the Trinity being sent by the Father and the mission of the third Person of the Trinity being sent by the Father and the Son. Those who accept a subordinate relationship of either the Son or the Holy Spirit (or both) to the Father follow the axiom, says Augustine, that "the one who sends is greater than the one sent." Augustine responds to this argument by first asking "In what manner did God send his son?" Augustine argues:

> Well, whichever way it was done, it was certainly done by word. But God's Word is his Son. So, when the Father sent him by

43. Augustine, *De Trinitate* 1.4.26 (p. 90).
44. Augustine, *De Trinitate* 2.4.28 (p. 92).

word, what happened was that he was sent by the Father and his Word. Hence it is by the Father and the Son that the Son was sent, because the Son is the Father's Word.[45]

What Augustine is arguing here is that because the Son is of the same divine substance, essence, or nature as the Father, when the Father wills and acts, the Son wills and acts harmoniously along with the Holy Spirit in the undivided unity of the Trinity. There is no relegation of one divine Person, such as the Son or the Holy Spirit, to another divine Person, viz., the Father, in the divine missions of the Son and of the Holy Spirit and hence in their being sent. Because all three of the divine Persons are consubstantial, i.e., of the same divine substance, the divine will is exercised and expressed by all three Persons without conflict. At the same time, each of the Persons can be designated as the subject of the divine action, and two of the Persons, viz., the Son and the Holy Spirit, can be designated as the objects of the divine action as evidenced by their being sent on behalf of believers. On the one hand, when speaking of the Son as an object of divine action he is "the Word [who] had been made in the fullness of time as the object of our faith." On the other hand, he is "the Word itself through whom all things have been made (John 14:21) [who] was being kept for the contemplation in eternity of minds now purified through faith." This being the case, Augustine can further contend:

> If, however, the reason why the Son is said to have been sent by the Father is simply that the one is the Father and the other the Son, then there is nothing at all to stop us believing that the Son is equal to the Father and consubstantial and co-eternal, and yet the Son is sent by the Father. Not because one is greater and the other less, but because one is the Father and the other the Son; one is the begetter, the other begotten; the first is the one from whom the sent one is; the other is the one who is from the sender. For the Son is from the Father, not the Father from the Son. In light of this we can now perceive that the Son is not just said to have been sent because the Word became flesh, but that he was sent in order for the Word to become flesh.[46]

Augustine further demonstrates a Neoplatonic interpretation of the Trinity making reference to the Son as "the Father's Word which is also called his Wisdom" and then implying a sort of divine emanation in the Son's being sent "because he is a certain pure overflow of the glory of God

---

45. Augustine, *De Trinitate* 2.2.9 (p. 103).
46. Augustine, *De Trinitate* 4.5.27 (p. 179).

(Wis 7:25)," which overflow does not indicate the Son's being unequal to the Father because "in this case what flows out and what it flows out from are one and the same substance," which is "like light flowing from light."[47] What Augustine is describing here is the Father's begetting of the Son with the Father's same infinite divine essence or substance in an eternal generation by means of the divine thought of the Father. As previously quoted, Aristotle reasoned in his *Metaphysics* that the eternal and unmovable substance thinks of that which is "most divine and precious and does not change" so that "it must be of itself that the divine thought thinks," which leads Aristotle to the conclusion that "the divine thought and its object will be the same, i.e., the thinking will be one with the object of its thought."[48] Aristotle speculates that the primary unmovable substance (God) eternally thinks the only thinking logically worthy of himself, viz., the idea of himself with which he is identical. In Christianity, the Father's eternal generation of the Son is a generation not only of the Father's same divine substance or essence but also of the divine personhood of the Son. Divine personhood, then, is the essence of God, but as the Father timelessly thinks or generates the divine image of himself he does not generate or beget himself, but, rather, he generates the complete divine essence, which is a complete Person other than himself—the Son. Everything that is in the Father is timelessly generated in the Son except being the Father. The generation of the Son by the Father includes the Father giving the Son the Holy Spirit as timelessly proceeding from him, i.e., the Son, just as the Holy Spirit timelessly proceeds from the Father. Says Augustine:

> Anyone who can understand the generation of the Son from the Father as timeless should also understand the procession of the Holy Spirit from them both as timeless. And anyone who can understand that when the Son said, "As the Father has life in himself, so he has given the Son to have life in himself" (Jn 5:26) he did not mean that the Father gave life to the Son already existing without life, but that he begot him timelessly in such a way that the life which the Father gave the Son by begetting him is co-eternal with the life of the Father who gave it, should also understand that just as the Father has in himself that the Holy Spirit should proceed from him, so he gave to the Son that the Holy Spirit should proceed from him too, and in both cases

---

47. Augustine, *De Trinitate* 4.5.27 (p. 180).
48. Aristotle, *Metaphysics* 12.9.1074b (p. 885).

timelessly; thus that to say that the Holy Spirit proceeding from the Son is something which the Son has from the Father. If the Son has everything that he has from the Father he clearly has from the Father that the Holy Spirit should proceed from him. But one must not think of any time in this matter which would include before and after, because there is absolutely no such thing as time there at all.[49]

Because God reveals himself in Scripture to be love (see 1 John 4:8), a further explanation of this procession of the Holy Spirit is that from the absolute love willed by the Father for his Son whom the Father begot as his perfect image, and the absolute love willed by the Son for his divine Father who begot him, proceeds the Person of the Holy Spirit. If the divine intellect is viewed as the agent of begetting of the Son by the Father, the divine will can be viewed as the agent of procession of the Holy Spirit by the Father and the Son. Thomas Aquinas tells us that within rational agents there are only two actions of the intellect possible that remain completely immanent, that is solely within the subject, viz., purely intellectual acts and acts of the will. Processions of the divine subject must remain completely within God and be of one or the other of these actions of the divine intellect. Says Thomas Aquinas:

> The divine processions can be derived only from the actions which remain within the agent. In the nature which is intellectual, and in the divine nature these actions are two, the acts of intelligence and of will. The act of sensation, which also appears to be an operation within the agent, takes place outside the intellectual nature, nor can it be reckoned as wholly removed from the sphere of external actions; for the act of sensation is perfected by the action of the sensible object upon sense. It follows that no other procession is possible in God but the procession of the Word and of Love.[50]

The only two processions possible in God are those of the Persons of first, the Word, i.e., the Person of the Son begotten by the Father and, second, the Person of Love, i.e., the Holy Spirit proceeding from the Father and the Son by means of their mutual willing of love. The problem that remains to be resolved is how the three Persons of the Trinity can be one God of one divine substance.

---

49. Augustine, *De Trinitate* 15.6.47 (pp. 438–39).
50. Thomas Aquinas, *Summa Theologica* Ia, q. 27, art. 5.

A SKETCH OF THE PERSONS, EVENTS, BELIEFS, AND PHILOSOPHIES 29

Augustine makes reference to the Greek word *hypostasis*, which literally means "that which stands under" or "that which stands within," so that Augustine tells us that those "who treat of these matters in Greek are accustomed to say '*mia ousia, treis hypostaseis*,'" which Augustine tells us is best rendered "one being or substance, three persons." As related to the Trinity, this means that there is one divine substance that is God and three distinct Persons who are God. Says Augustine:

> In very truth, because the Father is not the Son and the Son is not the Father, and the Holy Spirit . . . is neither the Father nor the Son, they are certainly three. That is why it is said in the plural "I and the Father are one" [John 10:30]. He did not say "is one" which the Sabellians say, but "are one."[51]

The Sabellians were modalists whose heresy denied the Trinity and claimed that there was only one person in God and that this one person presented or revealed himself in three different modes or ways, viz., as the Father who is the creator, the Son who is the redeemer, and the Holy Spirit who is the sanctifier. Augustine is arguing that when we speak of the Trinity as three distinct Persons we must use (as does Scripture) the plural for the verb "to be," "are."

HOW GOD CAN BE PERFECTLY SIMPLE AND STILL BE A TRINITY

But a critical problem still remains regarding there being three Persons in God and God's being perfectly simple and without parts or composition or divisibility of any kind. God has no accidents within his essence, existence, or personhood. God is independent of being acted upon or of receiving any essential being. God is his essence so that, in God, existence and essence are identical. God does not receive any essence from anywhere. God does not have nor does God possess his attributes, but, rather, God *is* his attributes, perfectly, completely, and absolutely. However, Augustine poses a difficulty regarding God's simplicity, his triune personhood, and subjectivity and asks:

> But if God subsists in such a way that he can properly be called substance, then something is in him as in its underlying subject, and he is not simple—he for whom it is the same thing to be as

---

51. Augustine, *De Trinitate* 5.2.10 (p. 197).

> to be whatever else is said of him with reference to himself such as great, omnipotent, good, and anything of that sort that is not unsuitably said of God.[52]

This problem is in part one of semantics, in that the use of the word "subsist" can be interpreted to necessarily mean, as Augustine suggests, that there is an underlying subject (or three subjects) in God. But if subjectivity as well as personhood is seen to be essential to God's being, then he simply is substantially a divine Person (or three divine Persons) without composition and exists as the one personal God who is united in being his attributes. Augustine adds to the same paragraph cited above that "for God to be is the same as to subsist, and therefore if the Trinity is one being it is also one substance." What is difficult to rationally explain is how God can be three Persons in one selfsame divine substance that is simple.

When considering the relations of the three Persons of the Trinity, Augustine finds himself in a conundrum. Because God in his simplicity is one Being without composition or parts, the problem arises that the relationship of the Father to the Son and of the Son to the Father is the only means of identifying who and what these divine Persons are. Further, to speak of a relationship requires there to be at least two substances that relate to each other and not only one selfsame substance or *homoousios* of which all three Persons of the Trinity are doctrinally pronounced to be. If from the Father there is a timeless generation of the Son as the selfsame divine substance that the Father is, there is no distinction explained of the substance of each of the persons that the Father and the Son must be. Says Augustine regarding the Father's begetting of the Son and yet both being of one substance:

> No, but surely this makes them even more of one and the same being; it means that the Father and Son are one and the same being, seeing that the Father's very "is" has reference not to himself but to the Son, and that he has begotten this being and by this being is whatever he is. So, neither of them is with reference to himself, and each is said with reference to the other....
> What it comes down to is this: every being that is called something by way of relationship is also called something besides the relationship.... So, if the Father is not also something with reference to himself, there is absolutely nothing there to be talked of with reference to something else.[53]

---

52. Augustine, *De Trinitate* 7.3.10 (p. 231).
53. Augustine, *De Trinitate* 7.1.2 (pp. 220–21).

To try to resolve this problem, Augustine speculates with the use of the predications of genus, species, and individual, but the use of these designations leads to conflicts over the divine substance and divine simplicity when the question arises whether to call the three Persons three beings, three substances, or three persons. After analyzing the use of these predications and the resulting deficiency of applying these to the Trinity, Augustine admits to an impasse (or what Aristotle calls *aporia*, meaning "no passage"). Augustine explains:

> So, if we try to explain those words in terms of genus and species and individual, why are the Father and the Son and the Holy Spirit not called three beings just as they are called three substances or persons? But as I said, I will pass over this.[54]

It was Thomas Aquinas who partially resolved this difficulty regarding the relationship of the three Persons of the Trinity by indicating that relationship in God must be of God's essence and that the divine essence is not distinct from the three persons who are related and yet distinct from each other. Relationships for creatures, on the other hand, are not part of a creature's essential being but are, rather, accidental to the essence of a creature. In God the divine substance, which is a unity, are the three Persons because in God's divine simplicity, says Thomas, "intellectual substance[s] is nothing else than person . . . in creatures relations are accidental, whereas in God they are the divine essence itself. Thus, it follows that in God essence is not really distinct from person; and yet the persons are really distinguished from each other."[55] But how are there three divine persons and not one within the one divine essence? As previously cited, Thomas Aquinas argues the divine processions can be derived only from actions that are immanent within God. The two immanent actions within God are the action of the intellect and the action of the will. Thomas Aquinas explains further beginning with a citation from Augustine:

> Now as there is no quantity in God, for He is great without quantity, as Augustine says (*De Trinitate*, i.1) it follows that a real relation in God can be based only on action. Such relations are not based on the actions of God according to any extrinsic procession, forasmuch as the relations of God to creatures are not real in Him. . . . Hence, it falls that real relations in God can be understood only in regard to those actions according to

---

54. Augustine, *De Trinitate* 7.3.9 (p. 232).
55. Aquinas, *Summa Theologica* Ia, q. 39, art. 1.

which there are internal, and not external processions in God. These processions are two only as above expounded (Q. 27, A.5), one derived from the action of the intellect, the procession of the Word; and the other from the action of the will, the procession of love.[56]

As real relation in God can be based only on action, and as the procession of the Word derives only from the action of the intellect, could it be the case that, just as the Person of the Word eternally generates from the action of the Father's intellect, so too could the action of the Son's same intellect involve a self-conscious affirmation of his Father begetting him so that he realizes his own identity as the perfect image of the Father, viz., God the Son? Can the Son eternally respond with an act of divine will in loving the divine essence intuited as the Father, and which divine essence is simultaneously and timelessly loved by the Father as his only begotten Son? It would then be the same that, with the spiration of the Person of the Holy Spirit proceeding from the willful love of the Father for the Son and of the Son for the Father, the third Person of the Trinity can respond with an act of self-conscious love (originating from the same divine intellect and will as that of the Father and the Son) that affirms the Holy Spirit's divine personhood and his relationship with the Father and with the Son in a bond of perfect unity as one God.

MADE IN GOD'S IMAGE, MAN IS A PERSON WITH UNDERSTANDING AND A WILL

Made in God's image, Augustine believed the personhood of man reflected God's triune personhood of the Trinity with spiritual faculties, including an intellect with which man can understand and make judgments concerning what is good and acceptable and a will with which man can follow the perfect will of God. In a paraphrase of Rom 12:2, Augustine writes:

> "Be reformed in the newness of your mind, that you may prove what is the good and the acceptable and the perfect will of God."
> Thus, You do not say, "Let man be made," but, "Let us make man"; nor do You say, "according to his kind," but, "to Our image and likeness." For when in newness of mind he sees and understands Your truth, man does not need any other man to

---

56. Thomas Aquinas, *Summa Theologica* Ia, q. 28, art. 4.

teach him to imitate his kind; but with You to teach him he sees for himself what is Your will, what is good and acceptable and perfect.... Thus, man is renewed onto knowledge according to the image of Him that created him, and having become spiritual, he judges all things—all things, that is, which are to be judged.[57]

Made in God's image and likeness, man's intellect begins to see, judge, and understand the perfection of God's truth. It is man's will that must choose to follow God's will in order to reach God. Unlike Aristotle, who uses reason and experience alone to understand the divine, Augustine utilizes reason and experience but ultimately relies upon faith to understand God as Creator. In his famous sermon that paraphrases a pre-Vulgate translation of Isa 7:9, Augustine writes: "I believe in order to understand; and I understand, the better to believe."[58]

Understanding from God's will what is good and acceptable and perfect begins with one's understanding of God as "most excellent Creator and Ruler of the universe," who in creating the human person with a physical body made him good, so that Augustine reflects that, even as a youth:

> I had an instinct for the care of my own being, a trace in me of that most profound Unity whence my being was derived; in my interior sense I kept guard over the integrity of my outward sense perception.... I had come to delight in the truth. I hated to be wrong, had a vigorous memory... delighted in friendship, shunned pain, meanness and ignorance.... Yet all these were the gifts of my God; for I did not give them to myself. All these were good and all these were I. Therefore, He who made me is good and He is my Good and in Him I shall exalt all the good qualities that even as a boy I had.[59]

So, Augustine considers that God, who is Goodness itself, created the universe and man good, and it is in man himself that goodness of God's moral order is reflected so that man can understand within himself those natural inclinations for self-preservation, for rational understanding of his perceptions, for seeking and delighting in finding the truth, and for delighting in friendship. And this moral order within man's human nature is not of his own making but transcends his own mind and will in that man did not put these inclinations within himself, but, rather, it was

57. Augustine, *Confessions* 13.22.32 (p. 309).
58. Augustine, "Sermon 43," 158 (p. 43).
59. Augustine, *Confessions* 1.20.31 (pp. 20–21).

the goodness of man's Creator who established immanently within man's human nature this transcendent moral order.

MORAL LAW IS WRITTEN ON EACH PERSON'S HEART

Before man can freely choose, he must reflect upon and accept the moral truth he is to pursue, which is found within himself. Augustine makes this position even clearer in his *Reply to Faustus the Manichaean*, written in AD 400, perhaps two or three years after he completed his *Confessions*. Augustine cites Rom 2:14–15, where Paul tells us:

> When the Gentiles who have not law do by nature what the law requires, they are a law to themselves, even though they do not have the law. They show that what the law requires is written on their hearts.

Augustine relates Paul's insight to Jesus's revelation that he came not to destroy the law but to fulfill it (Matt 5:17). But to what law was Jesus referring? Augustine speaks of three laws:

> One is that of the Hebrews, which the apostle calls the law of sin and death. The second is that of the Gentiles, which he calls the law of nature. . . . The third law is the truth of which the apostle speaks when he says, "The law of the Spirit of life in Christ Jesus has made me free from the law of sin and death."[60]

Augustine rejects the notion that Jesus is speaking of the disciplinary Mosaic laws imposed on the Israelites, but, rather, it is the Ten Commandments to which Jesus refers when, in Matt 5:17, he says: "Think not that I have come to abolish the law and the prophets. I have come not to abolish them but to fulfill them." This is the natural moral law that is written on men's hearts, as God has created man with this moral order internal to human nature. Says Augustine:

> If Jesus had gone on to speak of circumcision, and sabbaths, and sacrifices, and the observances of the Hebrews, and had added something as a fulfillment, there could have been no doubt that it was the law and the prophets of the Jews of which he had said that he came not to destroy, but to fulfill them. But Christ, without any allusion to these, speaks only of the commandments which date from the earliest of times: "Thou shalt not kill; Thou

---

60. Augustine, *Reply to Faustus* 19.2–3 (p. 239).

A SKETCH OF THE PERSONS, EVENTS, BELIEFS, AND PHILOSOPHIES   35

> shall not commit adultery; Thou shalt not bear false witness." These it can be proved, were of old promulgated in the world by Enoch and Seth, and other righteous men to whom the precepts were delivered by angels of lofty rank in order to tame the savage nature of man.[61]

Unlike the second law designated by Augustine as the law of the Gentiles, which is the law of nature, the third law is the law of the Spirit of life in Christ Jesus with which man is not created but must receive as a gift of faith and grace. But before faith and grace, there must first be an understanding and acceptance of the moral truth of the natural law written on men's hearts (in its most rudimentary form, the golden rule; see Matt 7:12). As such, the law of the Gentiles is something that all men can know through their natural inclinations and the use of their inborn rational understanding.

CICERO'S INFLUENCE ON AUGUSTINE

While not cited by Augustine, it is interesting to note that in the essay *On Duty* (*De Officiis*), Cicero reflects on man's natural inclinations in a manner similar to that found in *Confessions*, giving rise to the speculation that Augustine might have read this work before writing *Confessions*. Cicero (106–43 BC) was an eclectic Roman political philosopher whose primary concern in his writings was the cultivation of good citizens. He had ties with the Academics and tended toward a moderate skepticism but still accepted human nature as self-evidently good. Cicero based morality on rationally understood natural inclinations:

> From the beginning all species of living creatures have been endowed by Nature with the instinct to protect their own lives and bodies and avoid whatever seems likely to do them harm, and to find and secure whatever they need for life, such as food, shelter and the like. . . .
> There is, however, this great difference between man and beast. . . . Man . . . is endowed with reason through which he observes events and their consequences. He perceives the causes of things, understands a relation of cause and effect, draws analogies, and connects and combines the present with the future. . . . Through the same power of reason Nature links man to man, by their participation in speech and in social intercourse.

---

61. Augustine, *Reply to Faustus* 19.2–3 (pp. 239–40).

> Above all, she implants in him a special love for his offspring. She impels men too to meet and take part in social gatherings and festivals. Thus, they are driven to provide not only for their own comfort and livelihood, but also for that of their wives, children, and all others they hold dear and feel bound to protect. This responsibility stimulates their spirits, and encourages them to greater deeds.
>
> The thing most peculiar to the human race is its search and inquiry after truth. For, as soon as we are free from the cares of necessary business, we are eager to see, hear, and learn new things.... Hence, we see that the simple and unperverted truth appeals strongly to man's nature. To this craving for a sight of truth is added a desire for leadership. A mind naturally well developed is reluctant to obey anyone but a teacher of morals and wisdom, or, for practical reasons, a just and law abiding ruler....
>
> And through his great powers of nature and reason man is the one animal with a feeling for order, propriety, and moderation in word and act. In the same way, no other animal has a sense of beauty, loveliness, and symmetry in visible things. And nature and reason enable us to transfer these impressions from our eyes to our minds and to prize beauty, stability, and order even more in our thoughts and actions. So too, we are led to avoid any indecorous or unmanly deed, and any purely sensual thought or action. Out of these elements is formed and fashioned the goodness that is the topic of our inquiry, which is noble ... I truly say that by its nature it is worthy of every praise.[62]

Cicero, unlike Augustine, does not refer to God as the creator who endowed man with these natural inclinations and thus established the transcendent moral order. Cicero merely indicates that this endowment is the work of "Nature." However, without a Creator-God who is "the supreme and perfect Good" and who is "incorruptible"[63] there is no guarantee that man's natural order alone is the correct or sufficient order for man to follow. All things in nature, including man, from a blade of grass to the largest star are subject to corruption. Without God, man must rely solely on his natural inclinations or his practical reason and the sensibilities of human culture that develop within a given society. Cicero readily admits that in addition to natural inclinations, which are good if they enhance

---

62. Cicero, *On Duty*, 324–25.
63. See Augustine, *Confessions* 7.4.6 (p. 120).

benefits for society such as stability, order, and social intercourse, there are also deficient tendencies or bad inclinations in human nature such as impropriety, cowardliness, or unbridled sensuality that are to be avoided as nonbeneficial for society.

HUMANITY'S MOTIVES FOR DOING EVIL

For Augustine, the inclination to evil can be found motivating his own personal sins that he acknowledges throughout *Confessions*. This inclination to evil is not directly chosen by the human person but is rather the result of a fallen nature inherited from the original sin of our first parent, Adam. While sin that is deliberately and freely committed is an offense against the moral law placed in the human heart by God, a sinful inclination remains only a disordered urge or tendency to sin until a person knowingly and freely commits the evil act. The essence of every evil act is a rejection of the higher inclination in man to follow God's moral law written on the heart in order to satisfy the desires of a lower inclination, which lower inclination, while not evil in itself, becomes evil when a person gives it priority and chooses to act in accord with it over the dictates of moral law. Augustine speaks of a moral weakness that all men inherit, which acts as a distraction from the higher inclination to follow the moral law in order to provide satisfaction to one's lower inclinations. Augustine writes of this sinful weakness (referred to in moral theology as concupiscence) as a conflict with his good inclinations and as a type of "distraction [that] happened to me though I did not want it," so that "it is not I who caused it but 'the sin that dwells in me,' the punishment of the sin more freely committed by Adam, whose son I am."[64] It will be such a distraction to sin that will lead Augustine to his remarkable analysis in Book 8 of the conflict of the two wills that immobilizes his free choice to follow his good inclinations. But once the evil inclination in man to reject God and the moral order that God placed on each man's heart is acted upon, one has chosen in one's heart to sin.

Augustine speaks of the sin in man's heart of rejecting God and his moral order in order to delight in the rebellion of doing evil, which, in this case, was stealing pears with his friends:

---

64. Augustine, *Confessions* 8.10.22 (pp. 155–56).

> Our only pleasure in doing it was that it was forbidden. Such was my heart, O God, such was my heart yet in the depth of the abyss You had pity on it.[65]

What Augustine is investigating here is the intention or the goal or purpose for his actions. The most basic evil intention was for Augustine delighting in the love of evil itself for its own sake while knowing that it is evil. In the case of the pears he stole with his friends, Augustine will admit he stole the pears for two reasons, the first being that it was not because he and his friends wanted to eat them; in fact he and his friends ended up throwing the pears to the hogs. Rather it was the rebellious act of stealing in itself and knowing it was wrong that motivated the theft while not having as a real purpose gaining possession of the pears for the satisfaction of eating them. To assert one's ego in defiance of what one knows to be wrong was the enticement to commit the evil act. Says Augustine:

> We carried off an immense load of pears, not to eat—for we barely tasted them before throwing them to the hogs. Our only pleasure in doing it was that it was forbidden. Such was my heart, O God, such was my heart: yet in the depth of the abyss You had pity on it. Let that heart now tell You what it sought when I was thus evil for no logic, having no cause for wrongdoing save my wrongness. The malice of the act was base and I loved it—that is to say I loved my own undoing. I loved the evil in me—not the thing for which I did the evil, simply the evil; my soul was depraved, and hurled itself down from security in You into utter destruction, seeking no profit from wickedness but only to be wicked.[66]

That Augustine clearly knew that stealing the pears was wrong is made abundantly clear by his own confession:

> Your law, O Lord punishes theft; and this law is so written in the hearts of men that not even breaking of it blots it out; for no thief bears calmly being stolen from—not even if he is rich and the other steals through want.[67]

This confession provides the insight for understanding how Augustine could claim that he "loved the evil in me—not the thing for which I did

---

65. Augustine, *Confessions* 2.4.9 (p. 29).
66. Augustine, *Confessions* 2.4.9 (p. 29).
67. Augustine, *Confessions* 2.4.9 (p. 29).

the evil, simply the evil." Augustine could call his soul "depraved" because he chose the evil he knew to be wrong as it was instinctively understood within himself, and in so choosing, Augustine was taking delight in his defiance of his own natural moral sense and judgment of conscience. Such an act of defiance was an attempt to deaden his conscience and establish his own rule of conduct thus replacing what his Creator had endowed human nature to know, i.e., moral truth within himself. In effect, such an act of defiance may be the ultimate form of idolatry, viz., self-deification. As such, the love of evil within oneself may be the prototype of all acts of evil because every act of evil, when one knows it is evil, is a replacement of God with oneself and an attempt to recreate one's own nature according to one's own ego-centered designs.

Regarding the second reason for stealing the pears, Augustine explains that alone he would not have committed the theft, but his enticement to do wrong while knowing that it was wrong was aided and abetted by his friends who conspired together to do an evil act of theft. And this theft committed by Augustine and his associates was not for the purpose of gaining pleasure from eating the stolen fruit but for the thrill of all together doing what is evil, i.e., the stealing in itself done with the mutual approval, delight, and pressure of his peers. Augustine admitted:

> I would not have committed that theft alone: my pleasure in it was not what I stole but that I stole: yet I would not have enjoyed doing it, I would not have done it alone. O friendship unfriendly, unanalyzable attraction for the mind, greediness to do damage for the mere sport and jest of it, desire for another's loss with no gain to oneself or vengeance to be satisfied! Someone cries, "Come on, let's do it!"—And we would be ashamed to be ashamed.[68]

A possible interpretation of the sense of this last phrase could be that we should be ashamed to be so ashamed, indicating that the sense of shame is increased by our awareness of how great our shame is for committing an evil act while submitting to the pressure of others. There seems to be, then, a magnification of the love of evil within oneself when others acknowledge and encourage this evil openly and thereby reinforce the commission of evil acts. Peer pressure, which is often attributed to being a weakness of youth only, is actually a reality for anyone of any age who conspires to commit together and relish with others any act of evil.

---

68. Augustine, *Confessions* 2.9.17 (p. 34).

Augustine next joins this basic evil intention of satisfying the love of evil itself within oneself to the inclinations to enjoy inordinately the lower goods of human life in violation of the natural moral law written on the heart. While not denying the depravity of loving evil within oneself that brings one to "the depth of the abyss," Augustine also readily understands the inclinations of human nature to love the beautiful and pleasurable things of this world that, though not evil in themselves, may become evil when these inclinations are indulged inordinately in sinful violation of the transcendent moral law written on one's heart by the Creator. Says Augustine:

> There is an appeal to the eye in beautiful things . . . the sense of touch has its own powerful pleasure. . . . Worldly success has its glory and the power to command and to overcome: and from this springs the thirst for revenge. But in our quest for all these things we must not depart from You, Lord, or deviate from Your Law. . . . The bond of human friendship is admirable, holding many souls as one. Yet in the enjoyment of all such things we commit sin if through inordinate inclination to them—for though they are good, they are of the lowest order of good—things higher and better are forgotten, even You, O Lord our God, and Your Truth and Your Law.[69]

Augustine thus argues that all things including man's desires and inclinations are created good by God. Bad inclinations are the result of man's own deficient desire (inherited from Adam) to replace God's order of the good he created with man's own preference to impose his own order of goods—thus displacing the higher and better goods with lower goods in order to satisfy lower human passions for which a person develops an "inordinate inclination." When man freely chooses to do this, he sins. The tension between God-given good inclinations in man and the desire of man's fallen nature to replace the divine order of goods with man's deficient order of goods can immerse man in a stultifying conflict between two wills, "one carnal and one spiritual."[70]

---

69. Augustine, *Confessions* 2.5.10 (pp. 29–30).
70. See Augustine, *Confessions* 8.5.10 (p. 148).

CONFLICT BETWEEN THE TWO WILLS

Man has within his very being natural inclinations that vie for dominance. On the one hand, man yearns for the highest goods; he delights in the truth; has the moral law written on his heart by his Creator; and experiences the restlessness in his heart until he finds rest in God. On the other hand, man has a yearning for lower goods; he finds beautiful things appealing to his eye; experiences powerful pleasures from his sense of touch; and has ambitions for worldly success with its glory and power to command. Throughout life, man's mind is constantly choosing to pursue goods both higher and lower. As man makes choices, he tends to give priority to certain goods over others. Man will choose in a given instance to pursue a good of either his higher or lower inclination. Man's repeated choice for a certain good produces a habit, which can be defined as a pattern of actions that become easier to perform and harder to dislodge with this repetition of choice to pursue a certain good over others. However, man finds himself always experiencing both his higher and lower inclinations and at any given time can change his mind and attempt to pursue a good of the opposite inclination over the good to which he has become habituated. When this happens, man's will may become split and he may find himself unable to choose between the two goods with one whole will intact, resulting in the person finding himself caught and perhaps immobilized by a conflict of two wills within himself.

Speaking of the goods of the natural inclinations that vie for dominance within the person, Augustine states:

> If all these things attract us at the same moment, are not different wills tugging at the heart of man while we deliberate which we should choose? Thus they are all good, yet they are all in conflict until one is chosen, and then the whole will is at rest and at one, whereas it had been divided into many. Or again, when eternity attracts the higher faculties and the pleasure of some temporal good holds the lower, it is one same soul that wills both, but not either with its whole will; and it is therefore torn both ways and deeply troubled while truth shows the one way as better but habit keeps it to the other.[71]

Understanding one's habits is the key to understanding why there can develop a conflict of two wills tugging at the heart of man and preventing him from choosing one way or another with his whole will. For

---

71. Augustine, *Confessions* 8.10.24 (p. 157).

Augustine, it was his carnal will that desired the lower, temporal goods at the expense of his spiritual will's quest for truth and for God, as God had created man, and which carnal will solidified repeated actions of his past in pursuit of temporal goods so that these actions become vices. These vices imprisoned his divided soul into a slavery of offending the Creator, viz., sin. While it was Augustine's spiritual will that sought the truth and eternal life in union with God, the spiritual will was nevertheless stymied by the habits formed by his carnal will, so that even in praying for virtue he found himself in this quandary:

> I in my great worthlessness—for it was greater thus early—had begged You for chastity, saying, "Grant me chastity and continence, but not yet." For I was afraid that you would hear my prayer too soon, and too soon would heal me from the disease of lust which I wanted satisfied rather than extinguished. So, I had gone wondering in my sacrilegious superstition through the base ways (of the Manichaeans): not indeed that I was sure they were right but that I preferred them to the Christians, whom I did not inquire about in the spirit of religion but simply opposed through malice.[72]

Augustine's "disease of lust" motivated his choice to pursue women who would satisfy this lust, and his repeated choices throughout much of his early life led to his evil habit of lust that proved impossible for his spiritual will to overcome on its own. Further, reinforcing this habit of sin was his lingering acceptance of Manichaeism that Augustine found difficult to abandon (with its excusal of moral responsibility for evil committed) even when his rational philosophical investigations made transparent the contradictions and unfounded claims of this Manichaean cult. So too, with many bad habits a person may encounter associates who themselves are aiders and abettors of the vice. Breaking with Manichaeism also required Augustine to break with fellow "hearers" and the "elect" of the sect who all believed in a dishonest acceptance of an evil nature within all human persons that forced them to commit evil acts.

---

72. Augustine, *Confessions* 8.7.17 (pp. 152–53).

OVERCOMING SELF-DECEPTION WITH THE GRACE OF CHRIST

Ultimately Augustine had to admit to himself, and ultimately to God, an honest acceptance of his moral weakness so that his prayer for God's grace would be sincere and undivided. At the time of any person's conversion from vice, this honest acceptance of one's moral weakness must include an understanding of, and the ability to overcome, any person's inclination to deceive himself/herself. Augustine had to overcome his self-deception and freely and honestly confront and overcome his conflict of wills and his vice of lust, albeit with the necessary help of God through Jesus Christ. Augustine exclaims:

> I regarded it as settled that it would be better to give myself to Your love rather than go on yielding to my own lust; but the first course delighted and convinced my mind, the second delighted my body and held it in bondage. For there was nothing I could reply when you called me: "Rise, thou that sleepest and arise from the dead; and Christ shall enlighten thee" [cf. Eph 5:14]; and whereas You showed me by every evidence that your words were true there was simply nothing I could answer save only laggard lazy words: "Soon," "Quite soon," "Give me just a little while." . . . For the law of sin is the fierce force of habit, by which the mind is drawn and held even against its will, and yet deservedly because it had fallen willfully into the habit. Who then should deliver me from the body of this death, but thy grace only through Jesus Christ our Lord?[73]

While giving himself to God's love delighted and convinced his mind, yielding to his own lust delighted his body and held it in bondage. And yielding to his own lust led to the fierce force of habit with the mind held even against its spiritual will for which the mind was blameworthy, because it had carnally willed initially to succumb to the temptation of lust. What Augustine describes in the conflict of the spiritual will versus the carnal will necessarily involves an attempt of a person to deceive himself. On the one hand, a person may aspire to a virtuous life, to the pursuit of truth, and ultimately to the pursuit of union with one's Creator. On the other hand, each person inherits a fallen human nature with its concupiscence or inclination to satisfy lower human desires and goods at the expense of the virtuous life. Once habits of sin are acquired in violation of

---

73. Augustine, *Confessions* 8.5.12 (pp. 148–49).

the transcendent moral order written on the heart, the resulting conflict of the two wills cannot be resolved until the person honestly accepts the truth of his fallen nature and asks his Creator for help. Without accepting our inherited human weakness and the need for God's grace, one wallows in the delusion of self-reliance and self-mastery regarding our inclination to choose the lower good.

Augustine explains his own pretense regarding his own decrepit moral state and how it was the story (told by his friend Ponticianus) of St. Antony of Egypt who lived an eremitical life in the desert, i.e., dwelling alone devoting himself to prayer, meditation, and austere self-denial in search of God, that brought Augustine to honestly see himself as he really was. Augustine views this self-revelation as involving God's direct intervention, which forced Augustine to look at himself, as it were, "face-to-face." Ponticianus related to Augustine the inspirational effect that the life of this hermit had on himself and on his friends, some of whom dedicated their lives to God in prayer and sealed themselves with a vow of virginity. Augustine relates the effect that Ponticianus's report had on him:

> This was the story Ponticianus told. But You, Lord, while he was speaking, turned me back towards myself, taking me from behind my own back where I had put myself all the time that I preferred not to see myself. And You set me there before my own face that I might see how vile I was, how twisted and unclean and spotted and ulcerous. I saw myself and was horrified, but there was no way to flee from myself. If I tried to turn my gaze from myself, there was Ponticianus telling what he was telling; and again You were setting me face-to-face with myself, forcing me upon my own sight, that I might see my iniquity and loathe it. I had known it, but I had pretended not to see it, had deliberately looked the other way and let it go from my mind.[74]

Such a profoundly honest description of oneself can rarely be found in literature, be it biographical or psychological or philosophical. Augustine directly attributes this self-revelation of his true character to divine intervention. It was God, says Augustine, that forced him to see himself as he truly existed and to experience the self-loathing that resulted from this self-perception. Augustine tells us that it was God who stripped away Augustine's pretension as to his own identity and made him see himself as he really was. It would seem, then, that the conflict of the spiritual will

---

74. Augustine, *Confessions* 8.7.16 (p. 152).

and of the carnal will, which splits the mind and precludes the person from choosing with his whole will, involves a pretense or self-deception where a person refuses to will holistically because the person wishes to preserve an acceptable yet false image of himself as being virtuous while, at the same time, tenaciously holding on to a vice or vices that the person refuses to give up.

Chapter Two

Philosophical Perspectives That Contrast with Augustine's on God, Freedom, and the Moral Order

SARTRE AND HIS CONCEPT OF *MAUVAISE FOI*—BAD FAITH

IT IS IRONIC THAT in the twentieth century the phenomenologist Jean-Paul Sartre, an atheist, would provide an apt name and description of self-deception, viz., *mauvaise foi*, bad faith. Bad faith simply defined is lying to oneself. It is bad faith because the person is hiding the truth from himself and believing a falsehood. Sartre describes bad faith:

> Of course, for the person exercising bad faith, it is still a matter of covering up an unpleasant truth or of presenting some pleasant error as the truth. In appearance therefore, bad faith has the structure of a lie. But what changes everything is that in bad faith it is from myself that I am concealing the truth. Thus, the duality of the deceiver and deceived is not present here. On the contrary bad faith implies in its essence the unity of a single consciousness. . . . Bad faith is not undergone, nor does it infect us, nor is it a state. But consciousness itself takes on its bad faith. . . . From this it follows, first, that the person to whom one is lying and the person who is lying are one and the same person, which means that I must know—in so far as I am the deceiver—the truth that is hidden from me in so far as I am deceived.[1]

---

1. Sartre, *Being and Nothingness*, part 1, ch. 2.1, p. 90.

While this phenomenon of self-deception or lying to oneself is seen as a real possibility by both Augustine and by Sartre, their respective understanding of what man is and why he may lie to himself is radically different.

For Augustine (as we have already seen), a summary of human nature would include that he/she is endowed by his/her Creator with an immanent knowledge of a transcendent moral order known intuitively and through practical reason; this knowledge deals with matters of free choice and action. This transcendent moral order is known through innate inclinations within each person that prompt a person to pursue and give priority to higher goods including a quest for virtue, truth, and union with God. Lower goods including the satisfaction of bodily desires are understood intuitively by a person to be kept subordinate to the pursuit of higher goods; this understanding of higher goods includes an acceptance of the golden rule and the demands of natural moral law understood through the practical reason. When a person chooses to give priority to the satisfaction of bodily desires over the pursuit of higher goods, he/she violates the natural moral law placed within him/her by his/her Creator, and such violations can quickly develop into habits of sin. When a person at the same time attempts to acknowledge God's moral law within him/her but pretends not to see his/her own violation of it, or attempts to reject or alter parts of this moral law, he/she is lying to himself/herself. Instead of following God's transcendent moral law, that person tries to create his/her own moral order.

One might ask, if the moral law is known immanently, in what sense is the moral law transcendent? The moral law is not a matter of opinion, of whim, or of choice. It is first intuited instinctively as principles of right and wrong, which each person does not create. Rather, the moral law transcends, i.e., goes beyond each individual and does not vary from individual to individual. Augustine's students in Rome did not pay them for his teaching. He was rightly enraged because those students had wronged him, and he wanted retribution. The golden rule supplemented by the practical reason inclined Augustine to establish a universal moral axiom, even though at first Augustine was too absorbed by his own irritation to consider a moral rule that is applicable to others as well as to himself. The axiom in general states: "I don't want anyone wronging me; so, I must not wrong others."

However, for Sartre, in man "no taste or inclination is irreducible. They all represent a certain appropriative choice of being."[2] In other words, Sartre is saying that man has no necessary innate inclination, not even for self-preservation, to pursue virtue or to seek God. All man can do is to appropriate, i.e., choose to possess his own inclinations. Conscious man is a For-itself, that is, a being who is and must be constantly choosing, for the freedom to choose is all that the conscious man essentially is. And what the For-itself constantly tends to choose is to be an In-itself, that is any quality, characteristic, or thing (including virtues and vices), which constitutes the determined and essential being of the thing. But while the For-itself seeks to escape the angst of being a free consciousness without a substantive essence, it tends to choose to project an identity for itself as an In-itself. But the For-itself cannot have a substantive essence, i.e., an In-itself; the For-itself cannot be anything determined or substantive; the For-itself can only be its own free choices, i.e., its own freedom.

For Sartre, the For-itself is conscious of objects in the world through a process of negation, i.e., consciousness must negate the background of objects surrounding a chosen object in order to bring a chosen object into focus. So too, in order to freely choose the For-itself must negate (or, as Sartre puts it, nihilate) any identification with a substantive essence so as to choose a goal for itself not yet realized and ultimately unrealizable. Sartre tells us:

> Human reality was its own nothingness. To be, for the for-itself, is to nihilate the in-itself that it is. In these conditions, freedom can be nothing other than this nihilation. Through it, the for-itself escapes from its being, as from its essence; through it, for itself is always something other than what we can say about it, because it is at least that which escapes this very naming, which is always beyond the name we give to it, beyond the property we acknowledge it to have.[3]

Sartre is saying that the For-itself must nihilate the In-itself that the human reality is. The For-itself is conscious freedom, which can only remain free by nihilating or refusing to accept any identity of conscious freedom with any human condition, state of mind, instinct, emotion, or moral conscience that judges good and evil to be objectively real.

---

2. Sartre, *Being and Nothingness*, part 4, ch. 2, p. 796.
3. Sartre, *Being and Nothingness*, part 4, ch. 1.1, p. 577.

Without a substantive essential nature that was created in him by a providential God who directs man to a moral goal, Sartre argues that man must freely choose goals at his own whim by nihilating (what Augustine would identify as) innate inclinations, which Sartre sees as obstructing man's freedom. For Sartre, there is no creator God and there is no essential character to the nature of man; the human person lacks a substantive essence, and his capacity to choose to achieve such an essence, i.e., choosing to establish himself as an essentially substantive being, can never be fulfilled; and for the For-itself to choose to believe otherwise is bad faith. Sartre denies that the human person has a God-given nature with the moral law written upon his/her heart; man's freedom is set adrift to make choices that can never realize a divine purpose or goal because God simply does not exist. Says Sartre:

> Every human reality is a Passion, in that its project is to lose itself in order to found being and at the same time to constitute the in-itself as escaping contingency by being its own foundation, the Ens causa sui, which the religions know as God. In this way man's Passion is the opposite of Christ's, because man loses himself as man in order that God should be born. But the idea of God is contradictory and we lose ourselves in vain; man is a useless Passion.[4]

SARTRE'S UNDERSTANDING OF FREEDOM

For Sartre, then, man is free to choose and must choose because freedom is his only essence, albeit an essence that is never substantive but only a fleeting existence of making choices that are never realized. Failure to choose constantly, or pretending that one has through his choices brought about or caused the substantial essence of his being, constitutes bad faith, a lie man tells himself in spite of his ongoing experience of his own conscious freedom. For Sartre, the human person can never satisfy his/her desire or passion to have a complete substantive essence or to be the foundation for realizing himself/herself as an essential being. Therefore, Sartre concludes that a human is a futile or useless passion because he/she must freely choose to be what he/she cannot be.

But one might ask whether or not habits that result from repeated actions freely performed in the past that are difficult to change contribute

---

4. Sartre, *Being and Nothingness*, part 4, ch. 2.3, pp. 796–97.

to man's being a substantial character for which each person is responsible. In confessing his own sin Augustine said (as quoted above): "For the law of sin is the fierce force of habit, by which the mind is drawn and held even against its will, and yet deservedly because it had fallen willfully into the habit."[5] And, while Augustine would acknowledge that one can freely aspire to turn away from this fierce force of habit that perhaps has become a vice, it would take divine intervention to enable him to break this habit of sin. Augustine continues to say (from the quote above): "Who then should deliver me from the body of this death, but Thy grace only through Jesus Christ our Lord?" But unlike Augustine, Sartre denies God and grace, and Sartre would claim that man as a For-it-self is absolutely free to reject the ends or goals of his past actions and replace them with new and perhaps contrary ends or goals in the present—all this relying on a weak human nature dependent on habits and without reliance on divine help. According to Sartre, a person can then freely choose another goal or end in the present so as to project this goal or end onto the future in his attempt to create his own essence. Says Sartre, utilizing the biblical Adam as the prototype of all human persons:

> Adam is not defined by his essence, because essence, for human reality, comes after existence. He is defined through the choice of his ends. . . . In this way, Adam's contingency expresses the finite choice he has made of himself. But now it is the future, not the past, that acquaints him with his person: he chooses to learn what he is through the ends toward which he projects himself—i.e., through the totality of his tastes, his inclinations, his hates, etc. inasmuch as there is a thematic organization and an inherent meaning to this totality.[6]

While Sartre claims that for the human reality essence comes after existence (or as Sartre puts it in another way, existence precedes essence), nevertheless, according to Sartre's concept, the only essence that man realizes is a projection of himself based on his goals or ends chosen in present actions but directed toward the future. Man's tastes, inclinations, hatreds, etc., might be bound up with a "thematic organization," i.e., proclivities or habits are so organized within one's body so as to incline the person to act in a certain way; but, according to Sartre, nothing interferes with man's being defined by his free choices of goals, which man can and

---

5. Augustine, *Confessions* 8.5.12 (p. 149).
6. Sartre, *Being and Nothingness*, part 4, ch. 1.1, p. 613.

must choose, perhaps differently, at the ongoing present time. So too, in regard to one's past actions, one's essence is realized, to the extent that it can be realized, only insofar as upon this past the For-itself decides what this past's meaning is in relation to the ends or goals of the person's present choices. For Sartre, the past is over and is seen as an object, an In-itself that can be freely evaluated or assigned meaning as can any object through the conscious choice of the person. According to Sartre:

> I alone, in fact, am able to decide at each moment on the impact of the past, not by debating, deliberating, and evaluating in each case the importance of such and such an earlier event but, by projecting myself toward my goals, I rescue the past as well as myself and I decide on its meaning through my action.[7]

What Sartre stubbornly insists on is that there is nothing in the human reality that has or retains a substantive essence beyond the person's essence of freedom to choose to act and to project an end or goal onto past and future actions. Sartre maintains:

> To say that the for-itself has to be what it is, to say that it is what it is not by not being what it is, and to say that existence precedes and conditions its essence ... is to say one and the same thing: namely, that man is free. By the mere fact, indeed, that I am conscious of the reasons that solicit my action, these reasons are already transcendent objects for my consciousness; they are outside. I may try in vain to cling on to them; by my very existence I escape them. I am condemned to exist forever beyond my essence, beyond the motives and reasons for my action: I am condemned to be free. In other words, we cannot find any limits to my freedom other than itself or, alternately, that we are not free to cease to be free.[8]

For Sartre, man's freedom is absolute and without restraint in that man has no substantial nature created by God, and, moreover, man's repeated past actions and habits, both so-called virtues and vices, have no bearing on what man is. To claim that one is one's virtues and vices resulting from past actions is bad faith for Sartre. But without limits set by a God-given objective morality, man is free to choose lower goods and "nihilate" higher goods at his own discretion. The Ten Commandments are reduced to what a popular (but apt) cliché refers to as the "ten

---

7. Sartre, *Being and Nothingness*, part 4, ch. 1.2, p. 649.
8. Sartre, *Being and Nothingness*, part 4, ch. 1.1, p. 577.

suggestions." An explanatory statement of what happens when God is rejected and freedom is absolutized is provided by Fyodor Dostoyevsky's character the monk, the elder Zosima, in the novel *The Brothers Karamazov*, who, speaking of the upper classes, stated:

> They want to organize themselves scientifically, to devise a system of justice based on pure reason, not on Christ, as before, and they have already declared that there's no such thing as crime and that there is no sin. And, from their point of view, they are right—for how can there be crime if God does not exist?[9]

(A generalized restatement of the latter part of this quote that is commonly stated is: "If God does not exist, then everything is permitted.")

But is it not good faith to take responsibility for one's past actions, especially crimes and sins and their consequences, and to admit that it was one's own free choice in having performed these actions? Instances abound in *Confessions* where Augustine freely admits his guilt in his past actions. In one example Augustine states:

> And I so long was ignorant and loved vanity and sought after lying. . . .
>
> I read, "Be angry and sin not." And by this I was much moved, O my God, for I had by then learned to be angry with myself for the past, that I might not sin in what remained of my life.[10]

Is it not it bad faith, i.e., lying to oneself, to try to absolutely separate one's free choices of one's free conscious will in the present, i.e., one's For-itself, from the responsibility it has for one's past actions? Does not Sartre himself reveal a contradiction in his absolute separation of the freedom of the For-itself when he states (as quoted above) that man "chooses to learn what he is by means of ends toward which he projects himself—i.e., by the totality of his tastes, his inclinations, his hates, etc., in so far as there is a thematic organization and an inherent meaning to this totality"? Is not this a contradiction in Sartre to deny that the causes and motives of his past actions do not condition man to be inclined to act in a certain way in the present and provide a foundation upon which present choices are made? A person's tastes, likes, hatreds, and all his/her innate natural inclinations (such as self-preservation) exist as essential realities within himself/herself and are not absolutely separate from any person's ability

---

9. Dostoyevsky, *Brothers Karamazov*, 422.
10. Augustine, *Confessions* 9.4.9–10 (p. 169).

to freely choose as Sartre claims for the For-itself. A person's inclinations are an essential part of the basis upon which the free choices that the For-itself makes in the present and projects into the future. A person's created essence is always part of his/her existence in which he/she freely chooses to affect that essence for good or for evil.

SARTRE'S FREEDOM AND INABILITY TO ATTAIN A SUBSTANTIVE ESSENCE VS. AUGUSTINE'S FREEDOM OF THE PERSON AND RESULTANT RESPONSIBILITY

Yet, all concepts of God creating man with a determined nature as well as with freedom to choose are seen by Sartre as a rejection of all freedom and thus of responsibility. Sartre will reject the position of Gottfried Leibniz (1646–1716), who was an Enlightenment rationalist who argued that absolute power and moral perfection are attributes of God who chose to create the world to be the best of possible worlds; and, Leibniz argued, it is God who chose to create man as the best possible rational being. Sartre accuses Leibniz of falling:

> back into a necessitarianism that is completely opposed to the idea of freedom when he places the very formula of Adam's substance at the start, like a premise from which Adam's act will follow as one of its partial conclusions. . . . One result of this, indeed, is that the act is strictly necessitated by Adam's very essence. . . . And this essence is not chosen by Adam himself but by God. Therefore, it is true that the act committed by Adam follows necessarily from Adam's essence and hence that it depends on Adam himself and on nobody else, which is certainly one condition of freedom. But for Adam himself, Adam's essence itself is a given, Adam did not choose it; he could not have chosen to be Adam. In consequence, he does not in any way bear responsibility for his being.[11]

Whatever the premise of Leibniz regarding the essential substance of Adam and the act that was presumably necessitated by his God-given essence, Sartre ignores that in the biblical narrative Adam had a choice to obey or disobey God's command. Prior to sinning Adam was naked with his wife and yet felt no shame because he was without sin. Adam does bear responsibility for disobeying God's command, which had to be a

---

11. Sartre, *Being and Nothingness*, part 4, ch. 1.1, pp. 612–13.

free act of pride of mind, and as a result Adam incurred the consequences of a fallen nature, which included loss of innocence and subjection to death. Augustine tells us in his address to God: "If Adam had not fallen away from You, there would not have flowed forth from him the bitter sea of the human race, with the depths of its curiosity, the storms of its pride, and the restless tossing of its instability."[12] After Adam's disobedience the inclination to sin (concupiscence) enters the world and is bequeathed to his descendants, as evidenced by his first son, Cain, murdering Cain's brother Abel out of envy and resentment.

What must be said in further response to Sartre: man is finite and his freedom is finite. Man's choices are limited in part by his innate natural inclinations, both good and bad, and by how past choices affect these inclinations for better or worse. This is not to say that man cannot in the freedom of his conscious intellect conceive new choices to pursue. However, man's choices are always affected by his past choices, which, if and when they become habits, become difficult to change in spite of one's conscious deliberations. This is the specific cause of the division of the whole will into two wills, one spiritual and one carnal. Regarding his own past choices to lust, Augustine confesses that he was immobilized with his newfound spiritual will

> to worship You freely and to enjoy You, O God, the only certain Joy, but [I] was not yet strong enough to overcome the earlier will rooted deep through the years. My two wills, one old, one new, one carnal, one spiritual, were in conflict and in conflict wasted my soul.[13]

Sartre's position on human freedom can be countered in that it is not in keeping with the limitations of human experience. A person's habits do incline him to act with a certain behavior, notwithstanding that person's conscious capability to aspire to change that habitual behavior. Everything in human society points to this reality. Employers look to hire persons with definite capabilities, proven work habits, and proven skills and talents and not merely to hire those who aspire to be or declare that they will be great workers and will be assets to a company or organization. The judicial system judges a person's guilt or innocence based on his past actions, not on his future projections. There is a contradiction in Sartre's concept of freedom in that the person's free choices result in

---

12. Augustine, *Confessions* 13.20.28 (p. 306).
13. Augustine, *Confessions* 8.5.10 (p. 148).

man's being nothing but "a useless or futile passion." This is not freedom but a slavery to an ever-fleeting human existence where there is no substantial human essence that can be realized and thus no real freedom to realize one's ends or goals. All of human experience points to the need for a person to find help in overcoming vices that can be identified in his past and present actions, which vices bind him to unsavory behavior. But Sartre especially rejects the concept of divine help, of God's creation of a substantial human nature in man, and of God entirely as a real, existing, providential supreme Being.

DOES GOD EXIST?—SARTRE VS. AUGUSTINE REGARDING THEIR CONFLICTING CONCEPTS

In contrast to Sartre, Augustine accepts the existence of a providential God who created man as a free being with essential characteristics, including not only rational understanding but also a capacity to intuit absolutes of a transcendent moral order written on the heart and an innate yearning to be complete in union with God. For Augustine, divine help is that which is indispensable in breaking vices and developing virtues—no matter what Sartre maintains—because man's freedom is not absolute, as evidenced by his own incapacity to overcome his vices and to acknowledge responsibility for them and to follow God unequivocally. Augustine laments:

> But now the day was come when I stood naked in my own sight and my conscience accused me. . . .
> And I was in the grip of the most horrible and confounding shame. . . . What did I not say against myself, with what lashes of condemnation did I not scourge my soul to make it follow me now that I wanted to follow You! My soul hung back. It would not follow yet found no excuse for not following. All its arguments had already been used and refuted. There remained only trembling silence: for it feared as very death the cessation of that habit of which in truth it was dying.[14]

But obviously, to follow God first requires one's acceptance of the existence of God and also faith in his divine goodness and providence, which providence assures man's moral awareness and an ultimate destiny for man. For the atheist or for the agnostic, acceptance of the existence

---

14. Augustine, *Confessions* 8.7.18 (p. 153).

of God can perhaps be facilitated by refuting the arguments that claim to prove the nonexistence of God, such as Sartre's conception of God as *Ens causa sui*, or the "Being which is self caused"; such an argument Sartre considers contradictory. The presumed premise of Sartre's argument is that God is a For-itself, i.e., a self-conscious rational being who freely chooses to act and, in this case, to act to be his own cause. But for Sartre, the For-itself can only be its own free choices to act and never be or realize himself as essentially substantive. Moreover, the For-itself freely chooses by "nihilating" all that is to be rejected so that its goal that is to be projected is brought into focus. Sartre's articulation of this argument is the following:

> In order for something to found its own being, it must exist at a distance from itself; that implies a specific nihilation of both the founded being, and the founding being, and a duality that is a unity: we are back with the case of the for-itself. In brief, any endeavor to conceive the idea of a being that is the foundation of its being leads us, in spite of itself, to form the idea of a being that, contingent in so far as it is being-in-itself, is the foundation of its own nothingness. The act of causation through which God is causa sui—like any reclamation by something of itself—a nihilating act, to the precise extent to which the most basic relation is necessarily a return to itself, a reflexivity. And this original necessity, in turn, appears on the foundation of a contingent being: the precise being which is in order to be its own cause.... In brief, God—if he exists—is contingent.[15]

The fundamental deficiency in Sartre's argument is to begin his understanding of God as being a For-itself, which concept Sartre describes based on his own reflective experience of how a human consciousness is aware of anything, viz., through a discursive process of distinguishing (which Sartre calls nihilation) that begins with the negation of background objects so as to focus on the object chosen, which this negation brings into relief. A finite process of knowing in which the human consciousness moves away from certain surrounding objects (or in Sartre's description nihilates them), in order to found a chosen object to possess a certain essential substantive being, cannot be ascribed to an infinite Being who knows himself as he essentially is—viz., an omnipotent and self-subsistent supreme being. Simply put, if a being "must exist at a distance from itself" in order to be his own self cause, such a being is already

15. Sartre, *Being and Nothingness*, part 2, ch. 1.1, pp. 131–32.

a finite and contingent object for himself and it cannot be God. But God's consciousness and knowledge cannot will himself through a discursive process of movement from one object or topic to another, as is the case with a finite consciousness; but, rather, the divine consciousness is infinite and complete in himself, i.e., self-contained rather than self-caused, and must be aware and know who he is, and what everything else is all at once if he is truly infinite.

Further, if there is a God who is truly divine, there can be no contingency in God in that God is not the cause of his own being in the sense that Sartre implies, viz., an efficient cause that is the cause provided by an agent upon an exterior object. A person can move an object and thus be an efficient cause of the movement. But God does not move himself or act in any way as the efficient cause of his being. Rather, God must be what he is, the infinite, supreme Being that is free from all corruptibility, and hence free from all contingency or dependence. God must be what Aristotle calls "self-dependent actuality." To say that God is the cause of his formal being, or as Augustine says, God is the essential "supreme and perfect Good,"[16] is to state what God eternally and substantively is, viz., God's essence is his existence, and God's existence is his infinite incorruptibility.

IMMANUEL KANT—THE GREAT BUT SKEPTICAL ENLIGHTENMENT PHILOSOPHER ON THE LIMITS OF MAN'S KNOWLEDGE, GOD, AND THE MORAL ORDER

Augustine's concept of God as the "supreme and perfect Good," cited above, is from the following passage: "For no soul ever has been able to conceive or ever will be able to conceive anything better than You, the supreme and perfect Good."[17] This conception is open to that rebuttal of all ontological arguments for God's existence that claim that the definition of God's being and attributes necessarily includes the reality of God's existence. The most thorough refutation of the ontological argument is provided not by Sartre but by the Enlightenment philosopher Immanuel Kant (1724–1804), who makes the distinction between analytic judgments and synthetic judgments. Kant argues that whatever is judged to

---

16. See Augustine, *Confessions* 7.4.6 (p. 120).
17. Augustine, *Confessions* 7.4.6 (p. 120).

be predicated of a subject establishes a relation that is possible in two ways—the judgment is analytic or synthetic. Kant tells us:

> Analytic judgments . . . are those in which the connection of the predicate with the subject is thought through identity, while those in which this connection is thought without identity should be called synthetic. The former might be called elucidatory, the latter expansive judgments because in the former nothing is added through the predicate to the concept of the subject, and the concept is only analyzed and broken up into its constituent concepts which had all long been thought in it . . . while the latter add to the concept of the subject a predicate that had not been thought in it at all, and that could not be extracted from it by any analysis.[18]

Kant argues that if you speak of God as an omnipotent being because he is defined as being infinite, then one can judge analytically a given or assumed concept of God that provides a precise and coherent identity of God and from this accepted identity might be inferred further necessary and valid judgments. But, according to Kant, one cannot claim that this given concept of God as an infinite and omnipotent being also includes existence because existence is a reality that cannot actually be proven by any defined concept of God, but, rather, existence must be verified empirically based on one's senses. Kant thus argues against all ontological arguments for God's existence:

> If, then, I tried to think of being as the highest reality (without any defect), the question still remains as to whether it exists or not. . . .
>
> Whatever and however much, therefore, our concepts of an object may contain, we must always step outside it in order to attribute existence to the object. In the case of objects of the senses, this takes place through their connection with any one of my perceptions, according to empirical laws; as for objects of pure thought however, there's no means of knowing their existence.[19]

When Kant speaks of our perceptions grasping objects of the senses according to empirical laws, he is referring to sense perceptions providing the raw material of sight, sound, and touch being necessarily formed

---

18. Kant, *Critique of Pure Reason*, introduction, 4 (p. 43).

19. Kant, *Critique of Pure Reason*, Second Division, Transcendental Dialectic, 3.4 (p. 505).

into thoughts by the mind's understanding through its conditions and categories that are preexisting in the mind, i.e., a priori or before sense experience. Kant tells us that space and time are the subjective conditions by which the mind perceives external objects. Time is also a subjective condition of the mind's internal sense of having an ongoing identity throughout all of its perceptions. All of our sense perceptions are put together by the mind into various forms of judgments that determine the ways one understands what we experience through the senses. These forms of judgment were first called categories by Aristotle, and these categories—such as quantity, quality, relation, and modality—are for Kant the conditions of thought, and without these categories our sense data could not be understood. In other words, without the categories of the understanding the sense data would only result in a kaleidoscope of sight and a cacophony of sound without meaning except for the reaction of animal instinct. Yet, all of our certain knowledge of real existing objects must first come through the sensations of our sense experience and be understood by the categories that are the necessary conditions for thinking of objects and for verifying whether they really exist. Kant argues that when the thought of objects goes beyond the data of sense perception and ventures into "pure thought," there is no way to verify whether these objects of thought really exist.

Whereas the ontological proof for God's existence begins with a concept of God as the highest reality and argues that existence must be included in this reality, the cosmological argument for the existence of God begins with the observation of contingent changeable beings, each being caused by a prior being that is itself caused by a prior being. The cosmological argument holds that there must be a first cause of the whole series of causes that is not caused by anything else, because an infinite regression of causes in the past ultimately fails to explain any cause in the whole series of causes. Kant rejects as invalid the inferring of the existence of a necessary uncaused being based on sense observation of changeable, finite beings each of which is caused; one cannot produce a synthetic proposition about the nature of or the existence of a necessary uncaused being that cannot be directly observed or experienced by the senses. Kant rejects:

> the inference to a first cause, from the impossibility of an infinite series of causes, given above one another, in the world of sense. The principles of the use of reason do not allow us to draw this inference even in experience, while here we extend this principle

beyond experience (to a realm to which this series can never be extended).[20]

Kant argues that one cannot empirically experience with one's senses the data needed for the understanding to determine whether there is or is not an endless series of causes. Kant argues that all the cosmological argument does is to present the ontological argument of analyzing the concept of a necessary uncaused being and claiming that it is the first and uncaused cause of all contingent causes. The question then could be raised whether Kant's refutation of the ontological argument (and hence of the cosmological argument) for the existence of God renders Augustine's and Anselm's ontological arguments invalid. In a strict, scientific sense requiring complete certitude based on sense experience alone, the answer is yes. However, in the realm of probability it can be argued that there must be a cause beyond all contingent causes because all contingent causes are verified by our sense experience as being finite and corruptible; it defies our understanding of logically consistent progression to accept the speculative thesis that the whole series of finite, corruptible causes (which are the effects of still other finite, corruptible causes) is an infinite series. While not verifiable through sense perception, an ultimate spiritual reality beyond corruptibility is arguably the only convincing explanation for the causation of finite, corruptible beings. Further, the experience of this ultimate spiritual reality must be by definition beyond sense experience, though not necessarily beyond all experience.

Kant, who taught mathematics and physics at the University of Königsberg before becoming a professor of philosophy, demanded strict scientific, empirical proof for the certitude of any claim for God's existence. In pursuit of this scientific certitude Kant would only allow empirical evidence from the five senses of human experience to inform the conditions and categories of pure reason. From these five senses the empirical data are formed into concepts by the mind's self-consciousness utilizing the categories of judgment of which the mind's understanding is capable. For Kant, whatever does not come from these five senses is not allowable as evidence for the existence of God, the soul, or anything else that escapes sensible experience. Kant would rule out any data from inclinations, impulses, instincts, emotional, or mystical experience (and much less from religious faith) as providing any verifiable evidence for

---

20. Kant, *Critique of Pure Reason*, Second Division, Transcendental Dialectic, 3.5 (p. 511).

the existence of God, because such sources for Kant lack any apodictic reliability.

KANT'S REQUIREMENT OF EVIDENCE BASED ON SENSE EXPERIENCE AND THE CATEGORIES OF REASON VS. AUGUSTINE'S RELIANCE ON FAITH, REASON, AND EXPERIENCE THAT TRANSCENDS THE FIVE SENSES

For Augustine, there is a reliance upon reason but ultimately faith for the evidence from which he arrives at his understanding of God "since men had not the strength to discover the truth by pure reason and therefore, we needed the authority of Holy Writ."[21] Moreover, Augustine also relies upon what could be called nonsensual experience, as when his self-examination reveals to himself (as quoted above): "For Thou hast made us for Thyself and our hearts are restless till they rest in Thee."[22] An overwhelming personal experience of awe or angst or yearning or love may also lead one to accept the existence of a transcendent reality that is beyond the experience of the physical senses. On this basis then, one could conclude as does Augustine (as quoted above): "No soul ever has been able to conceive or ever will be able to conceive anything better than you, the supreme and perfect Good."[23] Through such nonsensual experience, synthetic evidence that God does indeed exist may be attained that could also provide a foundation for any analytical understanding of God.

Kant's arguments of the impossibility of proving God's existence continue with a third argument that Kant calls the physico-theological proof for the existence of God. This argument is rejected by Kant as also being based (at least partially) on the ontological argument. The physico-theological proof for the existence of God holds that both the orderly substance of all things in the world and how these substances are rationally arranged and interact points to a highest being who is both a creator and governor of the world, which is composed of conditioned (dependent), finite beings. But just as the cosmological argument for the existence of God looks for an uncaused cause of all things, which uncaused cause cannot be sensually experienced, the physico-theological proof for the existence of God looks for a highest being that creates and governs

21. Augustine, *Confessions* 6.5.8 (p. 101).
22. Augustine, *Confessions* 1.1.1 (p. 3).
23. Augustine, *Confessions* 7.4.6 (p. 120).

the world, and this highest being cannot be sensually experienced. Both these proofs rely upon a posited concept, as does the ontological argument, i.e., an unproven concept that is put forward or assumed to begin an argument, but, according to Kant, the subject of this argument, i.e., God, is not known with certainty to exist based on the five senses. Kant tells us:

> If the highest being should stand in that chain of conditions, it would be a member in the series, and would, exactly like the lower links above which it is placed, require further investigation with regard to its own still higher ground. If, on the contrary, we mean to separate it from this chain and, as a purely intelligible being, not include it in the series of natural causes, what bridge is then open for reason to pass over and reach it? For all laws determining the transition from effect to causes, nay, all synthesis and expansion of our knowledge in general, refers to nothing but possible experience, and therefore only to the objects of the world of sense, and can have meaning only in regard to them.[24]

What Kant will not consider is that the possible experience that provides the "bridge open for reason to pass over and reach the highest being," while not excluding the experience of the five senses, must also include the possibilities of inclinational, instinctual, emotive, and/or mystical experience. Man's most profound experience that leads to God does not come from the bodily senses alone but from man's deepest yearning, pathos, and angst. Augustine experienced being "naked in his own sight" with his conscience accusing him. Augustine tells us that he "preferred not to see myself. And *You* set me there before my own face that I may see how vile I was, how twisted and unclean and spotted and ulcerous. I saw myself and was horrified; but there was no way to flee from myself."[25] It was God who turned Augustine back toward himself to face the horror of what he had become. This experience would not be an argument based on synthetic judgments where there would be premises verifiable through sense experience. What Augustine describes is an undeniable encounter with God made possible only through the experience of "loathing" his own baseness and unworthiness. Arguments of pure reason that claimed that God cannot be known to exist because God is

---

24. Kant, *Critique of Pure Reason*, Second Division, Transcendental Dialectic, 3.6 (p. 518).

25. Augustine, *Confessions* 8.7.16 (p. 152).

PHILOSOPHICAL PERSPECTIVES THAT CONTRAST WITH AUGUSTINE'S 63

beyond "the objects of the world of sense" cannot dissuade those who have profound experiences of God's presence. Augustine tells us more of his own conversion after experiencing his own wretched vileness made transparent by God:

> Weeping in the most bitter sorrow of my heart . . . suddenly I heard a voice from some nearby house, a boy's voice or girls voice I do not know. . . . Repeated again and again, "Take and read, take and read." . . . I had put down the Apostle's book . . . I snatched it up opened it and in silence read the passage upon which my eyes first fell. "Not in rioting and drunkenness, not in chambering and impurities, not in contention and envy, but put ye on the Lord Jesus Christ and make no provision for the flesh in its concupiscences." I had no wish to read further, and no need. For in that instant, with the very ending of the sentence it was as though a light of utter confidence shone in all my heart, and all the darkness of uncertainty vanished away.[26]

This is the experience of certitude of God's presence and moral direction that transcends the limitations of pure reason based on sense experience.

Kant will, however, advance his judgment of the impossibility of the physico-theological proof for the existence of God to extending this impossibility to the positing of God as a creator. Establishing God as a creator would include God's creating the matter or substance of things in this world, says Kant, and this would require "proving an all-sufficient original being. If we wished to prove the contingency of matter itself, we must have recourse to a transcendental argument, and this is the very thing which was to be avoided here."[27] In other words, Kant is telling us that there is no way to experience the creation of matter by a creator; such experience would transcend the capacity of human sense experience.

While rejecting the notion of proving God as the creator of the world, Kant leaves open the possibility of there being an "architect" or an arranger of this world—a world that empirically displays definite order and harmony according to scientific laws that suggest the existence of such an architect. Kant explains:

> The purposiveness and harmony of so much of nature might prove merely the contingency of the form but not of the matter, that is the substance, in the world; for proving the contingency

26. Augustine, *Confessions* 8.12.29 (pp. 159–60).
27. Kant, *Critique of Pure Reason*, Second Division, Transcendental Dialectic, 3.6 (p. 522).

> of matter would require us to prove in addition that the things of the world would in themselves be incapable of such order and harmony according to universal laws, unless they were the product, even in their substance, of a higher wisdom; proving this would require very different grounds of proof.... The utmost, therefore, that could be established by such a proof would be an architect of the world.... Not a creator of the world to whose idea everything is subject.[28]

This is the closest that Kant will argue on the basis of pure reason for the possible existence of a God, but a God who is an architect and not a creator. In making this distinction Kant will separate knowledge of things empirically observed in this world, which he calls "knowledge of nature," from speculative knowledge, which relates to "concepts of an object which can never be reached in experience." All that Kant will allow is that the order and purposive form of things in the world and how things causally interact suggest the existence of an architect or governor, but even this conclusion transcends our sense experience. Therefore, says Kant, based on pure reason not only can one not prove the existence of a creator God; one cannot even infer with certitude the existence of God who is an architect or governor of the world because we lack actual sensual experience of such a being. Says Kant:

> If from the existence of things in the world we infer their cause, this inference is part not of the natural but of the speculative use of reason. The natural use of reason refers, as empirically contingent, not to the things themselves (substances), but only that which happens, that is, their states, to some cause; but it could know only speculatively that a substance itself (matter) is contingent in its existence. And even if we were speaking only of the form of the world, the manner of its combination and the changes thereof, and tried to infer from this a cause totally different from the world, then this would again be a judgment of merely speculative reason; for the object here is not an object of any possible experience. In that case, however, the principle of causality, which is valid only within the field of experience and is utterly useless, nay, even meaningless, one-sided, would be totally diverted from its proper destination.[29]

---

28. Kant, *Critique of Pure Reason*, Second Division, Transcendental Dialectic, 3.6 (p. 522).

29. Kant, *Critique of Pure Reason*, Second Division, Transcendental Dialectic, 3.7 (p. 528).

In saying that only through unexperienced speculative knowledge could one argue that "a substance (matter) is contingent in its existence" (a notion that Kant would claim to be unprovable), Kant is referring to the cause or creation of the material substratum of all things, i.e., matter itself, a long-time target of agnostic philosophers who especially reject the Christian concept of creation *ex nihilo* or creation of everything, including matter, from nothing preexisting. It is precisely the Christian concept of creation *ex nihilo* that Augustine accepts on the basis of faith as well as of reason. Augustine tells us that if God made:

> The earth, that is, the world and everything in it, out of some antecedent matter . . . or if he created them from matter that was formless. . . . Yet in no way are we to believe that the material of which we are speaking could by itself be co-eternal and coeval [of the same time or duration] with God. We are referring here to the material of which the world was made, be it formless, unseen, or whatever else might constitute the mode of its existence. The mode of being that it possesses, one which enables it to receive the forms of different things, it owes to Almighty God alone, by whose gracious disposition it not only has a form but becomes capable of receiving other forms as well. The difference between something already endowed with form and something that possesses form only potentially consists in this: what has been created already has form, while what is capable of receiving form has yet to receive it. The one who confers forms on things also confers the potential to receive form. . . . It is with absolute justification, then, that we believe God made everything out of nothing, for even if the world was created from some matter previously existing, that same material was created from nothing.[30]

Beyond the difficulties in proving God's existence, there is the added difficulty of explaining how God creates *ex nihilo* matter or already formed matter, i.e., from nothing preexisting, without resorting to pantheism. An answer to this latter problem might include the concept of God who thinks the divine thought of himself immanently, within himself, and God's necessary ability to think thoughts transcendentally that do not essentially relate to himself yet which divine thoughts extend beyond himself to include the creation of all things outside himself. Once again, Kant would reject such speculations as unprovable because such arguments are not based on premises that can be verified through sense experience.

---

30. Augustine, *Faith and the Creed*, 156–57.

Yet, Kant's philosophy has a certain element of unverifiability regarding the nature of scientific proof. Kant's philosophy is based in large part on what Kant called a Copernican experiment[31] in knowledge in which man's mind and its a priori conditions and categories of thought are the bases for how we can understand our sense experience and know the world around us. This occurs, says Kant, in man's understanding mind, which informs the way the world appears to us, rather than man's understanding conforming to the way the world actually exists in itself. For Kant the world is made understandable by the conditions and categories of the human mind, rather than the human mind conforming to the world as it really exists in itself. Further, what we understand and know about the world or an object in the world are sense appearances of the thing, or phenomena; we perceive and understand appearances and not the thing "as it really exists in itself," which Kant calls the noumenon. Things in themselves, noumena, are not experienced and are really unknowable but are considered by the understanding as the necessary means by which the phenomena or appearances of things are grounded so that in fact phenomena can appear to our senses. Kant tells us:

> It seems to be implied in our very concept that if we call certain objects, as appearances, beings of sense (phenomena), by distinguishing the mode in which we intuit them from the nature of those objects in themselves, then we may either take the same objects in their latter capacity . . . not [as] objects of our senses at all . . . [but] as objects merely through the understanding, and contrast them with beings of sense, calling them beings of the understanding (noumena).[32]

According to Kant, then, without the categories of the understanding structuring phenomena, such as the judgments of relation, which includes the category of causality, there can be no understanding that the appearance of subject B is brought about as an effect by subject A. We can know nothing of the appearing outside world and its objects without the a priori conditions and categories of the understanding structuring the sense perceptions that appear to us. While the noumena, or the unknowable things in themselves, are the necessary means by which the phenomena appear to us, there remains in Kantian thought a deficiency regarding that certitude on which science must rely, in that we never

---

31. See Kant, *Critique of Pure Reason*, preface to the second edition, 18.

32. Kant, *Critique of Pure Reason*, First Division, Transcendental Analytic, 2.3 (p. 258).

know for certain that what our understanding imposes on the world outside the mind is really the basis for absolutely predictable, scientific laws. All that Kant's transcendental idealism provides is verifiability and the necessity of the a priori conditions and categories of the understanding that render phenomena knowable but do not render knowable the real thing-in-itself. It could be argued that from Kant's philosophical perspective, an assumption is made that all we can ever know with certitude concerns appearances of the phenomenal world and not of the actual world.

It has been the philosophy of Immanuel Kant that has arguably dominated much of contemporary thought and led to the skeptical limitations of positivism—the modern philosophy that requires only empirical verifiability for acquiring knowledge of reality. Positivism has dominated our contemporary world and done much to erode Christianity in our time. Ironically Kant will argue that it is the limitations of pure reason that have opened the door for faith by rejecting the feasibility of rationally demonstrating God's existence. Kant claims:

> I am not allowed even to assume, for the sake of the necessary practical use of my reason, God, freedom, immortality, unless at the same time I deprive speculative reason of its pretensions to transcendent insights. Reason, namely, in order to arrive at these, must employ principles which extend only to the objects of possible experience and which, if in spite of this they are applied also to what cannot be an object of experience, actually always change this into an appearance, thus rendering all practical expansion of pure reason impossible. Hence, I had to suspend knowledge in order to make room for belief.[33]

Arguably such suspension of knowledge does not "make room for belief"; rather, it stifles belief by destroying that mutual support that faith and reason should provide in the pursuit of truth in the tradition of Augustine. However, it would be a mistake to maintain that Augustine believed that reason could provide a foundation for all aspects of Christian faith because, says Augustine, some and possibly much of Christian doctrine must ultimately rely upon faith alone and so a clear demarcation must be made regarding "to what extent reason comes to the support of religion, what lies outside the scope of reason and belongs to faith alone, what should be held first and last, what the whole body of doctrine amounts to, and what is a sure and suitable foundation of

---

33. Kant, *Critique of Pure Reason*, preface, second edition, 25.

Catholic faith."[34] By referring to "what lies outside the scope of reason and belongs to faith alone," Augustine does provide the ground for inferring that the noumena, i.e., the unknowable, does exist, at least for man on earth, regarding the supernatural kingdom of heaven whose mysteries the believer accepts in faith. Nevertheless, it is Kant's agnostic thinking that has helped facilitate the fragmentation of Christianity's impact on the modern world, on morality, and especially on faith in a divine order and purpose for mankind.

KANT'S MORAL ORDER THROUGH PRACTICAL REASON VS. AUGUSTINE'S RELIANCE ON REASON, INTUITION, AND SPIRITUAL "SEEING"

Regarding morality, Kant claims the reality of universal moral law is based on pure practical reason alone and mandates that it is rational man's duty to follow this universal moral law. The fundamental law of pure practical reason regarding this moral order, says Kant, is the following: "So act that the maxim of your will could always hold at the same time as a principle in a giving of universal law."[35] Kant's maxim can be judged to be a corollary to the golden rule in that any person in acting should act in a way that he or she would have others act toward oneself. Kant adds that "pure reason is practical of itself alone and gives to the human being a universal law we call the moral law."[36] Because the moral law is rational, necessary, and universal, it "applies to all finite beings that have reason and will" and carries with it a moral obligation binding on all human persons. Kant further tells us that this moral law is

> an imperative that commands categorically because the law is unconditional; the relation of such a will to this law is dependence under the name of obligation, which signifies a necessitation, though only by reason and its object of law, to an action which is called Duty.[37]

Kant amplifies this moral law by telling us:

---

34. Augustine, *Enchiridion*, "Origin of the Handbook" 4 (p. 274).
35. Kant, *Critique of Practical Reason* 1.1.1.7 (p. 28).
36. Kant, *Critique of Practical Reason*, 1.1.1.7 (p. 29).
37. Kant, *Critique of Practical Reason* 1.1.7 [5.32] (p. 29).

> It now follows of itself that in the order of ends the human being (and with him every rational being) is an end in itself, that is, can never be used merely as a means by anyone . . . without being at the same time himself an end, and that humanity in our person must, accordingly, be holy to ourselves: for he is the subject of the moral law and so of that which is holy in itself.[38]

What becomes more problematic for Immanuel Kant is the application of these abstract principles of moral law to the everyday problems of human life, with their contingencies and extenuating circumstances that make moral choices from which the human will must freely choose more difficult to know by relying upon pure practical reason alone. Kant rejects any reliance upon natural inclinations or impulses, which he denies have any rational grounds for moral obligation. For Kant, moral obligation does not arise from desire, impulse, or inclination at all but only from one's need to follow the moral law understood through pure practical reason.

The difficulty with Kant's moral theory is that he assumes that the human person understands the moral law and chooses to follow the moral law only on the basis of pure practical reason as if each human person chooses only with his rational intellect. To begin with, man is more than a rational being deliberating through the conflicting and confusing moral issues of everyday life only with his pure intellect utilizing pure reason. Man must and does rely upon his faith and inclinations and his moral habits, often times without the luxury of careful deliberation as to how to deal with immediate, everyday problems with moral implications that at once require prompt decision-making. Man's emotions, desires, and impulses no doubt need to be subject to moral training and rational restraints, but these human inclinations are a necessary part of the human person's decision-making. Augustine, as did Cicero, understood the importance of basic human inclinations and how they direct human persons in general ways to pursue moral goals. When the acceptance of a divine creator is a major factor in one's moral perspective, there comes with it an understanding that human nature, as well as natural law, are part of the human disposition to make moral decisions. This is not to denigrate the use of rational deliberation in understanding and following moral law, nor is it a denial of man's fallen nature or his deficient inclinations; rather, it is an insistence on understanding that the human person

---

38. Kant, *Critique of Practical Reason* 2.1.5 [5.132] (p. 106).

must rely upon more than his reason in understanding the moral order and in making moral decisions.

In the interest of fairness to Kant, it should be noted that on the basis of practical reason Kant will allow the possibility of God's existence as a means of sustaining man's obligation to follow the universal moral law. Kant does this in order to preserve the moral disposition of finite human beings who might find their grave obligation to their moral duty to observe the universal moral law more understandable and more doable with their acceptance of the existence of a supreme being who is the author of the obligation to follow the moral law:

> Now, it was a duty for us to promote the highest good; hence there is in us not merely the warrant but also the necessity, as a need connected with duty to presuppose the possibility of this highest good, which, since it is possible only under the condition of the existence of God, connects the presupposition of the existence of God inseparably with duty; that is, it is morally necessary to assume the existence of God.[39]

But Immanuel Kant is quick to add that for those who are skeptical about the existence of God:

> It is not to be understood by this that it is necessary to assume the existence of God as a ground of all obligation in general (for this rests, as has been sufficiently shown, solely on the other autonomy of reason itself). What belongs to duty here is only the striving to produce and promote the highest good in the world, the possibility of which can therefore be postulated, while our reason finds this thinkable only on the presupposition of a supreme intelligence; to assume the existence of this supreme intelligence is thus connected with the consciousness of our duty, although this assumption itself belongs to theoretical reason.... It can be called a hypothesis; but in relation to the intelligibility of an object given us by the moral law (the highest good), and consequently of a need for practical purposes.[40]

Kant, we have seen, makes his argument for rejecting proofs for the existence of God or there being any certitude of God's existence from the standpoint of reason alone based on the evidence, or lack thereof, provided by sensory experience alone. Augustine's argument for God's existence certainly includes sensory experience but also transcends the

39. Kant, *Critique of Practical Reason* 2.1.5 [5.125] (p. 101).
40. Kant, *Critique of Practical Reason* 2.1.5 [5.125] (pp. 101–2).

PHILOSOPHICAL PERSPECTIVES THAT CONTRAST WITH AUGUSTINE'S   71

empirical evidence of creation and involves a spiritual experience of the loving goodness of God's presence in his life. Expressing remorse for his life of vice, Augustine extols the lofty qualities of honor and beauty, which are beyond sensory experience:

> I did not realize that it belonged to the very heart of my wretchedness to be so drowned and blinded in it that I could not conceive that light of honor, and of beauty loved for its own sake, which the eye of the flesh does not see but only the innermost soul.[41]

Augustine tells us that even those blinded by sin and seeking to avoid God find themselves stumbling against him and perhaps experiencing his wrath. Such experience might transcend sensory experience but might also incorporate an unavoidable suffering of anguish and fear:

> Let the wicked in their restlessness go from Thee and flee away.... Where indeed did they flee to when they fled from Thy face? Or where dost Thou not find them? The truth is that they fled, that they might not see Thee who sawest them. And so with eyes blinded they stumbled against Thee—for thou dost not desert any of the things that Thou hast made—they stumbled against Thee in their injustice and justly suffered, since they had withdrawn from Thy mercy and stumbled against Thy justice and fallen headlong upon Thy wrath.... Let them therefore turn back and seek Thee because Thou hast not deserted Thy creatures as they have deserted their Creator. Let them turn back, and behold Thou art there in their hearts, in the hearts of those that confess to Thee and cast themselves upon Thee and weep on Thy breast as they return from ways of anguish.[42]

For anyone who experiences such anguish of heart and who turns back and seeks the Creator, there is likely no denying the reality of the existence of God from whom they flee. Anguish of heart can result in a kind of spiritual seeing of God's presence. But, for the critical rationalist like Immanuel Kant, emotional and psychological states of mind provide no evidence or certitude for the existence of the realities that are claimed to be their cause. The metaphysical problem with Immanuel Kant is his insistence on the existence of this world and universe being a noumenal world that is unknowable in-itself. When a philosophy leads human culture to tend to believe that all that human beings can be sure of is sense

41. Augustine, *Confessions* 6.16.26 (p. 114).
42. Augustine, *Confessions* 5.2.2 (pp. 75–76).

knowledge of appearances, and a rational intellect with only conditions, and categories of pure reason that subjectively order this world of appearances, then there is an accompanying tendency to view moral law as a matter of opinion even when there is a general acceptance of the golden rule. Even with the golden rule there can be arbitrary, subjective moral ends that can be in accord with one's own preference of what one chooses to pursue for oneself as well as for others.

If, as in the case of Augustine, good natural inclinations (excepting those distorted by our fallen nature) are viewed as God-given, they provide moral guidance for the individual or for society when pure reason alone proves incapable of doing so. But for Christian believers, there is an acceptance of a God-ordered creation that includes the ability of human persons rationally to understand natural law, as well as to understand natural law by a reliance on faith and God's revelation. This, of course, conflicts with Immanuel Kant's view of knowledge of only a phenomenal world and not of things as they are in themselves. Kant would claim that the only viable way to establish objective moral law is on the basis of man's being rational and not on objective realities whose origin is beyond human persons. The a priori categories that all rational human persons possess equip them to establish a rule of behavior that requires each person to act only in those ways that can be applied universally to every other rational person. Kant argues that "the maxim of your will could always hold at the same time as a principle in a giving of universal law."[43] As a principle of universal law this maxim provides a "categorical imperative" that binds all rational persons to a principle for moral conduct out of duty.

The difficulty with Kant's categorical imperative is that it succumbs to a subjectivity that each person potentially can assert as the maxim of his/her individual will. Even Kant's primary provision of his categorical imperative remains subjective, such as his contention that a person must be able to will so that the maxim he/she wills be also a universal moral law. Such a universal law would be determined by the subjective aspirations of the choices of each individual will notwithstanding the willingness of any individual to extend his action as morally permissible to any and all other persons. A person willing to choose to abuse drugs or to drink to excess, for example, could excuse his behavior by extending the same right to all other persons. However, for Christians or for

---

43. Kant, *Critique of Practical Reason* 1.1.1.7 (p. 28).

those who accept a transcendent moral order, the Kantian categorical imperative does not make the self-destructive action of this person (who abuses drugs or alcohol) serve as a maxim that is objectively and morally permissible.

A Kantian corollary of the categorical imperative mandates that persons be treated never as a means to an end but always as ends in themselves, because they too are rational persons subject to the same principle of universal moral law. While this corollary does contain a basis of moral objectivity, as an abstract principle, it lacks any connection to an understanding of natural law and how natural law developed (let alone any connection to an understanding of divinely revealed morality), so that this principle remains incapable of providing specific as well as universal moral direction for the acting person.

Augustine has already demonstrated his willingness to using rationality in applying an objective moral law as applicable to, and knowable by, all human persons. But Augustine bases his understanding of the moral law on God who created man with an immanent understanding of this law written on the human heart, and on man's ability to know God's presence in the world based on man's own experience of his need for God and on faith in God's revelation. This experience of the need for God has already been examined in Augustine's *Confessions* and shows itself as a yearning for God that does not abate until one finds God. Here, Augustine goes beyond Kant's pure reason that relies only on man's five senses to prove the reality of God, and, instead, Augustine also relies upon man's faith (as well as reason) and upon human instinctual and emotional intuition (aided by supernatural help) to produce a spiritual "seeing" needed to experience God's presence.

KANT'S TRANSCENDENTAL KNOWLEDGE AND HEGEL'S ABSOLUTE IDEALISM COUNTERED BY AUGUSTINE'S MAINTAINING GOD AS THE TRANSCENDENT CREATOR

As philosophy developed in the nineteenth century, the acceptance of the noumenon by Kant's transcendental idealism was questioned and rejected by some thinkers who espoused absolute idealism that conceives of all reality, both in the transcendental human mind before experience and in the exterior world after experience, as being objectively rational and knowable. If the noumenon as the thing-in-itself can be known and does not exist as unknowable, then neither do the categories of the understanding structure mere appearances or phenomena of things, but rather the categories then are not only structures for the human mind, but also these categories provide the structure of the real things-in-themselves that are perceived by our senses. We are then back to the realist point of view of Aristotle, used as a foundation to some extent by Hegel, who developed his absolute idealism with the view that the world and all things in it are rational, universal notions yet to be fully explicated by the rational mind. In the preface to his *Philosophy of Right* Hegel explains:

> What is rational is actual and what is actual is rational. On this conviction the plain man like the philosopher takes a stand, and from it, philosophy starts in its study of the universe of mind as well as the universe of nature.[44]

Although it is often argued that Immanuel Kant saved science from the radical skepticism of David Hume, it was Hegel who really placed science back on the verifiable foundation of a rationally structured world that corresponds in a unique "identity-in-difference" with a rationally structured mind. The concept of causality in the rational mind known a priori comprehends the real causality of things in the real world known a posteriori (after experience). With Hegel, the noumenon does not exist as an unknowable thing-in-itself. For Hegel, rather, the unknown (in distinction to the unknowable) is constantly being made known through the rational determinations of the conscious minds of men.

The importance of the world and the whole universe and all things in it as well as the rational structure of men's minds provide even more evidence for the physico-theological proof for the existence of God, at least God as an architect and governor. When Kant speaks of "the purposiveness and harmony of so much of nature," he is still referring to nature understood as a phenomenon, i.e., as nature appears to man and not as nature is in-itself. What Hegel argues, however, is that nature and everything in it is rational in-itself and hence subject to the laws of causality just as the mind understands through its category of causality; this categorical causality is applicable to objects that interact in the real world. As such, for the Christian when it is understood that the world is rationally constituted and governed by scientific laws that apply to

---

44. Hegel, *Natural Law and Political Science in Outline; Elements of the Philosophy of Right*, preface, 10.

things-in-themselves, there is a more compelling connection to an architect and governor of this world who created things-in-themselves and maintains these "purposive and harmonious" laws.

It can be objected, however, that Kant's counterargument still stands that a creator cannot be proven with certitude to exist because there can be no sense experience of such a creator. However, what Hegel's philosophy does provide is a rational ground for the feasibility of how God (assuming that he exists as a personal transcendent reality, which Hegel rejects) could create *ex nihilo* and how speculative reason (which Kant rejects as not being based on sense experience) could demonstrate this feasibility. If everything that exists is a concept or idea, then what science refers to as matter and its properties are nothing but universal concepts. Hegel writes his philosophy in esoteric and complex language, whereas the twentieth-century Princeton professor of philosophy W. T. Stace writes in his seminal work on Hegel in clear and understandable English:

> An object is not an object unless it stands in relation to a subject. The universe is nothing but the content of consciousness. If we deny these truths we land ourselves in the quagmire of contradictions connected with the theory of the unknowable. But if we admit them we are bound to admit also the objectivity of concepts or universals. For then the object is wholly and solely the object as we know it. And we know it only as a congeries [interrelated groupings or collections] of universals.[45]

Hegel accepted the concept behind all idealism, viz., that there is an identity between knowing and being, but he wished to explain how this identity is preserved while there is a distinction between the knower and the thing known. Hegel developed the concept of identity-in-difference, which Stace explains:

> But if subject and object are identical, they are also distinct. It is certain that, in some sense or other, the object stands over against me. It is the not-self.... But we may say at once that their identity is compatible with their difference. That the thing is identical with the thought,—this means that there is no absolute separation between subject and object, for the object is within the subject. That the thing is different from the thought,—this means that the subject expels part of itself, viz., the object, from itself, and opposes itself to it. This stone is certainly external to me. It is not me. This is the separation of knowing and being.

---

45. Stace, *Philosophy of Hegel*, 73.

> But the stone is still within the unity of thought. It is not external to me in the sense that it is something utterly outside thought, unknowable. This is the identity of knowing and being.... If the thing could break away completely from the unity of thought, it would become an unknowable thing-in-itself. And that is impossible.[46]

Because in Hegel's philosophy there is no thing-in-itself that is unknowable, each object exists as a rationally structured reality that is known through the rational consciousness of man. It is the rational consciousness of man (i.e., consciousness imbued with the a priori categories) that unifies the collection or congeries of universals of the object into a single idea that identifies the object's essential meaning. But once rational consciousness realizes that there is no absolute separation between itself, viz., the subject, and the determined object, then consciousness realizes also that there is no complete separation between the rationally structured object and the conscious idea that makes the object definable in the mind of the knower. Once it is accepted that there is no unknowable in the cosmos and that rational persons can collectively determine greater and greater knowledge of the world of nature and of the world of society, the philosophical mind can self-consciously conceive of knowledge as absolute. This means that for Hegel there are no limitations on man's mind coming to understand reason as the God-like spirit that progresses through history and allows rational minds to collectively comprehend through time every obscure object, question, or difficulty that may be encountered.

A problem remains, however, regarding the idea of God as reason itself that is immanently present in the minds of rational persons and especially in the minds of philosophers of absolute idealism. While absolute knowledge is supposed to be a realizable goal so that there exists nothing real that is not knowable (or can become knowable in time), fundamental and essential questions remain unanswered and mired in mystery regarding the basic laws of science generally. The question of why the material universe acts and changes according to precise laws uncovered by science can never be fully answered. Why does matter which can only be found as a formed substance even in its most primal state and is always in the state of ongoing change and transformation possess an atomic and molecular structure that is ordered so as to act in certain ways and not

---

46. Stace, *Philosophy of Hegel*, 73.

in other ways? If reason is immanent in the minds of men as well as in the structure of the entire cosmos and all things in it, from where does the logical structure of things receive their precise order and predictable capabilities in a constantly changing flow of energy transforming things, substances, lifeforms, and organisms that perdure, live, grow, and die, eventually giving rise to other forms of energy, substance, and life? It is a difficult acceptance to make that, even after allowing for survival of the fittest and an immensely long amount of time, atoms and molecules result into more complex substances, organisms, and even into intelligent beings. From the chaotic beginnings of the universe—a presumed big bang of primal energy—to the complexities of human beings, who discover and craft science and invent technology, there needs to be a more convincing argument than that of some materialists who would posit that reason is in the matter and in things themselves that evolve.

While the realist point of view argues that matter is only found as a formed substance that can be rationally analyzed and known, there are limits to human understanding that seemingly cannot be transcended. The author Lincoln Barnett writing in his book *The Universe and Dr. Einstein* (endorsed in a foreword by Albert Einstein) states:

> The factors that first led physicists to distrust their faith in a smoothly functioning mechanical universe loomed on the inner and outer horizons of knowledge—in the unseen realm of the atom and in the fathomless depths of intergalactic space. To describe these phenomena quantitatively, two great theoretical systems were developed between 1900 and 1927. One was the Quantum Theory, dealing with the fundamental units of matter and energy. The other was Relativity, dealing with space, time and the structure of the universe as a whole.
>
> Both are now accepted pillars of modern physical thought. Both describe phenomena in their fields in terms of consistent, mathematical relationship. They do not answer the Newtonian "how" any more than Newton's laws answered the Aristotelian "why." They provide equations, for example, that define with great accuracy the laws governing the radiation and propagation of light. But, the actual mechanism by which the atom radiates light and by which light is propagated through space remains one of nature's supreme mysteries.[47]

---

47. Barrett, *Universe and Dr. Einstein*, 17.

While science and technology continuously uncover new discoveries and innovations that reveal penetrating knowledge of things in themselves previously unknown, there remains in nature impenetrable mystery.

What is insightful in Hegel's philosophy is the concept of identity-in-difference between subject and object, which can be related to a transcendent God who can think the unification of congeries of universals in a given object that is a real unity distinct from himself. God then incorporates his rational designations of the universe and all things in it through his divine thought. Then the concept of creation *ex nihilo* is provided a rational grounding. If the true concept of reality is nothing but the universal ideas in the mind of God who knows the objective world and all things in it, then this concept can be extended to include the a priori categories of the human mind, which God knows and conceived for man's knowledge of the world that God's thought created and ordered.

Augustine describes the existence of the earth and all things in it and asks whether the things of earth are self-dependent, i.e., whether they are God:

> And what is this God? I asked the earth and it answered, "I am not He"; and all things that are in the earth made the same confession. I asked the sea in the deeps and the creeping things, and they answered, "We are not your God; seek higher." I asked the winds that blow, and the whole air with all that is in it answered, "Anaximenes was wrong; I am not God." I asked the heavens, the sun, the moon, the stars, and they answered, "Neither are we God whom you seek." And I said to all the things that throng about the gateway of the senses: "Tell me of my God, since you are not He. Tell me something of Him." And they cried out in a great voice: He made us.[48]

Augustine's main different difference with Hegel is his insistence on God's existence as a transcendent supreme being who created matter with an assigned form, without which form things simply would not exist as the rationally constructed beings into which they have developed and exist. Augustine's philosophy is a rational realism rooted in an acceptance of a transcendent God/Creator who revealed himself and whose revelation is to be accepted in faith as providing greater knowledge of God, man, and the universe. Augustine's commentary on the order and number constituting all things in the cosmos and on the nature of matter and form

---

48. Augustine, *Confessions* 10.6.9 (pp. 193–94).

ordained by God are found in the analysis of *On the Free Choice of the Will* in the next chapter.

HEGEL CONCEIVES OF THE TRINITY AS REASON DESCRIBED IN PICTORIAL TERMS; AUGUSTINE VIEWS REASON IN NEED OF DIVINE AUTHORITY TO REVEAL THE TRUE DEITY AS BEING THREE PERSONS IN ONE GOD

When Hegel comes to explaining God, he refers to metaphorical or pictorial language as being the preliminary, immediate, and nonphilosophical way in which a person of faith has conceived of reason as the Absolute Idea. For the Christian, the divine being is three Persons in one God who is transcendent to the human person's existence. But Hegel says that in referring to the triune God, there has been

> the elevation of [God's] existence into the sphere of figurative thought [*Vorstellung*]; just as in general, to take a concrete example, the "this" of sense, when transcended, is first of all the "thing" of "perception," and is not yet the "universal" of "understanding." . . .
>
> This individual human being, then, which Absolute Being is revealed to be, goes through in its own case as an individual the process found in sense existence. He [Christ] is the immediately present God; in consequence, His being passes over into His having been. Consciousness, for which God is thus sensuously present, ceases to see Him, to hear Him. . . . He has now arisen in Spirit, as He formerly rose before consciousness as an object existing in the sphere of sense. For consciousness which sees and hears Him by sense, is one which is itself merely an immediate consciousness, which has not canceled and transcended the disparateness of objectivity, has not withdrawn it into pure thought, but knows this objectively presented individual, and not itself, as spirit.[49]

What Hegel is telling us is that God is thought of figuratively or in a pictorial way by those who have religious minds. Hegel refers to Christ as accepted by believers as being "this individual human being, then, which Absolute Being is revealed to be" and as he who is essentially present before consciousness as "the immediately present God." For Hegel the

49. Hegel, *Phenomenology of Mind*, (CC). Religion, C Revealed Religion, 762–63.

Absolute Being is only fully conceived by pure thought as the "spirit" of reason. In short, Hegel does not accept a transcendent, personal supreme being who is three Persons in one God, but rather presents the Hegelian rational spirit as being pictorially expressed in Christianity as the divine Trinity. What is interesting about Hegel is that, similar to Porphyry in ancient times, who spoke of three *principia* composing the divine substance, Hegel views the Trinity as being portrayed in pictorial thought as the Absolute Idea with its three moments of rationality (the universal, the particular, and the individual) in which God reveals himself in the doctrines of Christianity as Father, Son, and Holy Spirit. Stace explains in his commentary on Hegel's *Encyclopedia of the Philosophical Sciences* in section 753 of "The Absolute Religion: Christianity":

> The Kingdom of the Father . . . is the doctrine of the nature of God as He is in Himself before the creation of the world. God, as such, is the Idea, the Notion. The Notion is threefold; and God is therefore threefold in Himself. As universal He is God the Father. The universal produces the particular out of itself, i.e., God the Father begets God the Son. The particular returning into the universal, is the individual, i.e., God the Holy Spirit.[50]

As Augustine found and welcomed rational justification for Christian belief in the neo-Platonic philosophers such as Plotinus and Porphyry, so too Hegel's explanation of the Trinity provides some rational basis for understanding God as he has revealed himself. For Augustine then, the basis for understanding truths of the faith is a reliance upon both reason and authority, i.e., upon reason and revealed Christian dogma (and of course upon experience). There are numerous instances throughout the Augustinian corpus where reason and authority are given as the foundation especially for knowledge of the faith in one transcendent and omnipotent God who exists as a Trinity of Father, Son, and Holy Spirit. In *Against the Academicians*, an early work written in 386, Augustine tells us that "no one doubts that we are prompted to learn by the twin forces of authority and reason. Therefore, I am resolved not to depart from the authority of Christ in any score whatsoever."[51]

Philosophy has and always will have an influence on the beliefs, practices, and culture in which human persons find themselves historically. So too, if Christianity is to increase its influence and practice, there

---

50. Stace, *Philosophy of Hegel*, 511.
51. Augustine, *Against the Academicians*, 3.5.20.43 (p. 92).

needs to be some philosophical basis for explaining the role of the church in the modern world and ultimately how man finds unity with God. Stace explains in section 755, "The Kingdom of the Spirit," how Hegel's philosophy (notwithstanding Hegel's rejection of a transcendent personal God) provides some rational grounding for this unity:

> God and man are one. There unity is now represented in this fashion, that the spirit of God is in man, not however in man as particular man, but in a community of men, the Church. The Holy Spirit is actually present in His Church. If the Kingdom of the Father was the Logical Idea, God before the creation of the world; and if the Kingdom of the Son was the Idea in its Otherness, nature; the Kingdom of the Spirit, as the third moment, the moment of individuality, is the unity of two foregoing. For the Church is, on the one hand, the pure spirit of God, but it is also, secondly, in the world, actually present. It is the kingdom of God upon earth.[52]

But in Hegel's philosophy, without a personal, transcendent, and providential God, the spirit of God in man is really the spirit of reason in man and thus arguably reduced to the rational spirit of man with no hope of salvation in union with a transcendent God. The kingdom of God on earth then becomes the godless city of man in which Augustine found much of the evils of this world—evils that man alone with all his rationality cannot dispel.

Ultimately, for Hegel, the Absolute Idea, all of reality, all that actually exists, is incorporated within the rational self-consciousness of philosophers of absolute idealism whose philosophy comprehends the identity of the knowing subject and the potentially all-knowable object. Stace tells us:

> The philosophic mind which should have attained omniscience would be nothing less than the mind of God. And it does not appear ridiculous to say that the purpose of the universe is the complete realization of the mind of God in actuality. The fact that Hegel should have regarded his own system as this final and absolute knowledge has no doubt an element of absurdity in it.[53]

---

52. Stace, *Philosophy of Hegel*, 513–14.
53. Stace, *Philosophy of Hegel*, 517.

However, Hegel cannot find rational grounds for accepting a personal and transcendent deity (beyond metaphoric representation) who is the Absolute Being from whom the actual, rational universe is conceived and created. And yet it follows from Hegel's concept of the identity-indifference between the subject knower and the object known, which precludes any absolute separation between the two, that the absolute subject could be God who continually conceives and hence creates and preserves the objective world and all things in it, including rational man. But this is not the inference made by Hegel or by Hegelians. Understanding God as the omnipotent, omniscient Creator who is at once a transcendent, personal, and providential God is considered as *Vorstellung* by Hegel, i.e., figurative or pictorial thought that does not rise to the level of self-conscious reason that can only be found in the minds of those philosophers, especially those who, like Hegel, have arrived at absolute idealism. For Hegel, within absolute idealism, which is really absolute reason, in the minds of philosophical persons there is a dialectical progression of the rational idea, which in its totality encompasses all of reality.

In Hegel's philosophy the Idea in itself is the Logical Idea, which contains hidden within itself its opposite, which is determined through deduction, viz., the Idea outside itself that is also called Nature. The synthesis of the Logical Idea and Nature is the Idea in and for itself or Spirit. Within each of the three categories of the Idea are subcategories that are dialectically deduced. Focusing on the third category of Spirit, there is the deduction of these three subcategories: Subjective Spirit includes anthropology, phenomenology, and psychology: the Objective Spirit includes morality, social ethics, and law; and the third subcategory deduced under Spirit is Absolute Spirit, which includes art, religion, and philosophy. With philosophy the Absolute Spirit reaches its highest expression, which metaphorically can be called God's self-conscious thought expressed by philosophers and most adequately expressed by Hegel.

But Hegel's is not a philosophy men could easily live by even if it is politicized as a type of statism or reduced to a scientific positivism. In Hegel's philosophy reason is absolute, and there is no ground for faith (except by metaphor) nor the possible existence of a providential God who cares for mankind. For Hegel, goodness is not the attribute of a transcendent, perfect God but is rather the realization of perfect reason. Evil is not the absence of the good that God created for each being. Evil, for Hegel, is the absence of the rational nature of each being. As Hegelianism applies to the nation state, with no caring God, the moral order is based on reason alone, which determines which states should go to war depending on real threats from foreign nations. On the basis in part of the human strength or deficiencies of their expendable citizenry and such factors as military and financial preparedness, leaders decide based on credible threats from abroad and vital self-interest whether their state should go to war and be successful or be subjugated. Hegel argues:

> War has the higher significance that by its agency . . . the ethical health of peoples is preserved in their indifference to the stabilization of finite institutions; just as the blowing of the winds preserves the sea from the foulness which would be the result of a prolonged calm, so also corruption in nations would be the product of prolonged, let alone "perpetual" peace. . . .
>
> This fact appears in history in various forms, e.g., successful wars have checked domestic unrest and consolidated the power of the state at home. Other phenomena illustrate the same point: e.g., peoples unwilling or afraid to tolerate sovereignty at home have been subjugated from abroad, and they have struggled for their independence . . . their freedom has died from the fear of dying.[54]

For Augustine, the Christian citizen of an earthly city is always subject to God's moral authority written on the human heart and revealed in divine revelation (and thus beyond reason alone). Still, the Christian must always strive to obey just laws and live harmoniously with those fellow citizens who are not Christian and who seek their advantage and self-interest solely in this earthly life. At the same time, Christians must obey the authority of the state of which they are citizens and work for the maintenance of peace and well-being within their nation and, to the best of their ability, with other nations. Augustine draws a contrast between those who are solely residents of the earthly city and seek its advantages, and those Christian believers who, while making good use of the temporal advantages of the earthly city, do not allow the goods of this world to deter their efforts to advance forward toward God and the heavenly city. Augustine tells us that, on the one hand "a household of men who do not live by faith strives to find an earthly peace in the goods and advantages which belong to this temporal life." While, in contrast, "a household of men who live by faith look forward to the blessings which are promised as eternal in the life to come," and while "such men make use of earthly

---

54. Hegel, *Natural Law and Political Science*, Third Part, Ethical Life, iii.324 (p. 210).

and temporal things like pilgrims: they are not captivated by them, nor are they deflected by them from their progress toward God."[55]

While both Christians and non-Christians make use of earthly peace, the Christian looks to be a resident of the Heavenly City in pilgrimage on earth and to direct earthly peace toward heavenly peace. Says Augustine:

> Even the Heavenly City makes use of earthly peace during her pilgrimage, and desires and maintains the co-operation of men's wills in attaining those things which belong to the mortal nature of man, in so far as this may be allowed without prejudice to true godliness and religion. Indeed, she directs that earthly peace towards heavenly peace.... For this peace is a perfectly ordered and perfectly harmonious fellowship in the enjoyment of God, and of one another in God.... This peace the Heavenly City possesses in faith while on its pilgrimage and by this faith it lives righteously, directing towards the attainment of that peace every good act which it performs either for God, or—since the city's life is inevitably a social one—for neighbor.[56]

For Augustine then, it is critical for the maintenance of peace on earth that there must be a respect for all peoples and no injury made among men in their pursuits of the necessities of life, while at the same time there must be a recognition of God and of one another in God, so that earthly peace reflects the peace of heaven. Augustine makes no promise of perpetual peace among men and among nations, but he does add regarding the peace of heaven:

> This peace is a perfectly ordered and perfectly harmonious fellowship in the enjoyment of God, and of one another in God. When we have reached that peace, our life will no longer be a mortal one; rather, we shall then be fully and certainly alive. There will be no animal body to press down the soul by its corruption, but a spiritual body standing in need of nothing: a body subject in every part to the will.[57]

But in Hegel's philosophy there is no peace of heaven, no spiritual body free from the corruption of a fallen nature, and little or no loving care of a transcendent, providential God whose divine plan includes eternal life for man in union with him. In Hegel's philosophy where Absolute Spirit

---

55. Augustine, *City of God* (trans. Dyson) 19.17 (p. 945).
56. Augustine, *City of God* (trans. Dyson) 19.17 (p. 947).
57. Augustine, *City of God* (trans. Dyson) 19.17 (p. 947).

is the spirit of reason alone, the individual person's life and existence is bereft of ultimate purpose and meaning.

The need for a person to find peace and, moreover, to live in the real world beyond the limitations of reason alone, and yet without rejecting reason, helped lead to the phenomenological movement, which sought to describe the whole gamut of human experience, which would not exclude man's emotive, religious, or mystical experience, especially in a world that had become more technologically advanced and even more capable of political upheaval, violence, and war.

ANTICIPATING MODERN PHENOMENOLOGICAL DESCRIPTION, AUGUSTINE NARRATES HIS SIGHT OF GOD AND GOD'S SIGHT OF HIM

Phenomenology as founded in part and developed by the German philosopher and mathematician Edmund Husserl (1859–1938) focused on clearly describing immanent conscious experience as it presents itself or is rather intended by consciousness, i.e., how consciousness is conscious of objects and their essential nature and even when consciousness is conscious of itself. As such, phenomenology reflects on conscious experience no matter its source—be it a belief, a fear, an anxiety, or even a hallucination, as well as a presumed real exterior object.

Unlike Kant's preoccupation with certitude of existence of an apparent being derived from sense experience structured by the categories of pure reason alone, phenomenology begins by suspending (not doubting/ not denying) any judgment about existence or nonexistence of the object of what consciousness is conscious of. This would include a suspension of philosophical, theological, psychological, sociological, or any scientific explanations of what consciousness experiences. Conclusions concerning the essential meaning and the existence (or nonexistence) of any phenomena are bound up with a process of carefully investigating and describing the modes of belief involved; these modes of belief include possibility, probability, certitude, or even imagination of the consciousness that experiences such phenomena. When he/she comes to a presumed experience of God, the phenomenologist will look at the essential nature of that experience of the awareness of God's presence without initially judging the real existence of the object of that experience. However, within a stream of conscious experience one could ultimately come to certitude regarding the existence of the source of the experience.

Phenomenological description can be applied to the experience of St. Augustine as he is quoted above, where Augustine says, in part:

> Let the wicked in their restlessness go from Thee and flee away.... The truth is that they fled, that they might not see Thee who sawest them.... Let them turn back, and behold Thou art there in their hearts, in the hearts of those who confessed to Thee and cast themselves upon Thee and weep on Thy breast as they return from ways of anguish.[58]

The phenomenologist would look at and describe the essential meaning of the experience of anguish of those who attempt to flee from assumed divine wrath. The essential meaning of this anguish of heart is then to be described in its primal givenness, albeit without initially asserting certitude of the cause of this anguish. For Augustine, it is obviously this repeated experience of divine presence within him that is the cause of the anguish he describes.

AUGUSTINE PREPARES THE WAY FOR MAX SCHELER'S "ALOGICAL" CONSCIOUS ACTS WITH HIS "YEARNING FOR GOD"

The German phenomenologist and professor of philosophy at the University of Cologne Max Scheler (1874–1928) investigated the essence of what he called the alogical of our psychic/emotive life and how "alogical" acts of the conscious person such as intuition, feeling, striving, loving, hating have an independence and originality built into the understanding and parallel to, yet independent of, the judgments of pure reason. Scheler asks whether there is:

> a pure intuiting and feeling, a pure loving and hating, a pure striving and willing, which are as independent of the psychophysical organization of man as pure thought, and which at the same time possess their own original laws that cannot be reduced to laws of empirical psychic life.... Since no one asked this question, no one asked whether or not there are a priori interconnections and oppositions among the objects and qualities to which those alogical acts are directed, or whether or not

---

58. Augustine, *Confessions* 5.2.2 (pp. 75–76).

there is an a priori lawfulness of these acts which corresponds to such interconnections and oppositions.[59]

Scheler argues that "ethics has" throughout the history of philosophy "been constituted either as absolute and a priori, and therefore rational, or as relative, empirical, and emotional." He further argues that "ethics can and must be both absolute and emotional" and that few philosophers have tried to insist on this view and reject the prejudice that emotions could not be the foundation for objective moral law. Scheler tells us that among those few who have rejected this prejudice "are Augustine and Blaise Pascal." Scheler interprets Pascal's concept that "the heart has reasons that reason does not know" to mean that "there is an eternal and absolute lawfulness of feeling, loving, and hating which is as absolute as that of pure logic, but which is not reducible to intellectual lawfulness." Scheler believed that there is an innate structure, order, and hierarchy of values within the whole emotional life of human beings that understands and interprets perceived objects as having distinct value meaning, which is uncovered in conscious experience but which does not rely upon rational judgment or analysis. Scheler came to the realization that:

> There is a type of experiencing whose "objects" are completely inaccessible to reason; reason is as blind to them as ears and hearing are blind to colors. It is a kind of experience that leads us to genuinely objective objects and the eternal order among them, i.e., to values and the order of ranks among them.[60]

An example that may clarify "values and the order of ranks among them" ("them" referring to "genuinely objective objects") could be the subject of abortion. Rational arguments may be given to justify abortion on such grounds as the mother being single, without financial support from the father, and already struggling to support another child; the mother struggling with an addiction and not being able to take care of herself, let alone a child; or a mother being a teenager and emotionally incapable of raising a child. However, anyone who witnesses on a sonogram a suction-aspiration abortion in the first trimester would see the results of a powerful vacuum tearing the baby's body from the mother's womb and into pieces, and unless the witness has already deadened his/her emotional feeling, he/she would experience an emotional repulsion at the destruction of the life of a tiny human being. This emotional repulsion

---

59. Scheler, *Formalism in Ethics and Non-Formal Ethics of Values*, 254.
60. Scheler, *Formalism in Ethics and Non-Formal Ethics of Values*, 254–55.

would be even more pronounced if the person witnessed a dilatation and evacuation abortion of a twelve-week fetus where a pliers-like instrument is inserted into the uterus by the abortionist, who seizes a body part and with twisting motion tears that body part from the baby's body until all the baby's body parts are removed. The nurse then must reassemble the body parts to confirm that all of them have been removed. Such a gruesome process would certainly evoke disgust and outrage in most persons who have not become inured to the procedure. On the basis of Scheler's description of emotive acts that detect objective value within a hierarchy of rank caused by an a priori capacity in every human person to evaluate objects as eliciting love or hate, one may conclude that the experience of witnessing such a gruesome procedure must result in the emotive judgment of the procedure as being loathsome.

When it comes to experience that transcends normal sense perception, the objects of this type of nonsensual experience can expand upon or exceed the data of the five senses with verifiable evidence of truly existent realities, which notion, of course, Kant would reject. A Kantian perhaps would also counter-argue that even if one grants that the experience of values in a presumed object is accepted as a possibility, there is no guarantee that that object which is experienced alogically really exists; not to mention, the object experienced may be identified subjectively to be God or something supernatural. What can be asserted about Scheler's "genuinely objective objects" and about the a priori, alogical acts of valuation that assess these objects as presenting a hierarchy of values is that this concept provides a foundation rooted in experience (transcending sense experience alone) of both an immanent and a transcendent moral order.

Augustine's influence on Scheler is apparent. In the beginning of his *Confessions* (as cited in the first chapter of this manuscript), Augustine anticipates the innate, a priori, alogical capacity in human persons to experience the need for God in the core of their being, which leads to an acceptance and verification of God's "genuinely objective" being. To repeat Augustine's prayer in regard to innate human yearning for God: "Thou dost so excite him that to praise Thee is his joy. For thou hast made us for Thyself and our hearts are restless until they rest in Thee."[61] This confirmation of God's real presence and personhood then exceeds the data of the five senses by providing the evidence of an ongoing,

---

61. Augustine, *Confessions* 1.1.1 (p. 3).

profound experience of restlessness and yearning for God, which the human person does not derive from reason, imagination, or willful assertion but, rather, is something that the person simply is aware that there is an inescapable presence within him/her that cannot be denied. Augustine had the foresight of seeing the importance of reflecting upon internal conscious experience as this experience clearly presents itself. Augustine expressed this foresight long before phenomenology became widely accepted by philosophers as a method providing legitimate descriptions of phenomena as they are directly experienced by consciousness without depending upon causal explanations provided by science or any academic disciplines, including purely rational philosophies.

What distinguishes philosophers like Scheler, Augustine, and Pascal from Immanuel Kant is their unwillingness to abandon a realist perspective that sees the world and all things in it, including human persons and their emotional life, as being morally ordered so that there is an objective reality that corresponds to human emotional apprehensions and instinctual inclinations as well as to rational conceptions. Further, in the thinking of many believers, God so created the human person that in instincts and emotions as well as in the rational mind there is an orientation to an objective moral order that God ordained and that this orientation remains unaltered by our fallen nature. The honest person of faith would conclude that man has both good inclinations with which he can perceive, understand, and possess a proclivity toward the moral law, and bad inclinations that incline him toward the seven capital sins. But sin so disorders God's moral objective order that Augustine confesses: "I can no longer support my good, until Thou, Lord who art merciful to my iniquities, shall likewise heal my weakness: redeeming my life from corruption and crowning me with pity and compassion, and filling my desire with good things."[62]

RUDOLPH OTTO'S INVESTIGATION OF THE "NUMINOUS" EXPERIENCE AND ITS REDUCTION OF A PERSON TO A "CREATURE FEELING"

An associate scholar of Max Scheler, Rudolph Otto, a religious philosopher with a phenomenological orientation, investigated this question of the existence of God, the supernatural, and all that is mysterious with his

---

62. Augustine, *Confessions* 1.9.11 (p. 239).

insightful examination of mystical experience. Also, a contemporary of Husserl and a German professor of comparative religions at Marburg-on-the-Lahn, Rudolph Otto (1869–1937) provided a description of the experience of the presence of the supernatural that he terms the "numinous," which, says Otto, reduces a person to a dependency, a "creature-feeling . . . which in itself indubitably has immediate and primary reference to an object outside the self."[63]

The word "numinous" defies a precise definition but is best understood by the religious emotions it evokes, which span a wide gamut. These religious emotions are brought on by an unnatural object called the numen by Otto, which object is shrouded in mystery. The expression that Otto uses to explain the numinous is "*mysterium tremendum,*" which could be translated "dreadful, fearful or terrible mystery." Otto provides several elements that describe the nature of *mysterium tremendum* beginning with the element of awfulness, which Otto identifies as "religious dread (or awe)." This has a primal form, viz., "demonic dread . . . with its queer perversion, a sort of abortive offshoot, the 'dread of ghosts.' It first begins to stir in the feeling of 'something uncanny,' 'eerie,' or 'weird.'"[64] The dread of the *mysterium tremendum* when it reaches an extreme evokes a feeling of horror that may even give way to shuddering. Otto tells us:

> For "shuddering" is something more than "natural," ordinary fear. It implies that the mysterious is already beginning to loom before the mind to touch the feelings. It implies the first application of a category of valuation which has no place in the everyday natural world of ordinary experience, and is only possible to a being in whom has been awakened a mental predisposition, unique in kind and different in a definite way from any "natural" faculty.[65]

The fear of which Otto speaks is beyond the natural fear that humans experience when they are confronted by a danger the nature of which they understand, such as a violent storm, confrontation with criminals or a wild animal, standing near a precipice, or facing the possibility of a collision. In each of these cases, a person understands the possible cause of harm and reacts with fearful precaution. But in the case of the *mysterium tremendum* there is no precise understanding of the nature of the object,

---

63. Otto, *Idea of the Holy*, 11.
64. Otto, *Idea of the Holy*, 14.
65. Otto, *Idea of the Holy*, 15.

i.e., the numen, which evokes dread and which presents a danger; this makes one shudder because the dread that one experiences is of a reality beyond the natural. Otto explains:

> That this is so is shown by the potent attraction again and again exercised by the element of horror and shudder in ghost stories, even among persons of high all-around education. It is a remarkable fact that the physical reaction to which this unique "dread" of the uncanny gives rise is also unique, and is not found in the case of any "natural" fear or terror. We say: "my blood ran icy cold," and "my flesh crept."[66]

At this stage of being conscious of the numinous, the *mysterium tremendum* is the experience of a dread object, which it would seem to be more accurately called preternatural rather than supernatural. That which is preternatural is a force or power exhibited in natural objects that exceeds the natural power of these natural objects. For believers, preternatural events are permitted by divine allowance or intervention often through spiritual beings such as angels or demons, who can act in this natural world using objects of nature in unnatural ways. Jonah's being swallowed in the sea by a large fish and after three days being spewed by the fish upon the shore (see Jonah chapter 2) is an example of a preternatural event caused by God in which a natural being is used to produce a divinely intended effect. Again, for believers, that which is strictly supernatural involves forces or powers directly caused by divine intervention that completely surpass the power of created beings. The miraculous restoration of life to a dead person (such as Peter's restoring Tabitha to life in Acts 9:40) or Christ's resurrection from the dead are supernatural events. Restoring Tabitha from the dead is clearly a manifestation of supernatural power caused by direct divine intervention, even though a mere man, Peter, is the agent who calls for this miracle and through whom it occurs.

It would seem that the numinous emotion of dread reaches the level of experiencing the supernatural when it transcends the unnatural fear of the demonic or ghosts and is replaced by a unique shudder at the presence of what could only be God. Otto tells us:

> Though the numinous emotion in its completest development shows a world of difference from the mere "daemonic dread," yet not even at the highest level does it belie its pedigree or kindred.... And this element, softened though it is, does not

---

66. Otto, *Idea of the Holy*, 16.

disappear even on the highest level of all, where the worship of God is at its purest. Its disappearance would be indeed an essential loss. The "shudder" reappears in a form ennobled beyond measure where the soul, held speechless, trembles inwardly to the farthest fiber of its being. It invades the mind mightily in Christian worship with the words: "Holy, holy, holy." . . . The "shudder" has here lost its crazy and bewildering note, but not the ineffable something that holds the mind. It has become a mystical awe, and sets free as its accompaniment, reflected in self-consciousness, that "creature-feeling" that has already been described as the feeling of personal nothingness and submergence before the awe-inspiring object directly experienced.[67]

Otto tells us that the "awe-inspiring object directly experienced" allows a person to experience further the *mysterium tremendum* through stages of development so as to constitute an "ideogram" or suggestive expression, picture, or symbol that represents or describes an idea or thing but not as a synonym or precise definition. Otto also refers to the *mysterium tremendum* as being "absolute over-poweringness" or "absolute unapproachability" of the numen, which reduces one to "personal nothingness" in the face of its "awful majesty." With this experience one approaches mysticism, which Otto tells us "leads to a valuation of the transcendent object of its reference as that which through plenitude of being stands supreme and absolute so that the finite self-contrasted with it becomes conscious even of its nullity that I am not, Thou art all."[68] This primal understanding of a God-like presence is thus realized when one has "a consciousness of the absolute superiority or supremacy of a power other than myself."[69]

At this point, one's experience of a God-like presence is marked by "the feeling of absolute profaneness" in the face of this "supreme and absolute plenitude of being," which absolute profaneness is

> accompanied by the most uncompromising judgment of self-depreciation, a judgment passed, not by [one's] character . . . but upon his own very existence as creature before that which is supreme above all creatures. And at the same moment he passes upon the numen a judgment of appreciation of a unique kind by the category . . . "holy," which is proper to the numen alone, but to it in an absolute degree. . . . This "sanctus" is not merely

67. Otto, *Idea of the Holy*, 17.
68. Otto, *Idea of the Holy*, 21.
69. Otto, *Idea of the Holy*, 21.

"perfect" or "beautiful" or "sublime" or "good".... It is the positive numinous value or worth, and to it corresponds on the side of the creature a numinous disvalue or "unworth."[70]

The religious experience of the numinous object or numen is that of a being supreme above all creatures, and this numen carries with it a holiness that includes and yet surpasses the "perfect," the "beautiful," the "sublime," and the "good." At the same time this experience of the holiness of the numinous object relegates the creature to a state of unworthiness, and yet simultaneously elicits from the person the highest praise to the divine being that has "the supremest right to make the highest claim to service and receives praise because it is in an absolute sense worthy to be praised."[71] Such a numinous being is "Augustus, 'august,'" i.e., marked by tremendous majesty and grandeur.

AUGUSTINE'S PHENOMENOLOGICAL-LIKE EXPERIENCE OF "FEAR AND HORROR" TOGETHER WITH "HOPE AND EXALTATION"

The experience of a God-like presence that Otto describes is that of a primal encounter or an original awareness of a divine presence possibly appearing to a person lacking in extensive religious teaching, faith, or worship. The experience of "the most uncompromising judgment of self-depreciation" thought by a creature before the most supreme, august being is not the experience of the Christian who, while aware of his sinfulness and unworthiness, entrusts himself to Christ's redemptive grace and God's mercy. At the level of the *mysterium tremendum*, which Otto describes, divinity is encountered with the shudder before the overpowering presence of the omnipotent being shrouded in mystery. While Otto is correct in saying that this experience of trembling to "the farthest fiber" of one's being is, or should be, never lost even in Christian worship, there—in Christian worship—this trembling is transformed into fear of the Lord, which is always accompanied by hope for God's forgiveness and the Redeemer's offer of salvation and the guidance of the Holy Spirit. Augustine relates that, by the time of his conversion shortly before his baptism:

---

70. Otto, *Idea of the Holy*, 51.
71. Otto, *Idea of the Holy*, 52.

> I was in fear and horror, and again I was on fire with hope and exaltation in your mercy O Father. And all these emotions found expression in my eyes and in my voice when Your Holy Spirit turned to us and said: "O ye sons of men, how long will ye be dull of heart? Why do you love vanity so much and seek after lying?" For I myself had loved vanity and sought after lying. And Thou, Lord, hadst already made Thy holy one wonderful, raising Him from the dead and setting Him at Thy right hand, whence He should send from on high His promise, the Paraclete, the Spirit of Truth.[72]

For Augustine, the experience of divine mercy and the Holy Spirit's prompting of a self-examination by the sinner so as to be rid of such corruptions as vanity and lying (as occurs when one attempts to justify one's own sin) places the Christian in an ongoing pursuit of truth and self-honesty. This pursuit marked by hope was understood by Augustine, who was well aware of his long-standing struggle against lust; for him, even after his conversion and baptism, which united him with God, there remained a danger of his falling back into this habit of sin. In his instruction on rules for interpreting sacred Scripture entitled *On Christian Teaching*, Augustine comments on the commandment to love with a pure heart taught by St. Paul (see 1 Cor 13:13) and especially the need for hope in maintaining a good conscience with genuine faith:

> So, when someone has learnt that the aim of the commandment is "love from a pure heart, and good conscience and genuine faith" [1 Tim 1:5], he will be ready to relate every interpretation of the holy Scriptures to these three things. . . . For when the apostle said "love" he added "from a pure heart," so that nothing is loved except what should be loved. He added "good" to "conscience" because of hope; for a person with the incubus [nightmare] of a bad conscience despairs of reaching what he loves and believes. Thirdly, he said "with genuine faith": for if our faith is free of untruthfulness then we do not love which should not be loved, whereas by living aright it is impossible for our hope to be in any way misguided.[73]

Augustine is emphasizing here the need for having hope in maintaining a good conscience in order to abide by the commandment to love. The honest person who is aware of his ongoing propensity to sin

---

72. Augustine, *Confessions* 9.4.9 (p. 168).
73. Augustine, *On Christian Teaching* 1.39.43–40.44 (p. 29).

needs hope in order to maintain such a good conscience, for without the hope that one can abide with the judgment of conscience, one easily falls into despair that he would ever be able to love with a pure heart. And the judgment of a good conscience requires faith, which ensures the intellect's truthfulness in acknowledging what should be loved and what should not be loved, so that one's hope guides one's conscience to live aright. The hope in maintaining a good conscience then relies upon faith in God's revelation providing the truth of what constitutes real Christian love. There must be continual growth in knowledge of the truth of the faith that God has revealed in Scripture in order for there to be a sound judgment of a good conscience, which is maintained by hope. Augustine later emphasizes this teaching on conscience in the same work:

> Good morals have to do with our love of God and our neighbor, the true faith with our understanding of God and our neighbor. The hope that each person has within his own conscience is directly related to the progress that he feels himself to be making towards the love and understanding of God and his neighbor.[74]

For the Christian particularly, "the hope he has within his own conscience is directly related to the progress he feels himself to be making towards the love and understanding of God and neighbor," because the Christian knows through faith that he faces judgment from Christ who "is expected to come from heaven as judge of the living and the dead." This judgment results in eternal damnation for the unrepentant wicked and eternal happiness for those judged to have lived lives of goodness. Faith, therefore, "instills great fear into the uncommitted, so that they may develop a serious commitment and yearn for him in lives of goodness rather than fear him in lives of wickedness."[75] As a result of divine judgment, conscience is strengthened by hope and made more acute in its judgment of the person's own actions, not only of his actions performed in the past, but also those actions he is planning to perform in the future, or is in the process of performing in the present. Conscience, for the Christian, therefore, facilitates the human person's participation in the transcendent moral order of which each person has immanent knowledge of the basic moral law (written on one's heart), which requires compliance—the extent of which conscience is always judging.

---

74. Augustine, *On Christian Teaching* 3.10.14–16 (pp. 75–76).
75. Augustine, *On Christian Teaching* 1.15.14–18.17 (p. 15).

For the Christian, the person himself/herself, the transcendent moral order, and each one's participation in it are created by God so that divine judgment is the critical factor in strengthening the role of conscience in a person's compliance with the moral law. Not only fear of damnation but also the promise of eternal happiness in union with God in heaven motivates this compliance with the moral law, including with the greatest Christian commandment, which is to love. Here, the Christian duty to love one's neighbor is bound up with his duty to love God, the Creator, for whom the Christian yearns for complete union, which results in complete fulfillment and happiness for the human person. The duty commanded by Christ to "seek first the kingdom of God and his righteousness" (Matt 6:33), which is to say to seek one's complete and eternal happiness in union with God, is inseparable from Christ's command to "love the Lord your God with all your heart, with all your soul, and with all your mind" (Matt 22:37). The distinction between Kantian and Christian morality is marked in this regard. Kant regards compliance with the moral law as a categorical imperative for the will to freely obey the moral maxim of pure reason ("act that the maxim of your will could always hold at the same time as a principle in a giving of universal law"[76]) for which each rational human person has a duty to comply, and which duty must be pure without admixture with, and separated from, one's pursuit of happiness. Kant states without equivocation:

> However, it can never be a direct duty to promote one's happiness, still less can it be a principle of all duty. Now, because all determining grounds of the will except the one and only pure practical law of reason (the moral law) are without exception empirical and so, as such, belong to the principle of happiness, they must without exception be separated from the supreme moral principle and never be incorporated with it as a condition, since this would destroy all moral worth just as any empirical admixture.[77]

Kant would have the human person divorce from his duty to obey the moral law the essential motive of all action, viz., the pursuit of happiness. Yet the moral law, when understood accurately and realistically to include the good, natural inclinations of human nature (which Kant also rejects as a ground for moral law), requires acting in reasonable

76. Kant, *Critique of Practical Reason* 1. 1. 1. 7, 5.31 (p. 28).
77. Kant, *Critique of Practical Reason* 1. 1. 3, 5:93 (p. 76).

compliance with our own good as well as the good of others. To do so (i.e., acting in reasonable compliance with one's own good as well as the good of others) is essential to acquiring one's happiness and hence the motivation to do good and to be happy coincide so that to be motivated by either, or both ideally, is hardly a danger to the moral worth of one's action. But understanding the full breadth of moral action also requires an acknowledgment of, and a reliance on, the Creator of the transcendent moral order and thus of the moral law. To this moral law all human persons are privy, as Augustine indicates in his *Reply to Faustus the Manichaean* (cited above), which includes part of St. Paul's passage from Rom 2:14–16 here given in its entirety: "For the Gentiles do by nature the things contained in the law; and not having the law they are a law unto themselves, who show the work of the law written on their hearts, while their conscience also bears witness and their conflicting thoughts accuse or even defend them on the day when, according to my gospel, God will judge people's hidden works through Jesus Christ."

Man's understanding of the moral law is, at the same time, rational and intuitive; it requires the use of one's natural inclinations and common sense to apply. Understanding the moral law is never just the application of abstract moral principles of pure reason to moral decisions demanded in everyday life. Moreover, one requires a recurring judgment of conscience to determine one's compliance with, and/or disobedience of, this moral law. In order to gain insight into what conscience is and how we are to use it, it is beneficial to examine the views of a nineteenth-century theologian and scholar whose explanation of conscience anticipated phenomenological description that developed in the twentieth century.

JOHN HENRY NEWMAN'S UNDERSTANDING OF CONSCIENCE AS AN INTERNAL "HEARING"; AUGUSTINE'S EXPERIENCE OF GOD IN "THE MOST INWARD PLACE . . . OF HEART AND LOFTIER THAN THE HIGHEST"

John Henry Newman (1801–90), who rose to prominence as an Anglican minister at Oxford, was known for his oratory and later as a leader in the Oxford Movement, which sought to bring the Church of England first back to certain forms of Catholic worship and later back to parts of Catholic doctrine. His attempts to reconcile Anglicanism with

Catholicism led to his being exiled from Oxford and his entry into the Catholic Church, where he was ordained a priest and later was raised to cardinal. Newman's views on conscience are nonsectarian for the most part and have appealed to many Christians of various denominations. What is most interesting about Newman's description of conscience is that in his view not only does conscience make us aware of a command to do good and avoid evil, but conscience also makes us aware of the commander, viz., God. Says Newman:

> Whether a man be born in pagan darkness, or in some corruption of revealed religion,—whether he has heard the name of the Savior of the world or not. . . . He has within his breast a certain commanding dictate, not a mere sentiment, not a mere opinion, or impression, or view of things, but a law, an authoritative voice bidding him do certain things and avoid others. . . . It is more than a man's own self. . . .
>
> This is conscience; from the nature of the case, its very existence carries on our minds to a Being exterior to ourselves . . . and to a Being superior to ourselves.[78]

Conscience, then, is not just a practical judgment of the intellect but is first received as an authoritative voice that provides the initial understanding of the moral law by which one is to judge. The person that listens to and encourages this voice within him/her receives at once an order to follow its direction, even if this direction is not clearly understood. The voice imposes a command to obediently follow what it ordains. What follows the reception of this authoritative voice is, quite naturally, a desire of the recipient to be more clearly aware of what is being commanded and especially to know who is commanding. Newman goes on to tell us:

> I say, without going on to the question what it says, and whether its particular dictates are always clear and consistent as they might be, its [the authoritative voice's] very existence throws us out of ourselves, and beyond ourselves to go and seek Him in the height and depth, whose Voice it is. . . . And in proportion as we listen . . . not only do its dictates become clearer, and its lessons broader, and its principles more consistent, but its very tone is louder and more authoritative and constraining. And, thus it is, that to those who use what they have, more is given. . . . They go on to the intimate perception and belief of one God. His voice

---

78. John Henry Newman, "Sermons Preached on Various Occasions," in Przywara, *Heart of Newman*, 45–46.

within them witnesses to Him, and they believe His own witness about Himself.[79]

Newman continues in the same work to warn that even as God is experienced in conscience, a person must be on guard to sift out whatever "comes from a merely earthly source," whenever "that true inward Guide commands."[80] Even saints who underwent deep mystical experience often found themselves in need of purification from the impure intrusions of their own fallen nature, the bad advice of others, or worse, the intrusion of a satanic-like influence. Newman tells us that when one has the gift of true docility to the voice of God, one's "conscience raises a desire for what it does not itself fully supply."[81] Openness to the divine presence found within one's conscience directs one to expand the formation of his moral knowledge beyond the natural law written on each person's heart by investigating deeper into the moral law that God reveals. Newman links the natural law known directly to the conscience of each person with the authority of the moral law found in divine revelation and known through faith:

> If the Author of Nature be the Author of Grace, it may be expected that, while the two systems of facts are distinct and independent, the principles displayed in them will be the same, and form a connecting link between them. In this identity of principle lies the Analogy of Natural and Revealed Religion. . . The case then stands thus:—Revelation has introduced a new law of divine governance over and above those laws which appear in the natural course of the world; and in consequence we are able to argue for the existence of a standing authority in matters of faith on the analogy of Nature, and from the fact of Christianity.[82]

For the Catholic Christian, as was Cardinal Newman, this formation of moral knowledge, upon which conscience must depend to increase the scope of the authoritative voice of God within the Christian, definitely

---

79. Newman, "Sermons Preached on Various Occasions," in Przywara, *Heart of Newman*, 46.
80. Newman, "Sermons Preached on Various Occasions," in Przywara, *Heart of Newman*, 46.
81. Newman, "Sermons Preached on Various Occasions," in Przywara, *Heart of Newman*, 47.
82. John Henry Newman, "Essay on the Development of Christian Doctrine," in Przywara, *Heart of Newman*, 93.

includes the moral direction provided by sacred Scripture and sacred tradition along with the moral teachings of the church's magisterium or teaching authority. Each person's participation and responsibility within the divine moral order increases as that person freely chooses to expand his conscience's ability to judge rightly; this happens when one increases his knowledge of the moral law. Hence, God speaks more clearly, more definitely, and more fully within the well-formed conscience of that Christian who diligently seeks to know God's will and the teachings of Christ and to follow them. Conscience, then, is an ongoing experience of the divine presence within us directing us on how to judge our actions. Newman tells us:

> Conscience is not a longsighted selfishness, nor a desire to be consistent with oneself; but it is a messenger from Him, who, both in nature and in grace, speaks to us behind a veil, and teaches and rules us by His representatives. Conscience is the aboriginal Vicar of Christ, a prophet in its informations, a monarch in its peremptoriness, a priest in its blessings and anathemas, and, even though the eternal priesthood throughout the Church could cease to be, in it the sacerdotal principle would remain and would have a sway.[83]

With a well-formed conscience the Christian realizes a fuller understanding of the transcendent moral order established by the Creator and the Christian's responsibility to live in accord with the moral law. What remains is for the Christian to realize his fullest participation in the transcendent moral order by following through with freely willed actions that are in accord with the moral law. What brought Augustine to accept Manichaeism as a young man was precisely his desire to excuse his disobedience of the moral law and thus placate his conscience with the belief that human persons cannot be held accountable for the evil actions they perform because evil forces within the body compel the person to act as he does. By embracing Manichaeism and ignoring the voice of his own conscience, Augustine fell into the depths of sinful habit from which only God could deliver him:

> But these fantasies of the Manichees I did believe. Alas, by what stages was I brought down to the deepest depths of the pit, giving myself needless labour and turmoil of spirit for want of the truth in that I sought You my God—to You I confess it, for You had

---

83. John Henry Newman, "Certain Difficulties Felt by Anglicans in Catholic Teaching: Conscience," in Hulsman, *Rule of Our Warfare*, 60

pity on me even when I had not yet confessed—in that I sought You not according to the understanding of the mind by which You have set us above the beasts, but according to the sense of the flesh. Yet all the time You were more inward than the most inward place of my heart and loftier than the highest.[84]

Augustine needed to turn continuously inward to God (who resided in his most inward place of heart—his conscience) for help and utilize his understanding of mind in order to realize the faculty of free will that separated him from the beasts so as to begin to be liberated from the fantasies of the Manichees, which had ensnared his mind and helped to lead to the enslavement of his body to lust.

---

84. Augustine, *Confessions* 3.6.12 (p. 44).

Chapter Three

An Analysis of Augustine's *On the Free Choice of the Will* with Contrasting Views of Other Philosophers and Theologians

INTRODUCTION TO *ON THE FREE CHOICE OF THE WILL*

UNDERSTANDING THE NATURE OF a will that is free is the subject of one of Augustine's major anti-Manichaean works, *De Libero Arbitrio Voluntatis*, *On the Free Choice of the Will*. Here Augustine sought to demonstrate the providential nature of God in creating man with a rational, immortal soul and with access generally speaking to knowledge of eternal truth and to man's knowing his primary responsibility to freely choose the highest good—God himself. *On the Free Choice of the Will* was begun by Augustine around 388, shortly after his baptism in 387, but was not completed until 395, some four years after being ordained a priest and shortly before he began his *Confessions*. While the work reflects Augustine's Christian faith, it does not extensively quote Scripture and approaches philosophically, as much as theologically, the answering of such questions as the cause of evil, what must be believed about God, why God gave freedom of will to human persons, and how the will can turn away from God and embrace evil.

It was, in fact, the question regarding the origin of evil that motivated Augustine to write *On the Free Choice of the Will* after discussions with his friend Evodius. Augustine was searching for a response to the answer given by Manichaeism (of which he was once an adherent), which posited that the nature of evil was a power co-eternal with God. Augustine later described this power as "some substance of irrational life [with] the nature of a supreme Evil." This supreme evil for the Manichaeans was a divisive and controlling force in man that stood in opposition to "the unity [in which] lay the rational mind and the nature of truth and the supreme Good."[1] For the Manichaean, human persons did not have a free will because they existed in a divided state with a supreme evil power creating and controlling the human body (as well as all physical things) and thus making a person enslaved to his/her bodily passions notwithstanding one's rational mind and will. The only liberation possible was for the supreme Good to lift the person into enlightenment by reabsorbing the rational soul, which purportedly was part of God and had been imprisoned in a physical body. In his refutation of Manichaeism, Augustine argues in *On the Free Choice of the Will* that evil does not lie in a supreme evil power but rather in man's free choice to be enslaved by bodily passions rather than abide by the eternal law of the incorruptible goodness of the one God whose eternal law "is stamped on us: it is the law according to which it is just for all things to be completely in order."[2]

On the Free Choice of the Will has been contrasted unfavorably by certain theologians and scholars with Augustine's later anti-Pelagian works such as *On Grace and Free Choice* (ca. 426). Such theologians claim that Augustine's earlier views so stressed man's freedom as to practically reject the need for God's grace. Pelagius (ca. 360–431) was most probably a lay theologian who denied the doctrine of original sin and claimed that the effect on mankind of the sin of Adam was merely bad example. Pelagius also argued that Christ's redemptive grace was not necessary for salvation and that man's free will was sufficient to be virtuous; Pelagius denied a need for actual grace, which is a temporary gift of divine intervention that strengthens the mind and will to avoid sin and pursue goodness. Ironically, it would be followers of Pelagius who would cite statements from *On the Free Choice of the Will* to support their own position. While Augustine, for his part, never outright denied man's God-given faculty of free choice of the will in any of his works, he also alluded to the human need for God's help even in this early treatise of *On the*

---

1. Augustine, *Confessions* 4.15.24 (p. 69).
2. Augustine, "On the Free Choice of the Will" 1.6.15–51 (p. 13).

Free Choice of the Will and explicitly emphasized in his later anti-Pelagian works the absolute need for grace to assist the will in accomplishing good and avoiding evil. Speaking of Adam, Augustine tells us in his later work On *Reprimand and Grace* (ca. 426–27):

> The First Man did not have this grace by which he would never will to be evil. But he definitely had grace (a) in which, if he had willed to continue, he would never be evil; (b) without which he could not have been good, even with free choice; but (c) which he could have abandoned through free choice. Therefore, God did not want Adam, whom He left to his free choice, to be without His grace, seeing that free choice is sufficient for evil, but hardly for good, unless it is assisted by the omnipotent Good One. And if Adam had not abandoned this assistance through free choice, he would always be good. But he abandoned it, and was abandoned. In fact, the assistance was such that he abandoned it whenever he willed to, and in which he could continue if he willed to—not that by which it would come to pass that he willed to. This is the first grace which was given to the First Adam.[3]

Thus, Augustine's view of man's free will is that man is free to accept and utilize God's assistance (grace) in doing good and avoiding evil; but if man freely refuses to accept God's help, he freely wills to fall into evil and be guilty of that evil. Moreover, grace will not usually force a person to accept grace nor forcibly prevent the person from refusing grace. Man's will remains free to choose to accept or refuse God's grace. In keeping with Augustine's development of thought, it is best to investigate first his earlier dialogue, *On the Free Choice of the Will*, and then to analyze his later anti-Pelagian treatises *On Grace and Free Choice*, *On Reprimand* (sometimes translated *Admonition*) *and Grace*, and *On the Gift of Perseverance*.

SUMMARY OF BOOK 1 OF *ON THE FREE CHOICE OF THE WILL*

Written in the form of a dialogue, *On the Free Choice of the Will* is more of a treatise by Augustine on free will rather than a dialectical development. Evodius, his questioner, provides his own insights and even objections in Book 1 but becomes less participatory as the work progresses. Evodius begins Augustine's work by asking whether God is the cause of evil. Augustine distinguishes two kinds of evil: one kind refers to a person doing evil,

---

3. Augustine, "On Reprimand and Grace" 11.31 (p. 212).

the other kind refers to a person suffering evil. Regarding the question of whether God is the origin of evil, Augustine answers on the basis of faith "that God is good (it is blasphemous to think otherwise), then He does not do evil."[4] Augustine then at the very start of his dialogue accepts Christian faith regarding God's existence and goodness; it would not be until Augustine wrote his *Confessions* two years after he completed *On the Free Choice of the Will* that he would proffer his ontological argument for God's existence. Augustine then argued (as quoted above in chapter 1):

> You [God] must be incorruptible whatever might be Your nature. For no soul ever has been able to conceive or ever will be able to conceive anything better than you, the supreme and perfect Good. Therefore, since the incorruptible is unquestionably to be held greater than the corruptible—and so I held it—I could now draw the conclusion that unless you were incorruptible there was something better than my God. But seeing the superiority of the incorruptible, I should have looked for You in that truth and have learned from it where evil is—that is, learned the origin of the corruption by which Your substance cannot be violated. For there is no way in which corruption can affect our God, whether by His will or by necessity or by accident: for He is God, and what He wills is good, and Himself is Goodness; whereas to be corrupted is not good.[5]

What Augustine does posit in *On the Free Choice of the Will* concerning God's nature and concerning what must be believed about God is that God is the Creator but does not create sin or evil. In *On the Free Choice of the Will*, begun only one year after his baptism into the Catholic faith in 387, Augustine does not rely upon the analysis of concepts concerning God as to what these concepts include or exclude, but rather appeals to the need for faith and pursuit of righteousness as the ground for accepting truth about God. Augustine argues in response to Evodius's inquiry about whether God is the cause of evil that God makes us understand what we need to believe, quoting Isa 7:9 (as translated from the Septuagint Greek and referenced in Augustine's "Sermon 43"; see *Catechism of the Catholic Church* §158): "take the course prescribed by the prophet Isaiah, who says: 'Unless you believe you shall not understand.'" And that which we are called to believe, says Augustine, is to hold:

---

4. Augustine, "On the Free Choice of the Will" 1.1.1.2 (p. 3).
5. Augustine, *Confessions* 7.4.6 (p. 120).

> God in the highest esteem [which] is surely the most authentic beginning of righteousness. Nor does anyone hold God in the highest esteem without believing that God is omnipotent, not changeable in even the least detail, the Creator of all good things, Who is more excellent than they are, the most just Ruler of all He has created.[6]

What is most significant regarding this initial and brief discussion of God is that Augustine is already placing God as the origin of the moral order found in creation. God created all things good possessing a suitability and appropriateness for each thing's being. God as "the most just Ruler" of all creation requires that all things created, including man, abide by and be treated according to this suitability and appropriateness for which he has ordered creation.

WHAT EXACTLY IS EVIL? CAN EVIL BE DEFINED? WHY DO MEN DO EVIL?

Regarding evil itself, Augustine in *On the Free Choice of the Will* does not proffer a precise definition of what evil is, or is not, as he does later in the *City of God* (quoted earlier in chapter 1) where he denied that evil has any nature of its own, but rather Augustine asserts that evil is the absence of good. Here, however, Augustine asks the questions why men do evil and what it is to do evil. There is already in *On the Free Choice of the Will* a recognition of particular evils such as "adultery, murder and sacrilege." What Augustine is seeking is the fundamental cause of evil that would provide an essential aspect of what evil is. Augustine proceeds to question Evodius concerning a particular evil, viz., adultery, and asks him for the reason why adultery is something evil. Evodius answers by appealing to the golden rule and stating that he knows adultery is evil because he would not tolerate it in regard to his own wife. In response to this argument, Augustine asks the following question of Evodius:

> What if someone's lust leads him to offer his wife to another, freely tolerating her being violated by him, and in turn desiring to have equal license with the other man's wife? Does he then seem to you to have done nothing evil?[7]

---

6. Augustine, "On the Free Choice of the Will" 1.2.4.11; 1.2.4.12 (pp. 5–6).
7. Augustine, "On the Free Choice of the Will" 1.3.6.17 (p. 7).

Evodius answers that such a person does a great evil. With this question and the obvious answer to it, Augustine provides a ready example of the limitation of the golden rule in providing the sole, principal foundation for establishing goodness and, at the same time, establishing the sole, principal foundation for establishing evil. As one principle of the moral order, the golden rule has a sure, important standing. But as the sole, principal foundation of the moral order, there is a deficiency found within it—any one person can be so corrupted as to tolerate a moral evil done to himself so as to indulge his disordered desire to perform a moral evil toward someone else.

Herein lies the great deficiency of Immanuel Kant's fundamental law of pure practical reason regarding the moral order. Says Kant (as quoted above): "So act that the maxim of your will could always hold at the same time as a principle in a giving of universal law."[8] As argued earlier in chapter 2 of this manuscript, Kant's maxim is a corollary of the golden rule in that one's action should be the basis for a maxim that serves as a universal law applicable to all persons. This concept is essentially related to the rule that one should do unto others (with the understanding of others as meaning all others and hence implying universality) as one would have them do unto him. There are of course various instances in which a certain kind of person would tolerate evil toward himself in order to practice that evil toward another as, for example, a person who has little regard for his own reputation lying about the reputation of another so as to discredit that other's social position. However, in fairness to Kant, it is necessary to add his qualification of the moral law, which was also quoted above: "It now follows of itself that in the order of ends the human being (and with him every rational being) is an end in itself, that is, can never be used merely as a means by anyone."[9] Still, there remains the problem of how to apply to human situations an admittedly abstract principle, which requires treating a person as an end and never as a means.

Rejecting the golden rule as the only grounds for proving that adultery is evil, Augustine looks beyond the nature of the act, without denying the evil of adultery in itself, to the motive committing the act. As in the civil law, judgment of a wrongdoer in the moral law involves the complex relationship among the factors involved in an action, viz., the nature of the act performed, the intention or motive of the person who acts, and

---

8. Kant, *Critique of Practical Reason* 1.1.1.7 (p. 28).
9. Kant, *Critique of Practical Reason* 1.2.2.5 (p. 106).

the circumstances that surround the action. Augustine will look for an evil desire motivating an action performed, and in the case of adultery, the evil desire will be lust understood in its specific sense. The term "lust" is also employed by Augustine in a more general sense to include any inordinate, disordered desire for a temporal good to the exclusion of a higher moral good. For example, lust for power can motivate one to destroy the reputation of another person so as to gain that person's position.

When asking Evodius for a convincing reason to establish that adultery is evil, Evodius can provide no answer, so that Augustine proposes the following explanation:

> Then perhaps lust is the evil in adultery, and you will run into more difficulties as long as you are looking for evil in the outward visible deed. Now to understand that lust is the evil in adultery, consider the following. If a man does not have the opportunity to sleep with someone else's wife but it is plain somehow that he wants to do so, and that he is going to do so should the opportunity arise, he is no less guilty than if he were caught in the act.[10]

In response to Augustine's explanation Evodius offers the following comments in agreement:

> Nothing could be more obvious. Now I see that there is no need for a long discussion to persuade me about murder, sacrilege, and in fact all other sins. It is clear now that nothing but lust dominates in every kind of evil doing.[11]

Lust as an evil motive can corrupt an otherwise good act in itself. For example, if a man were to help a woman who is an acquaintance to perform a task that she herself was unable to perform solely so the man could be near her and lust her, then an otherwise good act of charity would be corrupted into an evil act. On the other hand, however, to kill a man, for example, because he is verbally abusive toward his wife would still be an act of murder even if one's motive were to prevent ongoing verbal abuse of the woman. Augustine, however, will readily provide examples when homicide is justifiable and hence not murder, such as the killing of a robber who threatens to kill someone innocent, or the killing of a rapist by the victim before he completes his crime; or when, says Augustine:

---

10. Augustine, "On the Free Choice of the Will" 1.3.8.20 (p. 7).
11. Augustine, "On the Free Choice of the Will" 1.3.8.21 (p. 7).

> the law bids a soldier to kill the enemy, and if he holds back from this bloodshed he pays the penalties from his commander. Surely, we will not dream of calling these laws unjust—or rather, not to call them "laws" at all.[12]

Evodius further develops what Augustine teaches regarding duty and lust when he tells us:

> Furthermore, in killing the enemy a soldier is thus acting as an agent of the law, and thus easily does his duty without lust. Besides, the law itself, which was enacted for the protection of society, can hardly be accused of lust—a least assuming that the lawgiver, if he enacted the law of God's bidding (namely as eternal justice prescribes), was able to do so entirely free of lust.[13]

Here, it is Evodius who alludes to the distinction between divine eternal law and eternal justice and man-made temporal law, which can be corrupted by the moral limitations of the lawgiver but ideally should reflect divine eternal justice for its legitimacy. Such acts of justifiable homicide are not murder at all and are not evil but can be responsible and even dutiful acts. Pope John Paul II provides further support for this position in his encyclical *Evangelium Vitae, Gospel of Life*, regarding legitimate defense:

> Moreover, "legitimate defense can be not only a right but a great duty for someone responsible for another's life, the common good of the family or of the state" [*Catechism of the Catholic Church* §2265]. Unfortunately, it happens that the need to render the aggressor incapable of causing harm sometimes involves taking his life. In this case, the fatal outcome is attributable to the aggressor whose action brought it about, even though he may not be morally responsible because of a lack of the use of reason.[14]

IS EVIL DEFINED BY CIVIL LAW? CAN CIVIL LAW REFLECT DIVINE LAW?

Human law must take into consideration those conflicts in the human condition that necessitate qualifications and exceptions to what any given

---

12. Augustine, "On the Free Choice of the Will" 1.5.11.33 (p. 10).
13. Augustine, "On the Free Choice of the Will" 1.5.12.34–35 (p. 10).
14. John Paul II, *Evangelium Vitae*, 844.

law establishes. The moral law is reflected in civil law when the latter condemns homicide as a capital crime except in those instances when justifiable homicide is the case or, at least, renders the commission of a homicide as being noncriminal. The civil law, which is man-made, temporal, and reflecting man's practical reason, receives its ultimate justification from divine law that is God-made, eternal, and ordained by right reason. What Augustine begins to define and distinguish in *On the Free Choice of the Will* is eternal law and man's participation in eternal law through his knowledge and application of natural law and how both are ideally reflected in civil law. The civil law restricts a person's freedom to act in violation of certain parts of the natural law that can be reflected within a government's criminal code—this restriction is enforced by civil authorities under penalty of prosecution and punishment. The natural law, at the same time, restricts a person's freedom to act in violation of divine law (eternal law) under penalty of ultimate divine punishment.

Augustine as cited above in his *Reply to Faustus the Manichaean* refers to "the law of nature" or natural law as including the Ten Commandments found in sacred Scripture. Now here, in *On the Free Choice of the Will*, concerning the eternal law Augustine tells us to:

> Consider law referred to as "supreme reason." It should always be obeyed; through it good people deserve a happy life and evil people an unhappy one; and, finally through it temporal law is both rightly enacted and rightly changed. . . . [Here, Evodius asserts:] "I see that this law is eternal and unchangeable." [Augustine then answers:] Nothing in the temporal is just and legitimate which human beings have not derived from the eternal law. If a given society justly conferred honors at one time and not at another, this shift in the temporal law, to be just must derive from the eternal law whereby it is always just for responsible society to confirm honors and not for an irresponsible one. . . . So, to explain concisely as far as I can the notion of eternal law that is stamped on us: it is the law according to which it is just for all things to be completely in order.[15]

The eternal law, which Augustine says is "stamped on us," includes the law of nature, or natural law, which is written on all our hearts. We have already seen cited (in chapter 1 of this book) where Augustine refers to his having "an instinct" or inclination for such goods as "caring for

---

15. Augustine, "On the Free Choice of the Will" 1.6.15.48; 1.6.15.50; 1.6.15.51 (p. 13).

his own being," "delighting in the truth," and "delighting in friendship," which inclinations were all "gifts of my God."[16] Along with these goods, Augustine cites in his *Reply to Faustus the Manichaean* Rom 2:14–15, where Paul refers to the Gentiles doing by nature the things contained in the law so that the Gentiles "show the work of the law written on their hearts."

As the eternal law is God's order of all things created including man, there is a divine governance through which all things in the cosmos have a purpose and an end that God intended for their existence. But if God ordains in his eternal law that all things, including man, already have in their existence an ordered purpose or end, how is it that man can have reason and free will that any man can use to thwart God's purpose? Thomas Aquinas, utilizing his dialectical method, first cites Augustine and then proffers an objection to whether any law is natural to man; Thomas Aquinas then proceeds to answer the objection:

> Objection 1. . . . Because man is governed sufficiently by the eternal law: for Augustine says in *De Libero Arbitrio* that the eternal law is that by which it is right that all things should be most orderly. But nature does not abound in superfluities as neither does she fail in necessaries. . . .
>
> I answer that. . . Wherefore, since all things subject to Divine providence are ruled and measured by the eternal law . . . it is evident that all things partake somewhat of the eternal law, in so far as, namely, from its being imprinted on them, they derive their respective inclinations to their proper acts and ends. Now among all others, the rational creature is subject to Divine providence in the most excellent way, in so far as it partakes of the share of providence, by being provident both for itself and for others. Wherefore it has a share of the Eternal Reason, whereby it has a natural inclination to its proper act and end: and this participation of the eternal law in the rational creature is called the natural law.[17]

In the case of man, God has ordained human reason and free will to be operative in man's participation in the eternal law; this participation is called the natural law. The well-ordered person is free to choose wisely precisely because he/she can know the natural law instinctively because it is imprinted on the heart, so that the person can rationally distinguish

---

16. Augustine, *Confessions* 1.20.31 (p. 20).

17. Thomas Aquinas, *Summa Theologica* Ia IIae, q. 91, a. 2, obj. 1; Ia IIae, q. 91, a. 2, obj. 1, resp.

the ways to apply the natural law in his/her life toward himself/herself, toward others, and toward the world around him/her. Knowing the natural law and how to apply it first requires an awareness of the principles of the moral law imprinted on the heart, which the human mind rationally applies to practical, concrete situations. But, man also has irrational impulses that need to be controlled by man's rational mind and will in order to preclude deficient desires from dominating the person. Augustine tells us that "when reason (or mind or spirit) governs irrational mental impulses, a human being is dominated by the very thing whose dominance is prescribed by the law we have found to be eternal."[18] Man must follow the natural law in order to achieve the ordered purpose God intended for him.

Augustine inquires as to "how a human being may be completely in order within himself."[19] What disorders a human being is his enslavement to lust; and, says Augustine, "nothing makes the mind a devotee of desire but its own will and free choice" so that when a person chooses to lust the result is that "lust dominates the mind and drags it back and forth, despoiled of the richness of virtue, poor and needy."[20] In order to avoid the choice of lust, man must have understanding that can bring about "a more enlightened and perfect life in accordance with the light of the mind."[21]

KNOWING YOURSELF TO BE ALIVE, ACHIEVING SELF-MASTERY OVER LUST, AND ATTAINING WISDOM

In order to come to an understanding of how a human being may be completely in order within himself, Augustine proposes reflecting on the distinction between "being alive and knowing yourself to be alive."[22] "Knowing yourself to be alive" is not just a reflection upon one's bodily functions and capabilities but is also a basic type of self-awareness where the person realizes that he/she is a living, rational being who can know and understand his/her own inclinations, habits, and aspirations and knows that he/she is free to choose in accord with, or in opposition to,

---

18. Augustine, "On the Free Choice of the Will" 1.8.18.65 (p. 16).
19. Augustine, "On the Free Choice of the Will" 1.7.16.52 (p. 13).
20. Augustine, "On the Free Choice of the Will" 1.11.22.76–77 (p. 19).
21. Augustine, "On the Free Choice of the Will" 1.7.17.59 (p. 15).
22. Augustine, "On the Free Choice of the Will" 1.7.16.52 (p. 14).

the moral law stamped on his/her heart. Augustine refers to "the knowledge of life" as providing "a more enlightened and authentic life" because "nobody can know except those who have understanding, which itself is nothing but living a more enlightened and perfect life in accordance with the light of the mind."[23] "Knowing yourself to be alive" is the first step of coming to self-consciousness where the person is aware of and understands his inclinations, desires, and motives for freely choosing to do what he does and has done, and to his becoming aware of the person he has chosen to be. Knowing oneself to be alive awakens in the person the voice and judgment of conscience with its moral dictate to act in accord with the natural law imprinted on the heart and, at the same time, to perceive the Law Giver who is at once a Being exterior and superior to ourselves (as John Henry Newman informed us) but also a Being who is interior to ourselves and speaks to us "behind a veil."

As cited above, Augustine describes in his *Confessions* (written only shortly after *On the Free Choice of the Will* was completed) the experience of God inducing such a self-conscious reflection of conscience when he relates how the Lord "turned me back towards myself, taking me from behind my own back where I had put myself . . . [and] set me before my own face that I might see how vile I was, how twisted and unclean and spotted and ulcerous."[24] Augustine argues that knowing yourself to be alive is to know that you have reason and understanding and can control beings who are lacking in self-conscious reason, such as animals, whom men can train and command to perform certain acts. Whereas, on the one hand, the animal acts on instinct so that the capacities of its brain (such as they are in any given animal) follow the dictates of that instinct that dominates the animal's focus. Man, on the other hand, has the capacity to know that he is alive and thereby to reflect on himself self-consciously; this capacity provides him with the prerequisite for freely choosing what inclination to follow, be it a moral instinct imprinted on his heart and thereby the choice governed by virtue in accord with his rational nature, or the disordered, irrational instinct of lust in opposition to his moral instinct. If chosen, the disordered, irrational instinct tends to dominate one's reason and render one's free will unfree.

Augustine argues that reason must remain free to clearly understand that lust in all its forms robs the person of his self-mastery. Regarding the

---

23. Augustine, "On the Free Choice of the Will" 1.7.17.59 (p. 15).
24. Augustine, *Confessions* 8.7.16 (p. 152).

person who chooses virtue and rational self-control, Augustine states: "I call 'wise' those whom truth bids be so-called, namely those who have attained peace by subjugating lust to the mind's full governance."[25] Those who subjugate lust to the mind's full governance have a good will, i.e., "a will by which we seek to live rightly and honorably, and to attain the highest wisdom."[26] Augustine states further that the person who freely chooses disordered desire to dominate his reason "justly pays the penalties for so great a sin." Augustine tells us that when lust is freely embraced, virtue and truth are lost so that the person justly deserves to suffer in the present life:

> That reign of desires savagely tyrannizes and batters a person's whole life and mind with storms raging in all directions. On this side fear, on that desire; on this side anxiety, on that empty spurious enjoyment; on this side loss of something loved, on that ardor to acquire something not possessed; on this side sorrows for an injury he received, on that the burning to redress it. Whichever way one turns, greed can pinch, extravagance squander, ambition enslave, pride puff up, envy twist, laziness overcome, stubbornness provoke, submissiveness oppress— these and countless others throng the realm of lust, having the run of it.[27]

Augustine tells us that such a person who freely wills to abandon virtue and becomes a slave of lust is a fool who lacks a good will and deserves the penalties the person suffers, while the person who freely wills to live a virtuous and honorable life has a good will and is wise. Augustine asks, "What is so much in the power of the will as the will itself?" He proceeds to answer his own question by stating: "Anyone who does not have a good will certainly lacks the very thing the will alone would provide through itself."[28] Augustine unequivocally asserts here that the will is free in itself to choose goodness and avoid evil. However, Augustine is not claiming that the power of the mind and will to freely choose goodness is boundless given the limitations of human frailty. In Book 3, Augustine states that "the soul confronts the physical suffering that threatens to destroy its unity and integrity ... with reluctance and resistance" and that, like all living beings that can "feel the distress of pain,"

---

25. Augustine, "On the Free Choice of the Will" 1.9.19.69 (p. 17).
26. Augustine, "On the Free Choice of the Will" 1.12.25.83 (p. 21).
27. Augustine, "On the Free Choice of the Will" 1.11.23.78 (p. 19).
28. Augustine, "On the Free Choice of the Will" 1.12.26.86 (p. 21).

the soul avoids extreme pain and in so doing "avoids its fragmentation and pursues unity."[29] Man, like all living beings, is finite, and all the faculties of the soul including the mind and free will have limits, especially when a person is enduring extreme pain or torture. Augustine will later explicitly qualify all his assertions regarding freedom of will by adding that there is a definite need for God's grace in order for the person to endure suffering and for the will to choose the good and to carry out the good it chooses. But it is also necessary that a person's free will must always be ready to choose to act in accord with grace.

Granting that in the virtuous person wisdom governs the mind and the will is free to retain virtue and goodness so as to avoid becoming a slave of lust, Augustine will still ask whether such a person who is virtuous and just can be forced by another to become subjugated to lust. Augustine answers this question appealing to God's eternal law, which assigns to the mind and will mastery over lust and disordered, irrational desire. There is of course the case of a person who has become habituated to lust or to any of the seven capital sins so that the particular vice or vices can dominate the person's mind and will to the extent that the person can no longer exercise mastery over his/her evil impulses. This is not the case with those who are not habituated to vice, but who, nevertheless, possess the tendencies to vice that affect all human persons as a result of their inheritance of a fallen nature. Nonetheless, those who are not habituated to vice can still exercise mastery of their mind and will over lust and disordered desires. If the opposite were true, then man's very being would be completely disordered, and consequently the moral order in man would be much weaker or even nonexistent, and the immoral disorder in man would dominate the mind and will. Augustine reasons with Evodius that this latter point is not the case:

> Augustine: Do you think that lust is more powerful than the mind itself, which we know has been granted governance over lusts by eternal law? I do not myself think so. The weaker commanding the stronger would not be a case of being completely in order. Accordingly, I think the mind must be more powerful than desire for the very reason that it rightly and justly dominates desire.

---

29. Augustine, "On the Free Choice of the Will" 3.23.69.235; 3.23.70.238 (pp. 120–21).

> Well, can a just mind—a mind safeguarding its proper right and command—cast down from its stronghold and subjugate to lust another mind governing with equal justice and virtue?
>
> Evodius: By no means. . . . A mind that attempts to do this to another will fall away from justice and become vice-ridden, and thereby will be weaker than the other.
>
> Augustine: You understand quite well. Consequently, it remains for you to declare, if you can, whether you think anything is more excellent than a wise and rational mind.
>
> Evodius: Nothing but God, I think. . . .
>
> Augustine: That is also my view . . . . Whatever the nature may be that is appropriately superior to a mind powerful in virtue, it cannot be in any way unjust. . . .
>
> Therefore, since (a) anything equal or superior to a governing mind possessed of virtue does not make it the servant of lust, on account of justice, and since in addition (b) anything inferior to it could not do this, on account of weakness, as the points we have agreed on between us establish, we are left with this conclusion. Nothing makes the mind a devotee of desire but its own will and free choice.[30]

One might object here to Augustine's argument on the grounds that many human persons do not have minds powerful in virtue but, nevertheless, are not necessarily enslaved by lusts. There can also be those inferior in certain virtues who might still retain a powerful will in service to evil motives such as envy or anger. Such a person might even resort to intimidation to force another person to engage in evil behavior. Once evil behavior is indulged, even out of fear, there can result the beginnings of vice. However, a person not powerful in virtue (especially the virtue of fortitude) but at the same time not enslaved by any kind of lust can use his/her free will to move away from the intimidator and choose to bolster his/her courage to pursue virtue in the face of possible danger.

BEHAVIORISM, ITS ADHERENTS, ITS LIMITATIONS, AND AUGUSTINE'S EMPHASIS ON VIRTUE

Modern philosophies and scientific theories such as behaviorism that analyze the cause of human action would reject Augustine's conclusion

30. Augustine, "On the Free Choice of the Will" 1.10.20.71–11.21.76 (pp. 18–19).

that "nothing makes the mind a devotee of desire but its own will and free choice." Behaviorism is a type of psychological analysis of man and his actions that begins with a presumed scientific observation of the causes of man's behavior. According to behaviorism, events and situations in a person's life, especially when reinforced by ongoing environmental stimuli, account for why and how people act and react the way they do. Behaviorism tends to reject introspection or any attempt to explain human action based on a person's inner self, or mental states, or the operations of the mind. The concept of rational choice or free will tends also to be rejected in favor of learned stimuli response or conditioned reflex regarding how best to deal with problems, pressures, and occurrences in a person's life. Radical behaviorism tends to be reductionist and rejects beliefs, religious yearnings, or the intuition of values as opposed to responses to stimuli that result in learned behavior. Behaviorism tends to be a materialist philosophy that reduces the human person by making him/her solely a product of his/her genetic, instinctual, and neurological responses to the stimuli of one's immediate environment and personal experience.

The *Oxford Dictionary of Philosophy* in its entry "behaviorism" tells us:

> In psychology behaviorism associated with Watson and such researchers as Ivan Pavlov (1849–1936) was first of all a methodological view, counseling the avoidance of introspection and the subjective in favor of the scientific measurement of behavior and its causes. In later hands, particularly those of B. F. Skinner (1904–1990), the view became identified with a simplistic vision of the springs of human action, and with the prospect of control of action by relatively simple manipulation of the stimuli and patterns of reinforcement that are allowed to impinge on an agent. Skinner's belief [was] that the explanation of behavior through belief, intention, and desire is somehow unscientific, or the preserve of "mentalists."[31]

While behaviorism has become modified in recent years and developed into what is called functionalism, which holds that conscious states of the mind involve perceptions, rational analysis, intentional, or purposeful thought, emotional reactions, and choice, still all these activities of an agent organism depend upon, and are the result of, that agent's physical responses to the stimuli of a material environment. There is no credible acceptance in original behaviorism or in functionalism of man as a

---

31. Blackburn, "Behaviorism," 50–51.

spiritual being with his highest faculties being a rational conscious mind and a free will.

Generally, it is historically verifiable that philosophical and scientific views of man and reality have always exercised a sometimes subtle yet distinct effect on the culture of a people, including what values they accept (including aesthetic, social, and political values), what morality they practice, and what degree of vitality they experience in their lives. Without trust in, or yearning for, God, or a belief in the immortality of the soul, or an acceptance of eternal law and a transcendent moral order imprinted on the heart, the human person tends to be excused from moral responsibility, and human freedom is increasingly discounted. But along with the reduction in human responsibility comes a reduction in human worth, purpose, and ultimate meaning for human life. Instead of advocating the seeking of virtue and the avoidance of vice, behaviorism tends to excuse the human person's easy avoidance of discipline and restraint and to accept the lower desires, inclinations, and instincts of human nature at the expense of the pursuit of virtue and the higher goods that require perseverance and a good will.

Augustinian thought would tend to discredit modern behaviorism by contrasting against it the pursuit of virtue and higher goods through the free choice of a good will. Behaviorism expects the human person, through the reinforcement of environmental stimuli, to tend to pursue those lower goods of which Augustine speaks such as one's "glorious reputation, great wealth, and whatever bodily goods . . . that can easily be lost" so that the person is rendered "thoroughly unhappy even if he has all such goods in abundance."[32] Augustine unhesitatingly relates happiness with the person's freely chosen pursuit of the higher goods and virtue and relates unhappiness with the person's free pursuit of lower goods over the higher goods and of vice over virtue. Augustine's thesis is based on the belief, confirmed by lived experience, of eternal law, which is the providential divine plan of the proper, universal, and highest order of all things in nature, including man. Augustine makes this clear:

> Those who are happy (who must also be good) are not happy simply because they willed to live happily. Even evil people will this. Instead, it is because they willed to live rightly, which evil people are unwilling to do. . . . The eternal law . . . established firmly with unchangeable stability that deserts are in the will, whereas reward and punishment are in happiness and

32. Augustine, "On the Free Choice of the Will" 1.12.26.87 (p. 22).

unhappiness. Thus when we say that people are unhappy due to the will, we are not thereby saying that they willed to be unhappy, but rather that they are in a condition of will upon which must follow unhappiness, even against their will.[33]

As Augustine states above, those who are happy must also be good and will to live rightly. Those who will to live rightly reject the slavery of lust and vice and pursue virtue. It is logical for Augustine to have provided here in Book 1 of *On the Free Choice of the Will* a brief definition of each of the four cardinal virtues, so-called because they have traditionally been viewed as the "hinges" upon which the door to all other virtues swings open. These virtues include prudence through which virtue, says Augustine, "good should be pursued and things that are opposed to it should be avoided"; temperance through which virtue, says Augustine, moderateness is achieved as "the state that checks and restrains the appetite from things it pursues disgracefully"; courage, which is the virtue of bravery in which a person resists anything "inimical to his own most cherished good" and which he "does not love" and "is not pained by [its] loss and holds [it] as utterly worthless"; and justice, which is the virtue with which a person "cannot have ill-will towards anyone" so that "he would do injury to no one," which "can happen only if he gives to each his due."[34]

In stark contrast to behaviorism's insistence (in all its modified forms) that all thoughts, beliefs, emotive experience and choices of the human organism are results of conditioned responses to physical stimuli, the pursuit of virtue requires a rational conscious mind freely choosing to pursue a higher good over the satisfactions of bodily needs and desires. This is not to say that behaviorism is a philosophy and science that cannot provide some necessary truths and insights regarding man's need to respond to, and interact with, his environment. The response of human beings to their environment, given favorable or unfavorable stimuli, helps humans to survive and meet their physical and social needs. What is perhaps more evident to see and verify is the need of humans to interact with their natural environment. Man should not be completely isolated from the physical world of nature of which he is part. Man needs to experience the moon and stars, trees, wild animals, rivers and streams and to breathe clean air, and it is a grave error for man to live only in an artificial

---

33. Augustine, "On the Free Choice of the Will" 1.14.30.100–101 (pp. 25–26).
34. Augustine, "On the Free Choice of the Will" 1.13.27.89–93 (pp. 22–23).

environment where he is cut off from nature. Man is both physical and spiritual—a complex organism of body and soul. And it is a far greater error for man to be cut off from his spiritual life, or to ignore his yearning for God, and his need to bind with God through worship and religious experience—all of which behaviorism tends to ignore.

Augustine concludes Book 1 of *On the Free Choice of the Will* by contrasting two kinds of things: the eternal and the temporal, as well as two kinds of people whose goals in life are freely chosen by the will for either one or the other of these things—eternal or temporal, at the expense of the other. Speaking of "the power of eternal law," Augustine tells us:

> We have also explicitly and adequately distinguished two kinds of things, the eternal and the temporal, and again two kinds of people; some who follow and take delight in eternal things, and others who follow and take delight in temporal things. We have established that what each person elects to pursue and embrace is located in the will, and that the mind is not thrown down from its stronghold of dominance, and from the right order, by anything but the will. It is also clear that when a person uses something in an evil manner, the thing should not be blamed, but rather the person using it in that evil manner.[35]

As created beings, God provided us with temporal things to meet our physical needs and to provide enjoyment for legitimate physical desires. However, when a person freely chooses to turn aside from "divine and genuinely abiding things and towards changeable and uncertain things," a person sins against God, who created him/her with a will free to choose him first and foremost; but God is not the cause of our turning away from eternal things and deficiently choosing temporal things in violation of God's moral order.[36]

SUMMARY OF BOOK 2 OF *ON THE FREE CHOICE OF THE WILL*

Augustine begins Book 2 with Evodius asking why God gave free choice of the will to man seeing that, if he had not bestowed this capability, man would not able to violate God's eternal law. Augustine first provides Evodius with a succinct answer based on the following premises: that God

---

35. Augustine, "On the Free Choice of the Will" 1.16.34.114 (p. 29).
36. Augustine, "On the Free Choice of the Will" 1.16.35.116 (p. 29).

exists; that man's existence is from God and that God made man good; that God is the source of justice and rewards man's good actions and punishes his bad actions; and that God gave man free will to act rightly. Augustine tells us:

> [1] If a person is something good and could act rightly only because he willed to, then he ought to have free will, without which he could not act rightly.... The fact that a person cannot live rightly without it is therefore a sufficient reason why it should have been given to him.
>
> [2] Free will can also be understood to be given for this reason: If anyone uses it in order to sin, the divinity redresses him for it. This would happen unjustly if free will had been given not only for living rightly but also for sinning. How would God justly redress someone who made use of his will for the purpose for which it was given? However, when God punishes the sinner, what does He seem to be saying but: "Why did you not make use of free will for the purpose for which I gave it to you?"—that is, for acting rightly.
>
> [3] If human beings lack free choice of the will, how could there be good in accordance with which justice itself is praised in condemning sins and honoring right deeds? For what does not come about through the will would neither be sinning nor acting rightly. Consequently, penalty and reward would be unjust if human beings did not have free will. There ought to be justice in punishment and in reward, since justice is one of the goods that are from God.[37]

Augustine's answer is reasonable if one accepts the additional premise that God gave man the ability to know and understand what is right and what is wrong, what is good and what is evil; God also gave man the inclination for man to do what is good and avoid what is evil even if, at the same time, man has a moral weakness inclined toward what is evil. It will not be until the end of Book 3 that Augustine will explain how man has inherited a fallen nature from Adam, but that man still knows what is good and has the free ability to pursue this good. Nonetheless, at this point of *On the Free Choice of the Will*, Augustine provides a sufficient response to the question of why God gave man free will notwithstanding man's ability to do evil. The whole theme of Augustine's work is that there is a good, just God who established man with an understanding of the

---

37. Augustine, "On the Free Choice of the Will" 2.1.3.5–7 (pp. 29–30).

divine moral order and the ability to choose freely to act in accord with it. Moreover, as a result of man's actions, rewards for good actions and punishments for evil actions are just recompense. God made man to be his own agent with an autonomy founded in his rational understanding and free will.

A FURTHER COMMENT ON BEHAVIORISM

We find in the literature of certain behaviorists a rejection of man as being his own autonomous agent with a free will and, hence, deserving the rewards and punishments for either good or bad actions. B. F. Skinner provides a clear and distinct rejection of the Augustinian view of human persons as being endowed with free will and understanding that makes them responsible for the good they do as well as the evil they do. Says Skinner:

> Two features of autonomous man are particularly troublesome. In the traditional view, a person is free. He is autonomous in the sense that his behavior is uncaused. He can therefore be held responsible for what he does and justly punished if he offends. That view, together with its associated practices, must be re-examined when a scientific analysis reveals unsuspected controlling relations between the behavior and environment....
> Freud was a determinist—on faith, if not on the evidence—but many Freudians have no hesitation in assuring their patients that they are free to choose among different courses of action and are in the long run the architects of their own destinies.
> This escape route is slowly closed as new evidence of the predictability of human behavior is discovered. Personal exemption from a complete determinism is revoked as scientific analysis progresses, particularly in accounting for the behavior of the individual....
> By questioning the control exercised by autonomous man and demonstrating the control exercised by the environment, a science of behavior also seems to question dignity or worth.... A scientific analysis shifts the credit as well as the blame to the environment, and traditional practices can no longer be justified.[38]

---

38. Skinner, *Beyond Freedom and Dignity*, 21–23.

As we can see from Skinner's analysis, man's autonomy and free agency are rejected, for the most part, and replaced by an understanding of man and his behavior as being caused by his learned responses to the stimuli of his environment. For this extreme type of behaviorism man has little or no free will and is not responsible for the good or evil he performs. Moreover, there is a failure in this extreme behaviorism to acknowledge an innate moral order within human persons to which they owe obedience. For behaviorism, man is not responsible to God, will not deserve or be liable for rewards or punishments from God, but is subject to those who have the power to control or manipulate his environment. What behaviorism of this sort ignores is the innermost responses of man himself to his moral governor—his own conscience—and to his quest for truth, achievement, dignity, and God.

Behaviorists like B. F. Skinner are reductionists who seek to resolve all of mankind's problems by focusing on behavioral science, which investigates environmental stimuli shaping behavior. The major premise of these behaviorists is that man is only a physiological organism. What is rejected here is man's spiritual nature, which is incorporeal and involves man's intellectual faculties of a rational consciousness and a free will. What is further rejected by behaviorism is the human quest for spiritual and moral values such as goodness, benevolent love, empathy, compassion, honesty, and all other virtues and the quest for God and the ultimate knowledge of the cause and real nature of all reality. Practically speaking (and partially incorporating certain behaviorist premises) each person must choose among the various stimuli of the surrounding environment and pursue such stimuli, which encourage virtuous behavior. Human persons have moral as well as physiological/psychological limitations. But human persons also have a rational mind and a will free to choose to maximize moral behavior by avoiding stimuli that degrade the person and pursuing stimuli that uplift the person.

Returning to Evodius's question regarding why God gave free choice of the will to man, Augustine's succinct answer is that a person cannot live rightly without free will; this also includes an understanding of divine justice for the rewards for living rightly and the punishments for sin. After brief discussion of the reasonableness of accepting in faith the testimony of the authors of Scripture based on the prophet Isaiah's words "Unless you believe you shall not understand" (Isa 7:9; from an early, pre-Vulgate, Latin translation of the Greek Septuagint), Augustine extends the inquiry further by presenting the following three questions, for which he will seek an answer from a philosophical/rational perspective:

[1] How is it clear that God exists?

[2] Do all things, in so far as they are good, come from God?

[3] Is free will to be counted among these goods?[39]

With these three questions Augustine is searching for the ground for establishing God's reality and the truth of a transcendent moral order created by God. This moral order is known and freely acted upon by man without resorting to a cosmological argument. Augustine answers these three questions throughout Book 2 of *On the Free Choice of the Will* from a rational and philosophical perspective by proceeding introspectively with his investigation of man's consciousness and his pursuit of truth, which he had already begun in Book 1. There Augustine distinguished between man's merely living and man's knowing that he is alive. In Book 2, Augustine addresses Evodius: "I will ask you first whether you yourself exist. Are you, perhaps, afraid that you might be deceived by this line of questioning? Surely if you did not exist, you could not be deceived at all."[40] Augustine explains that if a person truly understands, he can know that he/she exists and is also alive and that he is not deceiving himself/herself. Augustine further says: "Existing, living, and understanding are three [distinct] things. . . . However, it is quite certain that one who understands both exists and is alive."[41] What places man above the mere existence of all things in creation and above merely being alive (life also found in animals) is that man also understands and thus self-consciously knows he exists and is alive. An animal is alive but does not self-consciously understand that it is alive. A stone exists but is not alive and has no understanding.

THE PHILOSOPHY OF DESCARTES

Before proceeding with the analysis of *On the Free Choice of the Will*, a digression into the philosophy of the Enlightenment thinker René Descartes (1596–1650) reveals a certain parallel with (as well as sharp deviations from) Augustine's dialogue. Descartes actually answers all

---

39. Augustine, "On the Free Choice of the Will" 2.3.7.20 (p. 34).
40. Augustine, "On the Free Choice of the Will" 2.3.7.20 (p. 35).
41. Augustine, "On the Free Choice of the Will" 2.3.7.22 (p. 35).

of Augustine's questions posed to Evodius. Descartes conceives of his "*cogito ergo sum*," "I think, therefore I am," on similar lines as Augustine's argument asserting that one must exist in order to be deceived. Descartes was a rationalist in a sense broad enough so as to include intuition. What Descartes sought to intuit was "what presented itself to my mind so clearly and so distinctly that I had no occasion to call it in doubt."[42] Descartes was seeking a first principle upon which an indubitable philosophy could be based—a principle that was free of falsehood and deception. In his *Discourse on Method* (written in 1637) he writes:

> Considering the fact that all the same thoughts we have when we are awake can also come to us when we are asleep, without any of them being true, I resolved to pretend that all the things that had ever entered my mind were no more true than the illusions of my dreams. But immediately afterward I noticed that, while I wanted thus to think that everything was false, it necessarily had to be the case that I, who was thinking this, was something. And noticing that this truth—"I think, therefore I am"—was so firm and so assured that all the most extravagant suppositions of the skeptics were incapable of shaking it, I judged that I could accept it without scruple as the first principle of the philosophy I was seeking.[43]

A philosopher's epistemology or theory or method of knowledge is important in examining that thinker's understanding of man's nature, especially man's intellect and will and his understanding of a moral order; once this epistemology is comprehended, a comparison with another thinker (such as Augustine) can be more readily accomplished. For Descartes, a systematic method of doubt pervades his philosophy in his quest for certain knowledge, and this systematic doubt is the obstacle that must be placated before there can be any understanding or acceptance of experienced truths regarding man's nature, intellect, and will.

Descartes's *Meditations on First Philosophy* (written in 1641 shortly after his *Discourse on Method*) is a treatise of six discourses concerning such topics as what can or should be doubted, the nature of the human mind, God's existence and perfections, and the distinction between, and connection of, mind and body. Descartes begins his first meditation by introducing a method of universal doubt in his search for a starting point of absolutely sure and doubtless knowledge based on one's awareness

42. Descartes, *Discourse on Method* 2.18 (p. 11).
43. Descartes, *Discourse on Method* 4.32 (p. 18).

of certain, distinct truth. What the reader discerns as he follows Descartes's thinking through the progression of each of these meditations is that there is a development of thought that is exploratory in nature and that does not initially establish conclusions that are necessarily immutable or sustainable. Certain positions that Descartes originally adopts he will later discard or at least greatly modify. Descartes reasons that he "should withhold [my] assent no less carefully from opinions that are not completely certain and indubitable than I would from those that are patently false."[44] Descartes will similarly reject the reliability of the senses as providing completely certain knowledge. Descartes reflects:

> Surely whatever I had admitted until now as most true I received either from the senses or through the senses. However, I have noticed that the senses are sometimes deceptive; and it is a mark of prudence never to place our complete trust in those who have deceived us even once.[45]

What Descartes's universal doubt led him to solely accept is what is clear, distinct, and absolutely certain innate knowledge, which alone can establish a doubt-free principle as a foundation for the sciences and for all truth. Initially, Descartes will even suspend acceptance of God as the omnipotent creator and source of all goodness and truth and entertain instead the possibility of his being deceived by an all-powerful being. Descartes opined:

> Accordingly, I will suppose not a supremely good God, the source of truth, but rather an evil genius, supremely powerful and clever, who has directed his entire effort at deceiving me. I will regard the heavens, the air, the earth, colors, shapes, sounds, and all external things as nothing but the bedeviling hoaxes of my dreams, with which he lays snares for my credulity. I will regard myself as not having hands, or eyes, or flesh, or blood, or any senses, but as nevertheless falsely believing that I possess all these things.[46]

Notwithstanding such possible deception, Descartes argued with the same observation given by Augustine to Evodius (above) that if you did not exist, you could not be deceived at all. Descartes observed that if "there is some deceiver or other who is supremely powerful and

---

44. Descartes, *Discourse on Method*, Meditation 1.18 (p. 59).
45. Descartes, *Discourse on Method*, Meditation 1.18 (p. 60).
46. Descartes, *Discourse on Method*, Meditation 1.22–23 (p. 62).

supremely sly and who is always deliberately deceiving me," then it can be concluded that "there is no doubt that I exist, if he is deceiving me." What Descartes further concludes is "this pronouncement: 'I am, I exist' is necessarily true every time I utter it or conceive it in my mind."[47] From this pronouncement Descartes will proceed to infer a precise, if definitely limited, understanding of what he and every rational person is, based on the *cogito, ergo sum*, "'I think, therefore I am'":

> What about thinking? Here I make my discovery: thought exists; it alone cannot be separated from me. I am; I exist—this is certain. But for how long? For as long as I am thinking; perhaps it can also come to pass that if I were to cease all thinking I would then utterly cease to exist. At this time I admit nothing that is not necessarily true. I am therefore precisely nothing but a thinking thing; that is, a mind, or intellect, or understanding, or reason—words of whose meanings I was previously ignorant. Yet I am a true thing and am truly existing; but what kind of thing? I have said it already: a thinking thing.[48]

Distinct difficulties will confront Descartes after his determining that he is certain that he knows that he exists because he thinks: what is the source of his (Descartes's) existence; and what is the source of the existence of other things (if they exist); and how can he be certain about the existence of anything else? For Descartes, the answer to these questions is bound up with the existence of God, and knowledge of the existence of God is bound up with one's clear and distinct idea of God. In answer to the question of what the source or cause is of his own existence, Descartes muses: "Why, from myself, or from my parents, or from whatever other things there are that are less perfect than God." But Descartes rejects this answer because he knows he doubts and cannot assure himself of his own origin, and neither can any other being that is finite and imperfect ultimately account for its own origin. For this reason, any intermediate source or cause of one's own existence must depend upon a being who is uncaused. If one were caused by an intermediate cause, then the question arises concerning this intermediate cause "whether it got its existence from itself or from another cause, until finally I arrive at the ultimate cause, which will be God." Descartes reasons (in a manner similar to Aristotle), "there can be no infinite regress here." Further, Descartes argues, "I am not dealing here merely with the cause that once produced me, but

---

47. Descartes, *Discourse on Method*, Meditation 2.25 (p. 64).
48. Descartes, *Discourse on Method*, Meditation 2.27 (p. 65).

also and most especially with a cause that preserves me at the present time."[49] Descartes thinks beyond the finite and imperfect to what is perfect and infinite and, in a manner similar to both Augustine and Anselm, conceives of "nothing more perfect than God, or even as perfect as God, [which] can be thought or imagined."[50]

Descartes searches to discover a fuller understanding of his idea of God so that it is intuited clearly and distinctly within him. The difficulty Descartes encounters is how can he, a limited being with limited ideas, have conceived of a being that is unlimited? Descartes speculates:

> I understand by the name "God" a certain substance that is infinite, independent, supremely intelligent and supremely powerful, and that created me along with everything else that exists—if anything else exists. Indeed all these are such that, the more carefully I focused my attention on them, the less possible it seems they could have arisen from myself alone. Thus, from what has been said, I must conclude that God necessarily exists. For although the idea of substance is in me by virtue of the fact that I am a substance, that fact is not sufficient to explain my having the idea of an infinite substance, since I am finite, unless this idea proceeded from some substance which really was infinite.[51]

The idea of an infinite substance found within a finite being who is also a thinking being aware of his own existence leads Descartes further to conclude not only that God exists but that he possesses all perfections and is without defect. Says Descartes, "There being in me an idea of the most perfect being, that is, God, demonstrates most evidently that God too exists," as this most perfect being is "a being subject to no defects whatever" and is consequently a being free from "all fraud and deception [that] depend on some defect."[52]

Descartes's argument is that the idea of an infinite substance being present within a person (Descartes himself) who is manifestly a finite substance must proceed from a substance that is infinite (viz., God). This argument is a version of the ontological argument that holds that God's existence is proven by the very idea of God as a most perfect being and must include his existence, because the lack of God's existence would be

---

49. Descartes, *Discourse on Method*, Meditation 3.50 (p. 79).
50. Descartes, *Discourse on Method*, Meditation 3.48 (p. 78).
51. Descartes, *Discourse on Method*, Meditation 3.45 (p. 76).
52. Descartes, *Discourse on Method*, Meditation 4.51–52 (p. 80).

a defect that is contrary to the very idea of God as a most perfect being. Descartes adds that as a finite being he could not be the origin of the idea of the most perfect infinite being. Further, Descartes also employs the cosmological argument for God's existence by arguing that there must be an ultimate cause for himself and for all intermediate causes that brought himself and all finite things into existence, or there would be an infinite regress of causes that cannot account for their own existence. Descartes argues, in a manner similar to Aristotle regarding the unmoved mover, that this ultimate cause must be God. However, Immanuel Kant argues that this cosmological argument is nothing but a restatement of the ontological argument, which holds that the positing of the idea of God as the most perfect being must include his existence. The cosmological argument holds that there must be an ultimate cause of all that exists that must be uncaused or there would be an infinite regress of causes. For both arguments Kant makes the same refutation, viz., both arguments rely solely on an idea of God, either as the most perfect infinite being or as the uncaused cause, yet both arguments lack empirical evidence of the existence (which can only be based on sense verification) of such a most perfect infinite being, or such an ultimate cause.

We have already discussed above Kant's rejection of the inference of the existence of the most perfect being proceeding from the idea of the most perfect being. Kant argues that such an inference is not valid because the mere concept of God cannot prove the existence of God, and neither can such a concept prove that God is the source of the idea of the most perfect being. Kant argues that God's existence requires empirical proof from one's senses. This argument can also be used, as we have seen, against Augustine's argument used in his address to God in *Confessions*, (also quoted above): "No soul ever has been able to conceive anything better than You, the supreme and perfect Good."[53] Kant's argument can also be used against Anselm's meditation *Proslogium*, which states concerning God "that there exists a being, than which nothing greater can be conceived, and it exists both in the understanding and in reality."[54] But if empirical proof is needed for absolute certitude that God exists, then it would seem that Augustine's, Anselm's, and Descartes's ontological proofs for the existence of God are all refuted.

53. Augustine, *Confessions* 7.4.6 (p. 20).
54. Anselm, *Proslogium*, 54.

However, as noted above, Kant's rejection of any data from inclinations, impulses, emotional or mystical experience is a rejection of evidence beyond that which is provided by human senses. While such data are rejected as not providing scientific proof for God's existence, it nevertheless presents evidence that appeals to our human experience. All scientific hypotheses and theories look to provide evidence of causation, and even when scientists cannot find conclusive evidence to establish a scientific law that is universally accepted, a theory or hypothesis may be established that demands further investigation. Man is constantly cognizant of the causation of things and events surrounding him in his everyday lived experience, and this experience demands that the human person search for an ultimate cause of himself and of all that exists, because an infinite regress of causes defies one's everyday understanding of how things happen.

In human experience instinctual, emotional, and mystical evidence will never satisfy the requirements of empirical, scientific investigation, but such data does supply strong motives for accepting the realm of what Rudolph Otto calls the numinous, or mysterious, in which man experiences himself as a unworthy creature before that which is supreme above all creatures. When Augustine speaks of that yearning in man that cannot be satisfied by anything but God himself, there is a strong motive for the acceptance of God. When John Henry Newman speaks of the commanding dictate of conscience revealing a Being who is exterior and superior to ourselves, there is a strong motive for accepting the existence of God. A similar argument can be made for what enters the mind of a rational man who perceives that the very idea of an infinite, all-perfect Being comes from, or is guided by, the divine and not merely man's imagination.

A summary of Descartes's determination of whether God exists might begin with Descartes first questioning—"what is the source or cause of his own existence?" Descartes reasons that as a finite and imperfect being he cannot be the ultimate cause of his own existence, and neither can his parents or any line of persons or things be the cause of his or their own existence, because they are all themselves finite and imperfect. Descartes reasons finally that there must be an ultimate cause that produced him and preserves him along with all other persons and things. Descartes comes to a clear and distinct idea of this ultimate cause as God who possesses all perfections (including existence) and who must be the infinite, independent, supremely intelligent, and all-powerful creator of everything that exists. Because Descartes knows he is finite and imperfect, he reasons there can be no way he could come to this idea of the most perfect being that is God unless God himself placed that idea within Descartes. Further, because deception is a defect, it cannot be found in the infinite perfect being that God is. God cannot be a deceiver and still be God. Therefore, the clear and distinct idea of the infinitely perfect and powerful creator must come from God and must be true.

Because God is the infinitely perfect and powerful creator "and he is not a deceiver," Descartes can have confidence in his God-given ability to perceive through the bodily senses so "that everything that I clearly and distinctly perceive is necessarily true."[55] However, it should be noted that not everything man perceives is perceived clearly and distinctly so that, says Descartes, "notwithstanding the immense goodness of God," by nature man "is composed of mind and body [and] cannot help being sometimes mistaken." Yet, Descartes asserts that he knows "that all the senses set forth what is true more frequently than what is false," especially "regarding what concerns the welfare of the body."[56] Moreover, Descartes reasons, from sense experience came "the ideas perceived by sense [that] were much more vivid and explicit and even, in their own way, more distinct than any of those that I deliberately and knowingly formed through meditation," so that Descartes had to conclude that these ideas perceived by sense did not come from himself but "that they came from other things."[57] Descartes concludes that not only much of what is perceived by the senses, but whatever is rationally demonstrated in the mind, "as in geometry," can be accepted without doubt, and:

> The certainty in truth of every science depends exclusively upon the knowledge of the true God, to the extent that, prior to my becoming aware of him, I was incapable of achieving perfect knowledge about anything else. But now it is possible for me to achieve full and certain knowledge about countless things, both about God and other intellectual matters.[58]

---

55. Descartes, *Discourse on Method*, Meditation 5.70 (p. 91).
56. Descartes, *Discourse on Method*, Meditation 6.88–89 (pp. 102–3).
57. Descartes, *Discourse on Method*, Meditation 6.75 (p. 94).
58. Descartes, *Discourse on Method*, Meditation 6.71 (p. 92).

DESCARTES'S FINAL REJECTION OF UNIVERSAL DOUBT

Descartes comes to a conclusion in Meditation 6, which is his final meditation, that "the hyperbolic doubts" entertained throughout the first five meditations "ought to be rejected as ludicrous." Descartes, it would seem, has come full circle in first accepting a method of universal doubt and then rejecting it. He explains that he could not be certain initially whether his perceptions were occurring while dreaming or while he was awake. At the end of his Meditations Descartes freely admits that he should not have "the least doubt regarding the truth of . . . all the senses, in addition to my memory and my intellect, in order to examine them," because "nothing is passed on to me by one of these sources that conflicts with the others."[59]

When Descartes speaks of his senses together with memory and the intellect passing on truths that are not in conflict and therefore are not to be doubted, he is speaking of the reality of conscious thought that is unified and harmonious in his "mind, that is, [in] myself insofar as I am only a thinking thing, I cannot distinguish any parts within me, rather, I understand myself to be manifestly one complete thing." As a thinking thing a person is united with any idea within him, including an idea of an external object perceived through the senses. Descartes emphasizes that the consciously rational "mind is not immediately affected by all the parts of the body, but only by the brain, or perhaps even by just one small part of the brain, namely, where the common sense is said to reside. Whenever this part of the brain is disposed in the same manner, it presents the same thing to the mind."[60] It is regrettable that in the Meditations Descartes does not define and precisely describe what this common sense is and what it actually does for the conscious mind where the goal is to clearly and distinctly understand the idea of each thing that is perceived. Each of the five external senses (seeing, hearing, touching, tasting, smelling) have organic structures and distinct neurological receptibility, with the data of their respective capabilities providing to the brain specific sensations of colors, sounds, tastes, smells, tactile feelings without there being consciousness of this data within the external senses themselves. For conscious perception to take place so that this perception can be grasped by the mind, a specific internal sense is needed that consciously relates and

---

59. Descartes, *Discourse on Method*, Meditation 6.89–90 (p. 103).
60. Descartes, *Discourse on Method*, Meditation 6.86 (p. 101).

unifies these sensations. The twentieth-century professor of philosophy at Catholic University William Wallace OP (1918–2015) tells us:

> The central sense, also known as the sensus communis (common sense) is necessary for consciousness of sensation, which is impossible for the external senses because their organic structure prohibits reflection on themselves. It [common sense] is also needed to explain comparisons between sensations of the various senses, comparisons that no sense can make since it does not know the objects of the other senses.[61]

Along with common sense (which has no capacity for retaining or remembering impressions gained from the external senses), there are several other internal senses that are necessary in the complex process of acquiring sense knowledge from the external senses. These internal senses include the imagination, which can produce and recall an image of a unified object (a phantasm) from which it is necessary for the mind or intellect through its cognitive powers to abstract an essential characteristic needed to grasp the meaning of the object. Another internal sense is the memory, which functions to retain various perceptions of the same object and which together with the cognitive powers can unify these perceptions of a material object, resulting in an understanding of a universal idea and definition of the object.[62]

One could reasonably ask at this point what significance or relevance the common sense and the other internal senses could have for understanding the free choice of the will. A short answer could be that, without discernment of what an object essentially is, there cannot be a rational choice to choose it in distinction to another perceived object. While the moral law is written on the heart, the will must understand in any of its acts what its chosen objectives are in order to choose freely. The common sense perceives an object through the respective sensations of the body's five senses and provides the needed consciousness of a unified object for the mind's reason to determine what this object essentially is, which determination, in turn, is needed for the will to make an informed choice regarding the object it chooses.

---

61. Wallace, *Elements of Philosophy*, 69.
62. See generally, Wallace, *Elements of Philosophy*, 69–71.

AUGUSTINE'S UNDERSTANDING OF THE INTERNAL SENSE; ITS RELATIONSHIP TO REASON

In Book 2 of *On the Free Choice of the Will,* Augustine investigates the common sense, which he calls the "internal sense," which perceives that it has five senses within the body even as it perceives the respective sensual data presented by each of these five senses. Further, the internal sense provides an awareness of how this data of each of these individual five senses can have a common relation to one object. Stated another way, through the internal sense there is a conscious awareness of one's own perceptions coalescing onto one perceived object, which awareness of a unified object is lacking in the individual bodily senses themselves. Man shares this capacity of the internal sense with many animals, but only man can go beyond this unified awareness of the interior sense by means of his reason, which can determine the essential meaning of a perceived object, whereas animals can only react instinctively to this perceived object. Augustine questions Evodius as to what the individual senses themselves perceive in the objects that they sense (e.g., the eye sees a plate of food, and the nose smells the food); then how is it that the sense data of each of the senses is combined so that there is a perception of one object? Restating this question, in both men and animals, if the eye cannot smell the food in its presence, and the nose cannot see the food before it, how is it that a conscious being is aware that what it sees and what it smells actually applies to the one same object? Augustine in his dialogue with Evodius explores the question:

> Augustine: Can we settle what pertains to each sense by means of any of the senses? Or what they have in common with one another, or some of them?
>
> Evodius: Not at all. These matters are settled by something internal.
>
> Augustine: This is not by any chance reason itself, which animals lack, is it? For I think it is by reason we grasp these things and know that they are so.
>
> Evodius: I think instead that by reason we grasp that there is an "internal sense" to which the familiar five senses convey everything. Surely that by which an animal sees is one thing, whereas that by which it pursues or avoids what it senses by seeing is another. The former sense is in the eyes, the latter within the soul itself. By it, animals either pursue and take up as enjoyable,

or avoid and reject as offensive, not only what they see but also what they hear or grasp by the other bodily senses. Now this [internal sense] cannot be called sight, hearing, smell, taste, or touch, but something else, whatever it may be, that presides over them all in common. We do grasp it with reason, as I pointed out, but I cannot call it reason itself, since it is clearly present in animals.

Augustine: I recognize it, whatever it is, and I do not hesitate to name it the "internal sense." Yet unless what the bodily senses convey goes beyond it, we cannot arrive at knowledge. We hold anything that we know as something grasped by reason.[63]

Augustine proffers a short summary of how this process of perception through the bodily senses proceeds and how the internal sense unites them. The internal sense provides the awareness of a perceived exterior object that reason, i.e., the rational operations of the conscious mind, can determine as having an essential meaning. First, there are physical objects that merely exist, and then there are the bodily senses that individually sense and report their respective data to the common sense, or as Augustine calls it, the internal sense. The internal sense, which exists and is also alive, combines or unites the data it receives from the individual bodily senses of which the internal sense is consciously aware, so that this diverse data is now perceived as applying to one common object. The internal sense, which perceives but cannot understand in itself, reports everything it perceives to the rational mind of the knowing human person, who not only exists and is alive, but also rationally and self-consciously understands. The rational understanding of the person makes determinations and universal abstractions of the object presented to it by the internal sense and thereby knows the object as an identifiable existent reality. Augustine abbreviates this process in this way:

> The following points are clear: (a) physical objects are sensed by bodily sense; (b) the same sense cannot be sensed by the selfsame sense; (c) physical objects are sensed by the internal sense through bodily sense, as well as bodily sense itself; (d) reason acquaints us with all the foregoing, as well as with reason itself, and knowledge includes them.[64]

---

63. Augustine, "On the Free Choice of the Will" 2.3.8.26–9.29 (pp. 36–37).
64. Augustine, "On the Free Choice of the Will" 2.4.10.41 (p. 39).

Augustine's last point, that reason acquaints us with reason itself and that this acquaintance includes knowledge, can be explained by the rational understanding that can reflect back upon its own determinations and examine its own functions, such as defining and judging what is presented to it from the senses through the internal sense. The internal sense is described by Augustine as "the whatever-it-is by which we can sense everything we know." The internal sense functions as "an agent of reason," which "presents and reports to reason anything with which it comes into contact," so that "the things sensed can be singled out within their limits and grasped not only through sensing but also through knowing."[65] It could be added that the rational understanding is self-conscious reason and is aware of its own rational processes and conclusions and can distinguish itself from its agents. Augustine makes this clear:

> Reason itself singles its agents out from the things they deliver. Again, it recognizes the difference between these things and itself, and it confirms that it is more powerful than they are. Surely reason does not grasp itself by anything other than itself (i.e., by reason), does it? How would you know that you have reason unless you perceived it by reason?[66]

Augustine is maintaining that man's reason not only recognizes the difference between things and itself but also that it can define the meaning of what a thing is from the distinctions that reason discerns regarding the thing. Further, the rational mind can judge that reason is superior to its agents, viz., the five senses that provide sensory data and the internal sense that perceives a unified thing, which reason defines because of its conscious understanding of what the thing essentially is. Augustine identifies the three gradations of being as including beings that merely exist, beings that are consciously alive, and rational beings that have self-conscious understanding. Beings such as animals that are consciously alive and have the internal sense are superior to beings that merely exist. And beings that have self-conscious understanding can judge themselves superior to beings that are only consciously alive. Human beings possess reason, which therefore elevates them above those nonrational animals that only possess the interior sense. While animals are consciously alive, they do not have self-conscious knowledge.

---

65. Augustine, "On the Free Choice of the Will" 2.3.9.35 (p. 38).
66. Augustine, "On the Free Choice of the Will" 2.3.9.36 (p. 38).

Augustine refers to man's reason as "the 'head' or 'eye' of the soul,"[67] which is the most exalted human faculty surpassing those of any other created being that merely exists or is consciously alive. These three gradations of being may be said to anticipate the Being that is superior to all that exists, is conscious, or is rational. Augustine refers back to the first of the three questions posed at the beginning of Book 2, viz.: "How is it clear that God exists?"[68] In order to answer this question, Augustine proffers to Evodius a somewhat astonishing challenge that if he (Evodius) could find something more exalted than human reason would he hesitate to call this, "whatever it is ... God?"[69] Augustine quickly justifies his challenge with the following question to Evodius: "If you find nothing above our reason except what is eternal and unchangeable, will you hesitate to say that this is God?"[70] Augustine will pursue this quest for God by means of a circuitous route throughout Book 2 of *On the Free Choice of the Will*.

AUGUSTINE ON HUMAN WISDOM

What Augustine establishes as clearly evident is that living conscious beings are finite and changeable, as are physical objects. While human reason can conceive of what is eternal and immutable truth, the rational human intellect itself is finite and changeable, at one time grasping eternal truth and wisdom, and at another, losing sight of both. Yet all reasoning beings can agree that certain truths can be known by all as being both eternal and unchanging. Numbers, ratios, and arithmetic calculations when done properly are eternally true and unchangeable, and, says Augustine: "Nor is there a flaw in it when anyone makes a mistake; it remains true and intact while the person is all the more in error unless he sees it."[71] Augustine is referring to the objective and unchanging truth of numbers, ratios, and arithmetic calculations, and links this truth to what Augustine will argue is the eternal and unchanging truth of wisdom, which he briefly defines as "the truth in which the highest good is recognized and grasped."[72] Further, Augustine has no problem link-

---

67. Augustine, "On the Free Choice of the Will" 2.6.13.53 (p. 42).
68. Augustine, "On the Free Choice of the Will" 2.3.7.20 (p. 34).
69. Augustine, "On the Free Choice of the Will" 2.6.14.54 (p. 42).
70. Augustine, "On the Free Choice of the Will" 2.6.14.55 (p. 42).
71. Augustine, "On the Free Choice of the Will" 2.8.20.80 (p. 46).
72. Augustine, "On the Free Choice of the Will" 2.9.26.100 (p. 50).

ing wisdom with happiness because he finds no doubt in accepting that "whatever the highest good is, human beings can become happy only when it is possessed."[73] Regarding his dialogue with Evodius in the early part of Book 2, the problem remains in determining whether wisdom is one and the same for all persons.

In addressing the problem of what wisdom precisely is and whether wisdom is one and the same for all persons, Augustine maintains that there are truths that are common to everyone who is open to the truth. For example, Augustine argues, "that the incorrupt is better than the corrupt, the eternal better than the temporal, the inviolable than the violable."[74] And for Augustine that which is incorrupt, eternal, and inviolable for humans is to be found in the cardinal virtues, which have true and unchangeable rules. The man of prudence (the cardinal virtue of practical wisdom) recognizes that the incorrupt should be preferred to the corrupt; and the just man (justice being a cardinal virtue) subordinates things of lower value to things of higher value and gives people that which is truly due them, while the man of courage (courage being another cardinal virtue) is not dissuaded from the moral high ground by misfortune. Augustine is persistent in his argument with Evodius over whether wisdom is one and the same for all persons:

> Just as there are true and unchangeable rules of numbers, whose intelligible structure and truth you declared to be unchangeably present in common to all who recognize them, so too are there true and unchangeable rules of wisdom ... and you granted that they are present and common to be contemplated by all who are able to look upon them.[75]

In order to complete the four cardinal virtues, three of which were mentioned by Augustine, temperance must be added, which is the virtue that moderates desire for pleasurable things and thereby enables any person to attain that self-control and inner peace that brings about a unity or wholeness in a person, which wholeness is the incorruptible quality of integrity. The person of integrity is most open to accepting what is true and unchangeable in pursuing the highest good and acquiring happiness. The word "integrity" is a derivative of the Latin word *integer*, which means an entirety or a complete unity or a oneness. The person with integrity is

---

73. Augustine, "On the Free Choice of the Will" 2.9.27.106 (p. 51).
74. Augustine, "On the Free Choice of the Will" 2.10.28.114 (p. 52).
75. Augustine, "On the Free Choice of the Will" 2.10.29.119 (p. 54).

honest and complete in himself and free from two-facedness or duplicity. With integrity, the connection between number and wisdom is given a certain foundation.

Augustine finds a profound link between wisdom and number, though he vacillates regarding the precise relationship between the two. What Augustine states with surety is that wisdom and number are linked in the known order of unchangeable truth and in the created order of changeable things. Regarding the link between wisdom and number and their unchanging truth, Augustine tells us:

> Even if we cannot be clear whether number is in wisdom or derives from wisdom, or whether wisdom in itself derives from number or is in number, or whether each can be shown to be the nature of a single thing, it is certainly evident that each is true, and unchangeably true.
>
> Consequently, you will not deny that there is unchangeable truth, containing everything that is unchangeably true. You cannot call it yours or mine or anyone else's. Instead, it is present and offers itself in common to all who discern unchangeable truths.[76]

Augustine here establishes the unifying reality of objective truth, which incorporates both wisdom and number within unchangeable truth that can be known and understood by rational persons. Augustine makes one of his few references to Revelation (found in *On the Free Choice of the Will*), which implies a divine source of both wisdom and number. Augustine tells us that "it is . . . said of wisdom in Scripture that it 'reaches from one end to the other strongly and puts all things in order sweetly' [Wis 8:1]." Augustine ventures an interpretation of this by adding "perhaps the power that 'reaches one end to the other strongly' is number, while the power that 'puts all things in order sweetly' is then called wisdom in the strict sense, although both powers belong to one and the same Wisdom."[77] Arguably, Augustine's reference to "one and the same Wisdom" is a reference to God, who is the source of all numeric order and of all wisdom. In Scripture, number and wisdom are understood by the faithful as revealed, unchanging truth, which truth is also believed to be discernible by all rational persons.

The revealed and unchanging truth of number and wisdom is seen by Augustine as found in the very nature of all existing physical things,

76. Augustine, "On the Free Choice of the Will" 2.11.32.129–12.33.130 (p. 56).
77. Augustine, "On the Free Choice of the Will" 2.11.30.124 (p. 55).

each of which has a discernible form that makes the object the existing thing that it is. Moreover, each form is discernible because it has a numeric ratio of atoms and molecules that structures the object as the precise existing thing that it is. Augustine directs the reader:

> Look upon the heavens, the earth, and the sea, and at everything in them, whether they shine down or creep below or fly or swim. They have forms because they have numbers. Take the latter away from them and they will be nothing. What is the source of their existence, then, if not the source of the existence of number? After all, they have being precisely to the extent that they are full of numbers.[78]

As God is the source of the unchanging truth of all numeric order, so too God is the source of all forms that provide the unchanging essence of each changing being that God created, including human beings themselves. Augustine proceeds to provide the evidence for answering the first of the three questions he presented to Evodius near the beginning of Book 2, viz.: "How is it clear that God exists?" Augustine argues that all changeable things must have a form, yet nothing can give form to itself, the obvious implication being that only an unchangeable eternal form could form things that are changeable. Says Augustine:

> Every changeable thing must be formable. (Just as we call what can be changed "changeable," I shall in like manner call what can be given form "formable.") Yet no thing can give form to itself, for the following reason. No thing can give what it does not have, and surely something is given form in order to have form. Accordingly, if any given thing has some form, there is no need for it to receive what it already has. But if something does not have a form, it cannot receive from itself what it does not have. Therefore, no thing can give form to itself, as we have said. . . . Thus it follows that mind and body are given form by an unchangeable form that endures forever. To this form was it said: "You shall change them, and they shall be changed; but you are the same and your years shall not fail" [Ps 101:27–28].[79]

---

78. Augustine, "On the Free Choice of the Will" 2.16.42.164 (p. 62).
79. Augustine, "On the Free Choice of the Will" 2.17.45.172–173 (pp. 64–65).

MATTER AND FORM

Augustine's reference to "an unchangeable form that endures forever" and that actually gives form to mind and body and to all things that exist and are changeable and are formable is, for Augustine, an acceptance of a personal and providential God who created and "gave numbers to all things, even to the lowliest" so that "all physical objects have their own numbers." But, says Augustine, God "did not give wisdom to physical objects, or even to all souls, but only to rational souls," so that the rational person can "discern the numbers that have been impressed on them [physical objects]."[80] In speaking of physical objects to which God gave each its own number(s), Augustine was referring to the dual nature of every changeable thing that exists in the universe, viz., all physical substances are a composite of matter and form. Augustine more lucidly expresses this concept in his *Confessions* where he states: "And it is true that anything subject to change suggests to our mind a certain formless element, by which it receives form which is changed and transformed."[81] Augustine is providing here an explanation concerning the nature of matter and form, where changeable matter through divine agency has a numerical essence impressed upon it at any given time. This does not negate the fact that ongoing changes within matter may transform the essence of an object from being of one distinct kind with its own number into being of another distinct kind of essence with a different number at any given time. The egg of a female human (with its own specific number) when united with the sperm of a male human (with its own specific number) can produce a living human embryo with its own specific number.

In saying that "all physical objects have their own numbers," Augustine was possibly considering the reality of small building blocks of matter, viz., atoms (as did the Presocratic Democritus, ca. 460–ca. 370 BC), which are numerically structured so as to form the essence of distinct physical substances. However, regarding rational souls, who have wisdom, Augustine contends that only the wise person understands that the unchangeable truths of number "transcend our minds and remain unchangeable in truth itself."[82] What Augustine is intimating here is that human minds, including the minds of wise persons, are changeable and finite, and yet the wise person can grasp and understand the unchangeable

---

80. Augustine, "On the Free Choice of the Will," 2.11.30.125 (p. 55).
81. Augustine, *Confessions* 12.19.28 (p. 274).
82. Augustine, "On the Free Choice of the Will" 2.11.31.126 (p. 55).

truths of number that establish the essential forms of changeable physical objects. How can this be? The human mind and will are the highest faculties of the soul, and, while not physical objects, the mind can abstract concepts of objects that are composed of a certain number and grasped by the mind's understanding; yet the human mind is subject to change and is finite. Augustine addresses the Creator in his *Confessions*:

> Your Knowledge is and wills immutably, Your Will is and knows immutably. It does not seem proper in Your eyes that immutable Light should be known by the mutable being which it illumines, as that Light knows itself. Therefore, my soul is as earth without water unto Thee, for just as it cannot of itself illumine itself, so it cannot of itself quench the thirst that it has. For with Thee is the fountain of life, and in Thy light we shall see light.[83]

God not only creates the mind with the potential to attain immutable knowledge but also activates and preserves this capacity in man. Yet the human person is mutable, finite, and incapable of enlightening himself/herself. The human person is composed of an intimate union of body and soul but with a human nature that is fallen and subject to deficiency and vice, which also subjects the mind and will to the propensity of deficiency and error, notwithstanding its capacity to attain immutable knowledge. Without God's help the human person cannot know immutable Light.

LUCRETIUS DENIES GOD AS THE SOURCE OF MATTER AND FORM

The theistic argument that God is the source of the forms that matter assumes had already been challenged five centuries earlier before Augustine by the Latin poet/philosopher Lucretius, ca. 100–55 BC, of whom it could be speculated that Augustine had some knowledge. Lucretius might be described as an ancient atheist, understood to mean that he had no acceptance of a transcendent supernatural Being or beings to whom the universe and all things in it owe their existence, design, order, or maintenance. Lucretius attributed to nature alone, in and of itself, all creative power to produce varying forms through the rearrangement of atoms or the elements constituting changeable matter:

---

83. Augustine, *Confessions* 13.16.19 (p. 301).

> This matter returns: what came from earth goes back into the earth; what was sent down from the ethereal vault is readmitted to the precincts of heaven. Death does not put an end to things by annihilating the component particles but by breaking up their conjunction. Then it links them in new combinations, making everything change in shape and color and give up in an instant its acquired gift of sensation. So, you may realize what a difference it makes in what combinations and positions the same elements occur and what motions they mutually pass on and take over. You will thus avoid the mistake of conceiving as permanent properties of the atoms the qualities that are seen floating on the surface of things, coming into being from time to time and as suddenly perishing.[84]

Regarding any conception of supernatural involvement of a divine being in the creative process, Lucretius quickly adds: "You will immediately perceive that nature is free and uncontrolled by proud masters and runs the universe by herself without the aid of gods."[85] It is safe to say that there is no sense of a personal or provident God or gods in Lucretius's cosmology. Lucretius holds that nature and natural laws control a material universe, i.e., a universe where all things are made solely of matter and where these laws of nature are behind and explain everything that comes into being, exists, possibly lives, and changes into something else.

What did Augustine say of "this matter," which according to Lucretius "came from earth [and] goes back into the earth" yet "was sent down from the ethereal vault"? While Augustine does speak of "formless matter," he nevertheless does not separate matter and form, because both belong together and were created "simultaneously," and however basic or primal the matter, it cannot exist without some basic or elemental form. For Augustine, everything that has being, exists, and changes must have form, or everything would cease to exist; and since things while formable cannot form themselves, they must receive their forms from the Creator who designed their numeric structure so as to constitute any given object. For Augustine, that God exists is manifest in the existence of all created things, each possessing its own distinct form that changes over time and becomes some other distinct thing or things with its/their own distinct form(s). Augustine reasons:

---

84. Lucretius, *On the Nature of the Universe*, 89–90.
85. Lucretius, *On the Nature of the Universe*, 92.

> All good things whatsoever, no matter how great or small, can exist only from God. What can be greater in Creation than intelligent life? What can be less then body? However much these things deteriorate and thereby tend to nonbeing, some form must nevertheless remain in them, so that they do exist in some way. Whatever form may remain in a deteriorated thing, it comes from that form which knows no deterioration, and it prevents the movements of these things—as they deteriorate or improve—from transgressing the laws of their own numbers.[86]

As all things that exist manifestly change, changes occur according to a transcendent plan of order whereby each changed thing assumes a new form in accord with laws governing its numerical and essential design. Matter alone cannot explain the rational order of the ways things change and assume a different form, and this truth is especially evidenced by intelligent human life. The transcendent plan of order in nature requires a Being who put things in order and arranges them according to a purposeful plan for all creation, especially for human persons. Augustine is answering his second question at the beginning of Book 2, viz., "Do all things, insofar as they are good, come from God?" Even things that deteriorate and change and organisms that die assume new forms that may provide resources or fertilize the soil so as to promote new life. All things God creates and forms ultimately work for the good of his creation.

AUGUSTINE'S VIEW OF CREATION IN CONTRAST WITH NATURALISM AND DARWINISM

But how did God create? Did Augustine believe in a simplistic creation of the universe and all that is in it where God directly created each entity and living being with its own distinct form and nature? This is not the view of Augustine, who argued that God's omnipotence did not preclude his creation of things according to a providential plan of development where the form of things contained potentialities that were actualized into other things through time. Even the casual observer must admit the process of development involved during the temporal course of nature. The acorn is the seed that germinates and becomes the oak tree. Scripture reveals that "unless a grain of wheat falls to the ground and dies, it remains just a grain of wheat; but if it dies, it produces much fruit" (John

---

86. Augustine, "On the Free Choice of the Will" 2.17.46.176–177 (pp. 65–66).

12:24). Augustine conceived of God creating things in a dynamic state of development explicit in his later work *The Literal Meaning of Genesis* (ca. 400), not published until 416. *The Literal Meaning of Genesis* is as much a speculative work of philosophy as it is biblical exegesis, and in it, Augustine explains that creation unfolded according to God's plan, where simpler forms of things possessed potentiality that become actualized into more complex forms:

> What it is our business ... to inquire about is how those causal formulae were set, with which he primed the universe when he first created all things simultaneously. Was it so that all things that came to birth in the way we see, whether shrubs or animals, would go through the different intervals of time appropriate to each species and its taking shape and its growth, were so that they would be fully formed forthwith, in the way it is believed that Adam was made without any growing pains in adult manhood? But why should we not believe that those formulae contained each potentiality, so that anything would be actualized from them that pleased the one who would make them?[87]

What Augustine observed with the development of the animal and plant kingdoms he also attributed to the creation of inanimate forms in nature, attributing to God's power and divine providence creation of certain substances from other substances according to natural processes. Augustine might not have been aware of the production of pearls within a mollusk such as an oyster, when a grain of sand or a bit of food or bacteria becomes embedded in the soft tissue within the shell of the mollusk, causing irritation, so that it secretes a mineral or protein substance to cover over the foreign object and protect itself, thus with the result of creating a gemstone of beauty. Diamonds are made from crystallized carbon that has been subjected to intense heat and pressure deep within the earth. The metamorphosis of an ordinary substance into a valuable object of beauty—a diamond—comes about through a change of carbon atoms under the right conditions. Augustine argues that God created certain things so that their formulae contained the potentialities to become actualized into different substances. Augustine speculates that God created so that:

> The elements of this material world have their distinct energies and qualities, which determine what each is or is not capable of,

---

87. Augustine, *On Genesis* 6.14, 25 (p. 350).

> what can or cannot be made from which. It is from these baselines of things, so to say, that whatever comes to be takes in its own particular time span, its risings and continued progress, its ends and its settings, according to the kind of thing it is.[88]

That God intended that what he created would be capable of evolving into other forms of things over time is definitely accepted by Augustine.

In the modern era, the philosophy of naturalism would generally hold that the universe and all it contains consists of matter only, and this matter is not derived from any supernatural source but is, rather, self-existing and self-operating according to its own laws, which can be scientifically examined and explained. Most modern theories of evolution espouse similar premises, but evolutionary theory need not dispense with the ultimate power of a supernatural Being as the source, designer, maintainer of nature or the laws of nature and any evolutionary process that might exist. The word "evolution" comes from the Latin *evolutio*, meaning unrolling or unfolding, and refers to the gradual and sometimes, sometimes not, orderly process of change of the universe and all living species within it. Inorganic evolution refers to the development of primal gases, stars, galaxies, solar systems, and planets all beginning perhaps with the "big bang." According to general evolutionary theory, from this inorganic beginning of the universe and after billions of years and under the right environmental conditions came the subatomic, atomic, and molecular changes, which marked the beginning of organic evolution of simple lifeforms, which eventually developed into a complex variety.

And since Darwin, most evolutionists accept the process of natural selection and its corollary of survival of the fittest. Natural selection is an operation of nature whereby organisms best suited for survival and thriving in their environment tend to perpetuate themselves and increase their number. "Survival of the fittest" is a phrase describing the process of natural selection and is often used synonymously with this process to refer to those organisms that best adapt to their environment and are most successful in reproducing themselves.

In a famous passage from his *The Origin of the Species*, Darwin refers to the laws of nature at work in the evolutionary process:

> These laws, taken in the largest sense, being Growth with Reproduction; Inheritance which is almost implied by reproduction; Variability from the indirect and direct action of the conditions

---

88. Augustine, *On Genesis* 11.17, 32 (p. 447).

of life, and from use and disuse; a Ratio of Increase so high as to lead to a Struggle for Life, and as a consequence to Natural Selection, entailing Divergence of Character and the Extinction of less improved forms. Thus, from the war of nature, from famine and death, the most exalted object which we are capable of conceiving, namely, the production of the higher animals, directly follows. There is grandeur in this view of life, with its several powers, having been originally breathed by the Creator into a few forms or into one; and that, whilst this planet has gone cycling on according to the fixed law of gravity, from so simple a beginning endless forms most beautiful and most wonderful have been, and are being, evolved.[89]

Darwin's reference to "Inheritance which is almost implied by reproduction" manifests an understanding of the passing on of traits from parents to their offspring, at a time when the scientific study of genetics was in its early stages in the late nineteenth century with Georg Mendel and others. What is of concern here is the understanding that genes are the vital means by which all species of animals that are reproduced, including "the production of the higher animals," pass on their traits. What is basically held in evolutionary theory is that there have been genetic mutations in animal species (over perhaps millions of years) that have resulted in the development of higher animals. Genetic pools of simple species of organisms with their recessive genes randomly emerging over dominant genes, when the opportunity arose, created new gene pools also resulting in differing, and perhaps improved, lifeforms. Natural selection and the survival of the fittest explain further how these improved forms of life became dominant. In general, for those naturalists and evolutionists who hold that matter is the only subsistent reality and that there is no spiritual or supernatural realm of being, mankind's existence (along with all organic existence) is solely explained by molecular changes that result in genetic mutations of organisms with improved traits that are best suited to adapt to their environments and are most capable of reproducing in numbers great enough so as to dominate their environments in the "Struggle for Life."

The theist, however, can still argue that the ability of matter to undergo molecular changes and genetic mutations so as to produce greatly improved forms of life requires a supernatural Creator, beyond nature itself, i.e., a Creator whose intelligent design made possible this formation

---

89. Darwin, *Origin of the Species*, 697.

of higher lifeforms and especially the creation of human life. The atheistic evolutionist, however, will claim that the only self-evident explanation of life is found in merely the material processes of nature. In response to Augustine's argument quoted above, that "every changeable thing must be formable.... Yet nothing can give form to itself, for the following reason. No thing can give what it does not have," the atheistic naturalist will point to matter as being the source of all form, including intelligent form, and not to a transcendent, supernatural God. Yet science itself can only partially trace the process of evolution and provide speculative causal descriptions of the subatomic, atomic, and molecular changes that needed to have taken place in order for organic evolution to take place.

Further, naturalism is at a loss to adequately explain how higher, intelligent animal organisms developed by means of matter alone and how evolutionary potential for the human species resulted in the general ability for abstract thought, for self-consciousness, and for each member of the species to freely choose objectives for his/her own good. The organic matter of the brain alone cannot provide evidence for how man can think self-consciously and choose freely. Nonetheless the rational soul is so intimately connected with the physical organ of the brain that what may happen to the brain can affect the faculties of rational thought and free choice. Still, from the standpoint of faith, the rational soul is primarily spiritual and continues to exist in a suspended state when the brain is comatose or severely damaged. So too, from the standpoint of faith, at death the rational soul is separated from the body to which it was intimately connected, often times in suffering and pain, and yet continues to live sometimes in glory in union with God. Writing in the *City of God* Augustine tells us:

> The death of the body ... is the separation of the soul from the body.... For a sensation of anguish, contrary to nature, is produced by the force that tears apart the two things which have been conjoined and interwoven during life; and this sensation persists until there is a complete cessation of all that feeling which was present by reason of the union of soul and flesh.... Death, generated in unbroken succession from the first man, is beyond doubt the punishment of all who are born of him. But, if it is undergone for the sake of godliness and righteousness, it becomes the glory of those who are born again; and, though

death is the wages of sin, it sometimes ensures that no wage is paid to sin.[90]

For Augustine, the soul is immortal, and when one lives a life of godliness and righteousness up to one's death one can receive glorification so that "no wage is paid to sin." This last clause is perhaps a reference by Augustine to the Catholic doctrine of purgatory in which state souls after death are purified from the vestiges of sin. Those who by the free choices of their lives die in "godliness and righteousness" can immediately be received into glory where they can share in God's goodness without the need for purification so that "no wage is paid to sin."

DESCARTES AND THE HUMAN WILL

The atheist phenomenologist Jean-Paul Sartre, while denying the existence of a rational soul, salvation, or even God, argues unequivocally that the nature of free choice must be the nihilation of the In-itself, i.e., any objectives, including obviously material objects, because the For-itself, i.e., consciousness, cannot find its essence in objective material things or in bodily processes or in emotional or instinctual states. The question arises: How can the For-itself escape from being essentially identified with material being if what the naturalist claims is true, viz., that consciousness, thought, and free choice are merely neurological impulses resulting from a brain of only organic matter? In speaking of free will, and returning to Descartes, he tells us that were he "to examine the faculty of memory or imagination, or any of the other faculties, I would understand that in my case each of these is without exception feeble and limited" in comparison with God's attributes; and that it is only with "free choice that I experience to be so great in me that I cannot grasp the idea of any greater faculty," so that the free will "is the chief basis for my understanding that I bear a certain image and likeness of God."[91] Descartes goes on to describe the act of willing as being a response to what the intellect presents to it as a reason or motive for action. Descartes acknowledges that what the intellect presents as a reason for the will to choose can be directed and prompted by God or by the person himself. So, Descartes states:

---

90. Augustine, *City of God* (trans. Dyson) 13.6 (p. 547).
91. Descartes, *Discourse on Method*, Meditation 4.57 (pp. 83–84).

> The will consists solely in the fact that when something is proposed to us by our intellect either to affirm or deny, to pursue or to shun, we are moved in such a way that we sense that we are determined to it by no external force. In order to be free, I need not be capable of being moved in each direction; on the contrary, the more I am inclined toward one direction—either because I clearly understand that there is in it an aspect of the good and true, or because God has thus disposed the inner recesses of my thought—more freely do I choose that direction. Nor indeed does divine grace or natural knowledge ever diminish one's freedom; rather, they increase and strengthen it.[92]

Descartes argues that there should not be hesitation or even indifference in choosing one way or another regarding a particular object or issue when one clearly understands the good and the true involved, or when God directs the mind to choose the right way. Descartes claims that indifference to freely choosing one way or another regarding a moral issue is a result of a defect of mind, that is, an inability to see clearly what is true and good, which leaves one deliberating about how to choose or not to choose. But what about choosing erroneously or choosing evil, or merely being slothful regarding a moral crisis? Descartes does not make clear that he believes that those who choose evil deliberately intend to do what is evil. Descartes provides an explanation that emphasizes a mistake of judgment rather than a deliberate act of an evil will or a slothful indifference to a moral problem. Says Descartes:

> What then is the source of my errors? They are owing simply to the fact that, since the will extends further than the intellect, I do not contain the will within the same boundaries; rather, I also extend it to the things I do not understand. Because the will is indifferent in regard to such matters, it easily turns away from the true and the good; and in this way I am deceived and I sin.[93]

Unfortunately, Descartes does not provide any ground for why the will extends itself further than the intellect and thus extends itself into errors caused by a lack of understanding. But what is missing in his analysis is an understanding of humanity's fallen nature and his/her capacity for vice and evil. A simple example can demonstrate the difference between committing an act out of slothful ignorance so that the act results in evil, and committing an evil act fully intending to achieve an evil goal. A

---

92. Descartes, *Discourse on Method*, Meditation 4.57–58 (p. 84).
93. Descartes, *Discourse on Method*, Meditation 4.58 (p. 84).

person who kills another while driving while intoxicated is guilty of negligent homicide under civil law. A person who commits homicide with premeditated malicious intent is guilty of murder (to some degree). The seriousness of the crime of negligent homicide, while great, is still not as serious as the crime of premeditated murder.

THE WILL'S FREEDOM; THE FREE CHOICE OF EVIL

As noted above, for Augustine, there is an inclination to evil that is inherited from the original sin of our first parent, Adam. It is evil to reject God's moral order by satisfying lower inclinations at the expense of the obligation to follow one's higher inclinations. In themselves the lower inclinations are given by God as lower goods that can be satisfied when done in accord with God's moral order. Sexual desire can be morally satisfied within matrimony with one's spouse when at the same time one expresses care and love. To satisfy craven lust is never justified. Anger can be justifiable when it is directed against injustices and expressed in a controlled manner. Anger that seeks violent reprisal against an adversary in order to satisfy one's hatred is not justifiable. One must choose to pursue the higher inclination and put the lower inclination within the bounds of God's moral law written on the heart. When one freely chooses to indulge in the satisfaction of one's lower inclinations in opposition to one's higher inclinations, the result is probably an act of evil. Evil is called sin when understood and committed as direct disobedience to the Creator's moral law written on the heart.

At the end of Book 1 of *On the Free Choice of the Will*, Augustine ties together evil and sin by redirecting Evodius to consider whether "evildoing is anything other than pursuing temporal things and whatever is perceived through the body ... as though they were great and wonderful" while "having neglected eternal things, which the mind enjoys through itself and perceives through itself and which it cannot lose while loving them." Augustine surmises that "all evildoings—that is to say, all sins—seem to me to be included under this one heading."[94] This discourse leads to Evodius asking Augustine at the very beginning of Book 2 to "explain to me why God gave human beings free choice of the will. If we had not received it, we surely would not be able to sin." Answering this question requires first answering the third of the three basic questions that

---

94. Augustine, "On the Free Choice of the Will" 1.16.34.115 (p. 29).

directed the entire inquiry of Book 2. The reader may recall that the first question is "How is it clear that God exists?" And the second question is "Do all things, in so far as they are good, come from God?" The third question is "Is free will to be counted among these goods?"

Instead of answering Evodius directly, Augustine draws out from him the following response to questions regarding our having our existence from God and regarding God's justice. Evodius freely admits that "it is clear that we belong to God" and that God is "most generous to us in his excellence, but also is most just in redressing wrongdoing." Further, Evodius acknowledges that "everything good is from God" and that "human beings can also be understood to be from God" and finally that "a human being qua human being is something good, since he can live rightly when he wills to."[95] Based on these premises that Evodius accepts, Augustine provides a substantiated answer to the third question regarding whether free will is to be counted among all the goods that come from God. Augustine provides a three-point response. First, if every person is good because he is from God and can act rightly by willing to act rightly, then every person "ought to have free will, without which he could not act rightly." Secondly, even though free will enables a person to live rightly or to sin and there are those who do use their freedom to sin, the result for the sinner is that "the divinity redresses him for it." This is just because the person could have acted rightly and avoided sin, but by sinning he/she needs to make just reparation to God.[96] Thirdly, if human persons lack free will, then they could not act rightly, or conversely, they could not sin, and consequently "penalty and reward would be unjust" because "there ought to be justice in punishment and in reward, since justice is one of the goods that are from God."[97]

AUGUSTINE AND FREE WILL AS A GOD-GIVEN INTERMEDIATE GOOD

Regarding Augustine's first (of a three-point) response to the question regarding whether free will is to be counted among all the goods that come from God, there is a need to clarify why free will is necessary to act rightly. Acting rightly means to deliberately, i.e., with rational, careful

---

95. Augustine, "On the Free Choice of the Will" 2.1.2.4 (p. 31).
96. Augustine, "On the Free Choice of the Will" 2.1.3.6 (p. 31).
97. Augustine, "On the Free Choice of the Will" 2.1.3.7 (p. 32).

consideration and voluntary willingness, perform or omit an action in accord with moral norms that begin with the moral law written on every person's heart. Acting rightly is to be distinguished from deliberately acting through one's physical (or psychological) power to bring about a result in violation of the demands of moral law. In either case, one freely chooses to act (or not act) so that deliberate action or inaction always requires free choice of the will. Without free choice there can be no deliberate action that is moral and hence right, or immoral and hence wrong.

Augustine's second response to the question whether free will is to be counted among all the goods that come from God is that, for those who use free will to sin (which is an offense against God and his moral law), God "redresses him for it." There is a need to clarify what it means to redress. To redress means to make up for or to repair the wrong done; this is a way of saying that to redress means to make reparation. God requires reparation from the sinner because of his/her failure to use free will rightly and without sin. Without the person's free choice to either act rightly or to act sinfully, God would not be just to redress the person and require reparation when the person chooses the latter, i.e., sinning.

Augustine's third response to the question of whether free will is to be counted among all the goods that come from God is that "there ought to be justice in punishment and in reward" because "justice is one of the goods that are from God." This response is very similar to the second response in that both responses are based upon God being just in both redressing the sinner and rewarding those who act rightly. However, some clarity and distinction can be derived through a concise definition of what justice is. Justice is giving everyone his or her rightful due, which in turn involves what a person owes to God and to his/her neighbor. In civil law one who freely chooses to violate the legal rights of another can be found guilty of criminal wrongdoing and suffer the penalties provided by the laws of state. Under civil law one could be found not guilty of a serious crime such as murder by reason of insanity if it can be shown that one was not capable of freely choosing to violate the other's right to life; or conversely, one can be found guilty of premeditated murder when one freely chooses to plan and carry out one's killing of another person. Any attempt to minimize or deny free will may well result in a weakening of self-responsibility among society's citizenry; diminished self-responsibility can lead to persons committing more crime and thus to greater social disorder.

So too, according to Augustine, under divine justice rewards or punishments are allotted to a person according to that person's actions based on his/her deliberate free choice to sin and to offend God. Free will can be counted among those goods that come from God and are just, because only with free will can a person be assessed as having guilt or innocence, virtue or vice, benevolence or malevolence. Free will is an essential element to God's moral order, so that both virtue and vice transcend man in that man is not the creator of his nature or of this moral order, and yet at the same time this moral order is found immanently within man—the basic moral law is written on man's heart. Free will determines whether a man will choose to obey (and thereby act rightly toward) or choose to disobey (and thereby sin against) his Creator.

Free will is a good that comes from God, and God gave man free will to live rightly, and no one can live rightly without free will. The question remains, however: How great a good is free will? Augustine answers this question by distinguishing three levels of goods that give evidence of "the abundance and the greatness of God's goodness [which] has furnished not only great goods, but also intermediate and small goods."[98] Small goods are given by God to enable persons to live their life fully as God intended for human life. Among small goods would be the human eye, which allows us to see the beautiful things of God's creation, to live productive lives to support ourselves and others, to aid in our rational understanding and pursuit of truth, goodness, and ultimately God. Among the intermediate goods is freedom of the will, because only with the free will can we live rightly by our own choice. With freedom of the will, man can turn toward the unchangeable goods and toward God. However, freedom of the will remains an intermediate good, because with it a person can choose to turn away from God and choose evil by choosing changeable goods over unchangeable goods. Says Augustine:

> Thus, it turns out that the good things desired by sinners are not in any way evil, and neither is free will itself, which we established should be numbered among the intermediate goods. Instead, evil is turning the will away from the unchangeable good and towards changeable goods. Yet, since this "turning away" and "towards" is not compelled but voluntary, the deserved and just penalty of unhappiness follows upon it.[99]

---

98. Augustine, "On the Free Choice of the Will" 2.19.50.102 (p. 69).
99. Augustine, "On the Free Choice of the Will" 2.19.53.200 (pp. 70–71).

Among the great goods are things that are unchangeable, such as truth, the pursuit of virtue, the quest for the happy life, all of which are found in the pursuit and ultimately the attainment of God. But we cannot attain God solely on our own because of our proclivity to fall into sin, sin being a turning away from God. Augustine tells us at the end of Book 2:

> But since we cannot rise of our own accord as we fell of it, let us hold on with firm faith to the right hand of God stretched out to us from above, namely our Lord Jesus Christ; let us await him with resolute hope and desire Him with burning charity.[100]

Augustine is suggesting here that ultimately our free will (without which we cannot live rightly) is in need of Jesus Christ and his redemptive grace in order to reject sin, persevere in faith, and live in accord with God's will. It is an act of free will to beg God's help and abide by his grace.

SUMMARY OF BOOK 3 OF *ON THE FREE CHOICE OF THE WILL*

In Book 3, the final book of *On the Free Choice of the Will*, Evodius begins the discussion by questioning how it is that the movement of a person's free will away from God and away from the greater unchangeable goods toward lesser changeable goods comes about. Evodius acknowledges that nothing can be called "mine" more than one's will because it is through the will that each one individually, personally, and with responsibility chooses to move in one direction or another. Evodius also acknowledges that only when one chooses with a voluntary will can he/she be found praiseworthy or blameworthy. However, Evodius encounters a difficulty regarding God who gave us free will and, at the same time, has a necessary foreknowledge of all that will happen in his creation, including how each person will choose to turn toward God and the unchangeable goods or turn away from God and toward lesser changeable goods. If God's foreknowledge is absolute and unavoidably necessary, then what God knows will happen in the future will necessarily happen. If God knows that a person will turn away from him and sin, then it may seem that it would necessarily be the case that God's foreknowledge would obliterate man's freedom and cause that person to sin.

---

100. Augustine, "On the Free Choice of the Will" 2.20.54.205 (pp. 71–72).

WHAT DOES GOD FOREKNOW, AND HOW DOES HUMAN FREE WILL COMPORT WITH THIS?

Considering God's justice and God's foreknowledge of man's sins, Evodius proceeds to ask Augustine the following three questions: How can "God justly punish sins that necessarily happen?"; How can it be otherwise "that future events that God foreknows do not happen necessarily?"; and How is it that "whatever necessarily happens in His Creation is not to be imputed to its Creator?"[101] Augustine provides short, conclusive answers to these three questions. Regarding the first question Augustine states: "God justly punishes sins, namely because He does not do the things He knows will happen."[102] In short, it is the sinner who freely commits the sin and deserves the punishment. In answer to the second question, Augustine states: "God, although He does not force anyone into sinning, nevertheless foresees those who are going to sin by their own will."[103] Augustine's response to the third question is that "whatever necessarily happens in His Creation is not to be imputed to its Creator."[104] Two pages later Augustine reinforces his argument that God is not to be blamed for man's evil, which necessarily happens because God has given man the ability to necessarily make things happen: "God did not force them to sin merely because he gave to those whom He made the power whether they would so will."[105]

A more comprehensive explanation of how it is that God foreknows everything that will be, including how a person sins, not by necessity but by his will, and how punishment consequently is just, can be found based in Augustine's understanding of eternity. This understanding is partially explained in Augustine's *Confessions* where he states that "whatever comes into being and ceases to be, begins at the moment and ends at the moment when the eternal reason—which has in itself no beginning or ending—knows that it should begin or end."[106] God is the eternal reason, and unlike a being in time, he has no beginning and no end, no past and no future, but is an ever-present immutable now. Writing in Book 12 of

---

101. Augustine, "On the Free Choice of the Will" 3.4.9.37 (p. 80).
102. Augustine, "On the Free Choice of the Will" 3.4.11.40 (p. 81).
103. Augustine, "On the Free Choice of the Will" 3.4.10.39 (p. 81).
104. Augustine, "On the Free Choice of the Will" 3.5.12.42 (p. 81).
105. Augustine, "On the Free Choice of the Will" 3.5.14.53 (p. 83).
106. Augustine, *Confessions* 11.8.11 (p. 239).

Confessions, Augustine expresses the following prayer of praise to God in anticipation of divine union with him:

> You said in the ear of my spirit that the creature . . . is not co-eternal with You: You are its sole delight and it tastes of Your delight in purity unfailing: never and in no way does it lose its quality of mutability, yet, being ever in your presence and held to You with other love, having no future in anticipation nor passing away into any past for memory, it suffers no variation and its being is not spread out over time.[107]

God is not subject to change but everything in time is subject to change, as time is the measurement of change. When the soul of man (while finite and mutable in itself) is held in the divine presence, that soul experiences no future and does not retreat into any past but is held by God in an eternal now of loving union.

God is immutability, and hence God is essentially eternal because there is no change of time in eternity. So too, God's knowledge is perfectly eternal, i.e., God's knowledge is absolute and unchanging; yet God's knowledge is prescient in relation to we who live in time, which is to say God has foreknowledge of future events, i.e., future events relative to we who live in time. In no way does God's eternal being preclude his creation of rational beings such as angels and men, who have free will and can cause things to happen in the present. And God's eternal knowledge of us, including his foreknowledge of how we will use this faculty of free will in the future, does not violate our free will in any way. Writing in his *City of God*, Augustine tells us:

> Even if a certain order of causes does exist in the mind of God, it does not follow that nothing is left to the free choice of our will. For our wills are themselves included in the order of causes which is certain to God and contained within His foreknowledge. For the wills of men are causes of the deeds of men, and so He Who has foreseen the causes of all things clearly cannot have been ignorant of our wills among the those causes, since He foresaw them to be the causes of our deeds.[108]

Returning to Book 3 of *On the Free Choice of the Will*, Augustine discusses in a long monologue why God does not withhold the bestowal of his goodness on a person by not creating such a person whom he

---

107. Augustine, *Confessions* 12.11.12 (p. 266).
108. Augustine, *City of God* (trans. Dyson) 5.9.9 (pp. 201–2).

foreknows is going to sin and will persist in sin. Augustine argues that human persons have immortal souls and faculties of reason and free will, which place them in God's created order on a higher level than animals or even the galaxies, stars, and heavenly bodies. God in his goodness allows the human person to turn away from sin and pursue the highest goods. Notwithstanding the failure of some persons to find ultimate happiness in God and their willingness to remain ultimately unhappy without God (while possibly enjoying a false, temporary happiness in sin), he allows them to be preserved in their existence and freely choose their pursuits, even if those persons choose to keep sinning until the end of their lives. In this, God is to be praised for preserving his order of creation and not blamed by those who believe that it would be better if God did not allow evildoers to exist. Augustine asks why God should not be praised for all that he has created, including rational beings who were given free will, viz., angels and men, both those who have chosen evil as well as those who have chosen good. Says Augustine:

> Why should God not be praised? . . . Even though He made those [good angels] who were going to abide in the laws of justice, he also made other souls which He foresaw would sin—indeed, ones which He foresaw would persevere in their sins. Yet these souls are better than [things] which cannot sin because they have no rational and free choice of the will.[109]

Augustine insists on the higher value of the human person over all other physical creations, animate or inanimate, because only the human person has a rational soul with free choice. And only the human person (or angels) can possibly attain eternal union with God. While other Christian thinkers will attest to God's promise of salvation in union with him being a possibility for human persons, not all accept the concept so clearly stated by Augustine in *On the Free Choice of the Will* that it is necessary for man's free will to choose to pursue God or to turn away from him. There will be in Augustine's later works a greater emphasis on the necessity for God's grace in order for a person to do good and avoid evil, grace given by God gratuitously. But nowhere in *On the Free Choice of the Will* does Augustine discount the need for man to choose freely to search for God (for whom all persons yearn), to freely seek the truth that God reveals, and, by implication, to cooperate with God's help (grace) in order to be saved. Two of the most important Protestant reformers,

---

109. Augustine, "On the Free Choice of the Will" 3.5.15.56 (p. 84).

Martin Luther and John Calvin, reject this notion of man's freedom to cooperate with grace and attribute all of man's good works and certainly man's salvation to God's action alone.

PREDESTINATION AND CALVIN'S POSITION

Regarding salvation, John Calvin taught that God's foreknowledge was dependent upon his will to predestine each and every individual to eternal life or to eternal death, so that one could conclude that each person was created for one or the other divinely ordained fate. Writing in his definitive and final edition of *Institutes of the Christian Religion*, published in 1559, Calvin states:

> The predestination by which God adopts some to the hope of life, and adjudges others to eternal death, no man who would be thought pious ventures simply to deny; but it is greatly cavilled at, especially by those who make prescience its cause. We, indeed, ascribe both prescience and predestination to God; but we say that it is absurd to make the latter subordinate to the former. . . . By predestination we mean the eternal decree of God, by which He determined with Himself whatever He wished to happen with regard to every man. All are not created on equal terms, but some are preordained to eternal life, others to eternal damnation; and accordingly, as such has been created for one or other of these ends, we say that he has been predestinated to life or to death.[110]

To say (as does Calvin) that God by his own eternal decree of predestination created and preordained some to eternal life and others to eternal damnation is to ascribe to God's omnipotence a superiority over his attributes of justice, mercy, and love. In God, however, there is no such division. To assert God's power to limit or obliterate his attributes is self-contradictory. God's attribute of goodness, including his bestowal of justice and mercy toward his creatures, cannot be denied or limited by an arbitrary designation of the meaning of his omnipotence. God's justice and his omnipotence are not in conflict, and, while his ways to man can be inscrutable, there can be no self-contradiction of the truth of the perfection of God's Being. Moreover, the moral order that God impressed on all his creation and the moral law that God wrote on each person's

---

110. Calvin, *Institutes* 3.21.5 (p. 206).

heart would be disordered if he were to create certain persons who were preordained to suffer eternal damnation without their ever receiving a will that would have a free choice to follow God's moral law and be saved, or to persist in sin and be damned.

The theological confusion concerning the understanding of God's omnipotence and his justice and mercy had its roots in the breakdown of faith and reason that occurred during the late Middle Ages with the rise of skepticism. The skeptical philosophy of the late Middle Ages, which helped lead to the breakdown of faith and reason and which, generally speaking, influenced the early Protestant thinkers, was that of nominalism (from the Latin *nomen*, meaning "name"). Nominalism basically held that *no* essential characteristic inheres within an object so that this object cannot be conceptually grouped together with other objects that seem to share their own essential characteristic universally, i.e., in common. For nominalists all that objects may have in common are apparent qualities for which rational human persons assign names that link them together. But in reality, according to nominalists, there is no universal concept that can be abstracted from objects designating what those objects essentially are. For nominalists, there are only what appears to be characteristics among certain objects that are intuited by us as being similar, which apparent characteristics seem to distinguish these certain objects as different from the apparent characteristics of other objects. Nominalism reduces man's comprehension of reality to only a knowledge of the appearances of relationships of individual things that are grasped intuitively through the senses as being similar.

WILLIAM OF OCKHAM

When applied to ethics, the reductionist perspective of nominalism presents a serious problem regarding man's capacity to recognize and apply moral law. This difficulty became apparent in the writings of William of Ockham, ca. 1285–1349, a Franciscan philosopher/theologian who lectured at Oxford. Often referred to as the "Prince of the Nominalists," Ockham is famous for his dictum referred to by historians of philosophy as "Ockham's Razor," which states: "entities should not be multiplied without necessity." This means that the simplest explanation with the fewest assumptions or principles regarding an object, a phenomenon, an event, or whatever is to be explained is more likely to be the most accurate explanation. Ockham's philosophy was highly skeptical and rejected any conclusive proof for the existence of God through reason alone. Ockham's theology tended toward fideism, which holds that religious truth must be based on faith alone and not on rational understanding of such issues as the causes of the universe or of man's being. Fideism would rule out the acceptance of any presumed innate moral knowledge, because morality can be determined only by what God has revealed. From a standpoint of faith, Ockham tended to emphasize God's omnipotence in all things, including establishing and even changing moral law. God alone establishes the moral law, and, according to Ockham, God can impose an obligation as to what is the nature of the moral law that we are to follow so that God by his own will can change commandments regarding what is good and evil, and God could even ordain that man will act without freedom. Writing in his commentary on the *Sentences of Peter Lombard*, Ockham states:

> By the very fact that God wills something, it is right for it to be done.... Hence if God were to cause hatred of Himself in anyone's will, that is, if he were to be the cause of the act (He is, as it is, its partial cause), neither would that man sin nor would God; God is not under any obligation, while the man is not (in this case) obliged, because the act would not be in his own power.[111]

In stating that when God wills something it is right to be done, Ockham is arguing that God could reveal anything he wanted to reveal as his moral law at any time because of his omnipotence. What Ockham is implying is that human persons must accept God's revelation in faith and obey it without regard to its rational consistency or to the innate human understanding of what is right and wrong. This could, of course, be in contradiction to what is already found in Scripture, which reveals that the Gentiles, who do not have the law, "show that the demands of the law are written in their hearts" (Rom 2:15). In effect, Ockham is claiming that a contradiction within God himself is possible in that God's omnipotence could be in conflict with his own veracity and with the immutability of his moral law written on the hearts of the human persons he created. The twentieth-century scholar and professor of the history of philosophy at Heythrop College at the University of London Frederick Copleston provides the following description of Ockham's teachings on morality:

---

111. Copleston, *History of Philosophy*, 3:104, citing William of Ockham, "4: Sentences," 9, E–F.

> Because according to Ockham, there is no natural or formal repugnance between loving God and loving a creature in a way which has been forbidden by God, God could order fornication. Between loving God and loving a creature in a manner which is illicit there is only an extrinsic repugnance, namely the repugnance which arises from the fact that God has already forbidden that way of loving a creature. Hence if God were to order fornication, the latter would be not only licit, but meritorious. Hatred of God, stealing, committing adultery, are forbidden by God. But they could be ordered by God; and if they were, they would be meritorious acts.[112]

The problems involved in such a theology/philosophy as that of Ockham's are profound, and chief among them is the moral confusion that would result when human society can no longer rely at all upon human moral instincts and practical reason to determine good and evil. Not everyone at any historical time, and certainly not in contemporary times, would hold to Christian revelation as the sole guide to moral behavior even though it is incumbent on every person to search for the full truth, especially in matters of good and evil. But certainly, if divine revelation were open to arbitrary change by God, then Christian believers would tend to see themselves in a hopeless morass of moral contradictions, which could have devastating consequences for the whole human race. What Ockham, and nominalism in general, tend to reject is a transcendent moral order created by God that is immutable and is capable of basically being known by all persons despite human mutability. God's transcendent moral order is immutable because God himself is the source of that moral order and that moral order reflects the immutable goodness of God himself even as it applies to the mutable beings that God created. Misinterpretations of God's Being must be guarded against with right reason as well as premises of revealed faith, or they can lead to insurmountable contradictions. Augustine tells us:

> Now any error that masquerades as divine authority is best refuted by the following line of reasoning. It is proven to believe or maintain that there is (a) some changeable species apart from God's Creation, or (b) some changeable species in God substance.[113]

---

112. Copleston, *History of Philosophy*, 3:105.
113. Augustine, "On the Free Choice of the Will" 3.21.60.205 (p. 114).

The above passage is a rare instance when Peter King's translation possibly does not provide a clear and distinct an understanding of Augustine's meaning. Perhaps a better translation of this passage is found in the Anna S. Benjamin and L. H. Hackstaff version of *On Free Choice of the Will*, which states:

> Any error that assumes the guise of divine authority is refuted chiefly by the following reasoning: it is an error, if it is shown to affirm or maintain either that there is any mutable form apart from God's creation, or that there is any mutable form within the substance of God.[114]

By maintaining, as does William of Ockham, that God's omnipotence enables God to change his essential goodness (as reflected in his commandments) is to claim that there is a changeability or mutability in God's substance, which, as Augustine points out, is a falsehood regarding God's immutable essence. God does not have parts, nor is he a compound, and nor is he subject to time and space or to movement or change. God is eternal, i.e., he exists all at once beyond time and change, and he is essentially uncaused. Using Aristotle's term, God is pure actuality, i.e., he is pure existence and eternal reality that is not capable of being acted upon by a cause. Augustine adds that God is unchangeable simplicity itself in that he is essentially his own existence where his attributes are identical with his being, and, therefore, God's attributes are in a unified harmony with himself so that no one attribute is in conflict with the other. Writing in his *City of God* while reflecting on the Trinity, Augustine explains:

> There is then one sole Good, which is simple, and therefore unchangeable; and that is God. By this Good all good things were created; but they are not simple, and for that reason they are changeable. They are, I say, created, that is to say, they are made, not begotten. What is begotten by the simple Good is itself equally simple, identical in nature with its begetter. . . . What is meant by "simple" is that its being is identical with its attributes. . . .
> The reason why a nature is called simple is that it cannot lose any attribute it possesses, that there is no difference between what it is and what it has.[115]

---

114. Augustine, *On Free Choice of the Will* (trans. Benjamin and Hackstaff), 135.

115. Augustine, *City of God* (trans. Bettenson) 11.10 (pp. 440–41). (Note: this is an earlier translation of the *City of God* different from the translation used throughout this text. The passage cited here is being quoted because of its relatively greater clarity.)

Because God's moral order reflects God's absolute Goodness, it is as God is, viz., immutable. God is in his simplicity identical with his unchanging attributes, and these attributes cannot be in conflict within God's being. God's veracity is an unchangeable attribute that cannot be in conflict with God's omnipotence, so that God's basic moral order written on a person's heart is unchangeable, even though that person is mutable and capable of violating this basic moral order because of one's free will. But it is also because of this moral order of which each person has immanent knowledge that the person is able to freely choose with self-responsibility between good and evil. Without the immanent knowledge of the basic moral order written on one's heart, a person would not be responsible for choices of good and evil. So, too, with the nominalist philosophical/theological perspective of Ockham, there is an acceptance of the mutability of both the moral order and man's basic knowledge of the moral law that tends to render certain persons who do not know or who do not believe in God's revelation incapable of right judgment of good and evil. Moral confusion and a deficiency of self-responsibility can result from an acceptance of nominalism. Moral clarity and an acceptance of self-responsibility follow from an acceptance of Augustine's analysis of the free choice of the will found in *On the Free Choice of the Will*.

If all persons know the basic moral law and have free choice of the will to follow the moral law, why do humans routinely disregard it and too often violate it in a serious way? The answer to this question is touched on by Augustine toward the end of *On the Free Choice of the Will*, where the author discusses the sin of Adam. Augustine tells us:

> With complete justice it pleased God, Who regulates all things, that we be born of that first union with ignorance and trouble and mortality, since when they [Adam and Eve] sinned they fell headlong into error and distress and death, in order that His justice in punishing us would be apparent at the origination of the human race, and later on His mercy in setting us free.[116]

Original sin caused a series of events that affected the whole course of human history. All persons inherited from Adam, from whom they descended, the bad effects of his fall from grace. These effects were the divinely ordained, justifiable punishment for the sin committed by the first human being for his personal offense against the absolutely and infinitely perfect supreme Creator. These effects included a breakdown of the

---

116. Augustine, "On the Free Choice of the Will" (trans. King) 3.20.55.186 (p. 110).

amicable relationship between mankind and the natural world. Dealing with the rest of creation became burdensome, so that human beings had to toil and struggle to meet the needs of their survival. Sickness, aging, and eventual death became the plight of every person. But there was also the loss of humanity's original virtue and holiness and its friendship with God, which broke the original created order God intended among all human persons and also among all human persons and the rest of creation. Augustine while still lost in sin spoke of his own early attraction to vice and yet to his simultaneous pursuit of a relationship with God. At that time, Augustine "was deliberating about serving the Lord my God," yet he acknowledged how he did "not wholly will" but "was not wholly unwilling" to serve God. Augustine further describes the debilitating effect of original sin on his own soul and concludes (in a passage partially quoted in chapter 1 of this text):

> Therefore, I strove with myself and was distracted by myself. This distraction happened to me though I did not want it, and it showed me not the presence of some second mind, but the punishment of my own mind. Thus, it was not I who caused it but the sin that dwells in me, the punishment of the sin more freely committed by Adam, whose son I am.[117]

While admitting that he had reason and free will and the inclination to seek God and live a virtuous life, Augustine also admitted the inclination to sin, which, whenever allowed to take hold, results in "lust [that] dominates the mind and drags it back and forth, despoiled of the richness of virtue, poor and needy."[118] Augustine came to the realization that he must freely choose to ask God for divine help in order to undergo a conversion from his habits of sin, which had been prompted by that threefold concupiscence that 1 John 2:16 warns against and to which Augustine refers as "the lust of the flesh, the lust of the eyes, and the pride of life."[119]

HUMAN FREE WILL AND GUILT FOR CHOICES MADE

In light of Augustine's understanding of original sin and its punishments inherited by all the descendants of Adam—ignorance, suffering, death of the body, and the spiritual death of the soul motivated by the threefold

---

117. Augustine, *Confessions* 8.10.22 (pp. 155–56).
118. Augustine, "On the Free Choice of the Will" 1.11.22.77 (p. 19).
119. Augustine, *Confessions* 10.30.41 (p. 212).

concupiscence and realized when a person freely chooses to sin—a question can naturally arise regarding man's guilt. If original sin is only the personal sin of Adam, which all persons inherit but do not commit, and if man's propensity to sin is also inherited, how can human persons be blamed for their actually sinning? Returning to Book 3 of *On the Free Choice of the Will*, the following question arises from those who refuse to accept responsibility for their own transgressions:

> Suppose Adam and Eve sinned. What did we unhappy people do, on our part, to be born with the blindness of ignorance and the torments of trouble? First, not knowing what we should do, we fall into error—and then, once the precepts of justice begin to be revealed to us, we will to do these things but we cannot, held back by some sort of necessity belonging to carnal lust.[120]

Augustine had already addressed this contention that "some sort of necessity belonging to carnal lust" causes us to sin. This occurred in a previous instruction to Evodius in Book 1 where Augustine stated:

> Since (a) anything equal or superior to a governing mind possessed of virtue does not make it the servant of lust, on account of justice, and since in addition (b) anything inferior to it could not do this, on account of weakness, . . . we are left with this conclusion: Nothing makes the mind a devotee of desire but its own will and free choice.[121]

The free will while subject to the influence of original sin remains for Augustine the fundamental cause of one's turning toward or away from God, or of one's pursuit of virtue, or of its surrender to vice. In his *Confessions* Augustine provides a fuller explanation of how virtues and vices are developed as habits orienting the future behavior of persons. What is increasingly emphasized in Augustine's later writings is the need to ask for, and to cooperate with, God's grace in order for man's free will to reject sin. Yet, Augustine introduces a new difficulty in Book 3 in assessing the relation of the will to sin by stating, "Whatever the cause of the will is, if it cannot be resisted there is no sin in yielding to it."[122] The question looms: Can it be the case that carnal lust cannot be resisted?

Obviously not all persons have a "governing mind possessed of virtue." Regarding the fallenness of human nature, Augustine acknowledges

---

120. Augustine, "On the Free Choice of the Will" 3.19.53.180 (p. 109).
121. Augustine, "On the Free Choice of the Will" 1.11.21.76 (p. 19).
122. Augustine, "On the Free Choice of the Will" 3.18.50.170 (p. 107).

that humankind's inheritance of the effects of the sin of Adam is a "just penalty" imposed by "the omnipotence and the justice of God" because Adam's original sin is essentially an offense against the Creator's infinite Being by a human creature who is a finite being. Mankind inherits the penalty of ignorance, leading each person into accepting falsehoods that, in turn, may lead to lustful actions and the penalty of "trouble"—suffering resulting from sin. At this point in *On the Free Choice of the Will*, well into Book 3, Augustine is making a slow but certain transition from writing mostly philosophy to a greater inclusion of Christian theology. This will not become fully explicit until he writes his next major work, *Confessions*. A fuller explanation of God's infinite justice, not present in *On the Free Choice of the Will*, is that it lies in harmony with his infinite mercy so that God sent his infinite divine Son to assume the finitude of human nature and provide victory over ignorance, lust, and sin and over trouble, suffering, and death. Only Christ, who is true man, could vicariously take the place of Adam and of every human being so as to atone for original sin and all consequent sins of the human race. Only Christ, who as a human being is a divine Person whose atonement has infinite merit, superabundantly satisfies the reparation needed to counterbalance the infinite offense of the creature's original sin and all consequent sin against the infinite Creator. Through his redemption or buying back of the human race, Christ merited the salvific grace for each person to find forgiveness of their personal sins toward which the original sin has inclined all persons. Each person despite his/her fallenness and weakness can still search for the one (Christ) who might not as of yet be known but who brings wisdom and healing from sin. Speaking of those who do complain that their ignorance and concupiscence necessarily make all persons prisoners of lust and hence not free, Augustine declares:

> Perhaps they would have a legitimate complaint if there had existed no one among human beings who triumphed over error and lust. But there is one, present everywhere throughout the Creation that serves Him as Lord, who calls out in many ways to the person who has turned away; who instructs the person who believes; who comforts the person who hopes; who encourages the person who persists; who helps the person who strives; who gives heed to the person who prays for forgiveness. Accordingly, it is not counted as a fault of yours that you act in ignorance against your will, but rather that you do not search for what you do not know; nor [is it counted as a fault] that you do not bind

up your wounded members, but rather that you reject the one willing to heal you—these are properly your sins.[123]

The sins that properly belong to a person include not searching for what one does not know yet yearns for and then not accepting the One willing to heal the sinner. What Augustine admits toward the end of *On the Free Choice of the Will* is the limitation of human freedom. While not denying the free choice of the will, Augustine qualifies man's free choice to act rightly by saying that "obviously we are speaking of it [free choice] as human beings were originally made."[124] However, even in a person's fallenness, that person has the free choice "to investigate advantageously matters of which it is disadvantageous to be ignorant" and the free choice "to confess humbly his weakness, so that He Whose support is unerring and effortless supports the person who investigates and confesses."[125] Augustine is saying here in these passages in Book 3 that while each human being is prone to sin, which is extremely difficult to overcome because of ignorance and concupiscence, each person nevertheless has the instinctual propensity to seek God and truth and to seek God's human voice on earth, who provides the wisdom and strength to overcome weakness and sin. This freedom to choose God and truth, especially in the Person of Jesus Christ (who is only occasionally named in *On the Free Choice of the Will*), is incumbent on every person so that those who willfully reject the search for truth, who reject the teachings of Jesus Christ while knowing in faith his revelation is true, who arrogantly refuse to acknowledge their own moral failings, or who fail to accept God and God's help are guilty of offending their Creator. Free choice of the will and moral responsibility remain in all members of the human race, who are tainted with physical and moral weakness.

AUGUSTINE ENTERTAINS FOUR THEORIES ON THE ORIGIN OF THE SOUL

As further evidence of Augustine's transition from a more purely philosophical approach in analyzing the free choice of will to the inclusion of a theological perspective that may impact this freedom, Augustine engages in a speculative discussion of how souls may come into the world by

123. Augustine, "On the Free Choice of the Will" 3.19.53.181 (p. 109).
124. Augustine, "On the Free Choice of the Will" 3.18.52.179 (p. 109).
125. Augustine, "On the Free Choice of the Will" 3.19.53.182 (p. 109).

entertaining four distinct theories. Augustine conjectures that: "[1] Souls come from a stock. [2] Souls come about anew in each individual born. [3] Souls already exist somewhere and they are sent by God into the bodies of those who are born. [4] Souls already exist somewhere and they do descend of their own accord into the bodies of those who are born."[126] Regarding these four theories, Augustine is quick to add that, because of the complexity and obscurity of this problem of how souls come into the world, "Catholic commentators on Scripture have not yet untangled and clarified this question," or at least, Augustine admits, that he has yet to discover such a clarification. Augustine cautions further that those who struggle with this question should not think anything "false or unworthy of the substance of the Creator";[127] nor should there be a prohibition against "anyone who has the ability [of] investigating in accordance with divinely inspired Scripture."[128]

The first of these theories that "Souls come from a stock" refers to the propagation of the soul as being the same as the propagation of the body, meaning that each body is a product of a supply or stock of potential bodies that could come from a parent body, and so too each soul is a product of a supply or stock of souls that could come from God or a parent soul. One Catholic commentator who did untangle and clarify this question regarding the origin of souls, and who rejected this first theory, was St. Peter of Alexandria (who was bishop of Alexandria, one-time head of the famous catechetical school in Alexandria, and who died a martyr ca. AD 311). He wrote:

> God said, "Let us make man to our image and according to our likeness." It is clear from this that man was not formed by the conjunction of the body with some pre-existing type. For if the earth, at a command, brought forth the other animals endowed with life, how much more certain it is that the dust which God took from the earth received vital energy from the will and operation of God.[129]

What Peter of Alexandria is saying is that the revelation that man is made in the image and likeness of God negates the notion that man's soul was a preexisting, life-giving substance that sprang from earthly sources as do

---

126. Augustine, "On the Free Choice of the Will" 3.21.59.200 (p. 113).
127. Augustine, "On the Free Choice of the Will" 3.21.59.201 (p. 113).
128. Augustine, "On the Free Choice of the Will" 3.21.62.214 (p. 116).
129. Peter of Alexandria, "The Soul," in Jurgens, *Faith of the Early Fathers*, 1:259–60.

the life-giving substances that animate animals. Man, on the contrary, has a vital energy, i.e., a soul that is directly created and enjoined to a body by the will and operation of God. Man's soul, therefore, based on these premises, could not have proceeded from any physical source, or even from an animal's preexisting, life-giving substance. Man's soul must come directly from God because the soul is made in his image and likeness.

A further exposition of this passage from Genesis—"made in God's image and likeness"—cannot obviously refer to the human body but, rather, most likely refers to man's personhood reflecting God's Person. The essence of personhood is having a rational intellect and a free will, which are the highest faculties of the human soul. Because a person is his/her own agent, a person has the power to willfully bring about a conceived effect on himself/herself or on another person or thing, he/she limitedly reflects God's agency, which has the omnipotent power to create both material and spiritual being and to will any possible effect according to his divine plan. What Genesis reveals is that the human soul does not come into existence by emanating from, or being procreated by, another soul as does the soul of an animal, which is propagated by the parents of that animal. The vital energy received from the will and operation of God refers to the direct creation of man's soul by God.

Even more clear is a letter entitled *Against John of Jerusalem* written by Augustine's contemporary and colleague Jerome, in which Jerome writes:

> Whence did Cain and Abel, the first offspring of the first human beings, have their souls? And the whole human race afterwards, what do you suppose is the origin of their souls? Was it from propagation like the brute animals, in such a way that just as body comes from body so too soul is generated from soul? ... But certainly... God is engaged daily in making souls, God, for whom to will is to have done and who never ceases to be the Creator.[130]

God's "engagement in daily making souls" referred to by Jerome is an obvious reference to God's directly creating the soul and is most in keeping with the second theory listed by Augustine that "souls come about anew in each individual born," provided there is an understanding that God directly creates the soul and brings about through the soul the animation

---

130. Jerome, "Against John of Jerusalem," in Jurgens, *Faith of the Early Fathers*, 2:201.

of the body to which it is joined. This teaching became a doctrine of the Catholic Church, which states:

> The unity of soul and body is so profound that one has to consider the soul to be the "form" of the body: i.e., it is because of its spiritual soul that the body made of matter becomes a living human body; spirit and matter, in man, are not two natures united, but rather their union forms a single nature.
>
> The Church teaches that every spiritual soul is created immediately by God—it is not "produced" by the parents—and also that it is immortal: it does not perish when it separates from the body at death, and it will be reunited with the body at the final Resurrection.[131]

AUGUSTINE ON CREATION OF THE SOUL

What did Augustine say about the origin of the soul? In *On the Free Choice of the Will* Augustine focuses on the nature of, and the limitations of, human freedom as well as man's moral responsibilities. He does not venture to explain explicitly how the human soul comes into the world. However, Augustine does provide definite indications of the great importance of the human soul in God's created order in that God's plan for creation includes the most elevated place for those human souls who use their free choice of the will to seek God over transient material goods. Augustine tells us that in the human view of God's plan of salvation, "the Creator of the soul is praised on all sides for implementing the capacity for the highest good," and God is praised for "assisting our progress; perfecting and satisfying those who make progress," and also God is praised even for "ordaining the most just damnation of the sinner." Most informing is Augustine's assertion that "God did not create the soul as evil just because it is not yet as great as it received the power to become."[132] As Augustine has already argued, God does not create anything evil, and so the soul, which is directly created by God, must have been created good. The question arises: How does a good soul contract original sin? There is a certain element of mystery involved in answering this question, but the possible solution to this problem lies in God's plan to directly create the human soul profoundly enjoined to a human body so that the original sin

---

131. *Catechism of the Catholic Church* §§365–66.
132. Augustine, "On the Free Choice of the Will" 3.22.65.221–22 (p. 117).

propagated by Adam to all his human offspring through the human body is transmitted to the soul at the moment the soul is enjoined to the body.

In Augustine's reference of God creating the soul, there is a clear implication of God's direct creation of the soul that could comport with Jerome's explicit assertion that "God is engaged daily in making souls." Augustine restates again "that very trouble the soul is given" is caused by the human person's "slower and carnal part." Then the Doctor of Grace articulates the importance and priority given to the human soul by God:

> On account of that very trouble the soul is given a warning call to call upon Him Who helps in its perfection, the one Whom it perceives is the author of its inception. The upshot is that the soul becomes more dear to God, seeing that it is raised up to be happy not through its own powers but instead through the mercy of Him from Whose goodness it has its being. The soul is more dear to him from Whom it exists precisely to the extent that it finds secure peace in Him, and to the extent that it more richly enjoys His eternity.[133]

The fact that Augustine asserts that the soul can perceive God as "the author of its inception" implies that Augustine means that the soul was directly created by God and not propagated through another soul or by some other preexisting means.

The remaining two theories on the origin of the soul about which Augustine speculates both argue that "souls already exist somewhere," which contention introduces a split within, or a fragmentation of, the integrated unity of the soul and the body that forms not two natures but a single nature. Whether preexisting souls "are sent by God into bodies of those who are born" as asserted by the third theory, or whether preexisting souls "descend of their own accord into the bodies of those who are born" as asserted by the fourth theory, the problem remains that the profound, integrated unity of soul and body is missing. In both these theories, an artificial union of soul and body is assumed, which can easily lead to the acceptance of some sort of theory that posits a transmigration of souls where a specific immortal soul can pass at the death of one of its bodies into another body.

In philosophy, transmigration of souls or reincarnation is called "metempsychosis," from the Greek *meta*, meaning "beyond," and *empsychos*, meaning "animate." The origin of the concept can be traced to

---

133. Augustine, "On the Free Choice of the Will" 3.22.65.223 (pp. 117–18).

Eastern religions such as Hinduism, which accepts the belief of *samsara*, which means "the wheel of rebirth." Hinduism accepts the existence of the soul as immortal. Hinduism teaches that upon the death of the body, the soul (unless it attains salvation) is reborn into another body, possibly human or animal, according to the law of karma, which means action and its consequences and which refers to the choices one makes in the present life. Good actions in a person's life can lead to that person's soul being born into a higher level of existence in the next life, whereas bad actions can have the opposite effect. Plato (427–347 BC) probably was acquainted with Eastern religious thought, and in one of his major works, *The Republic*, he provides a mystical account of the ongoing life of the immortal soul after the death of the mortal body. Writing in the last book of *The Republic*, Book 10, Plato provides a somewhat vague and mythical description of the transmigration of souls that emphasizes the importance of one's virtuous choices in the present life, which have consequences in the reincarnation of the soul in the next life:

> Souls of the passing day beginneth another cycle of mortal life that leads to death. No Destiny shall cast lots for you, but you shall all choose your own Destiny; let him who draws the first lot first choose a life, and thereto he shall cleave of necessity. But Virtue knows no master; as each honors or despises her he shall have more or less of her. The blame is for the chooser; God is blameless.
> ... The interpreter threw the lots before them all, and each one picked up that which fell near him... After this again he laid out the models of lives on the ground before them, many more by number than those present, all sorts and kinds of them; there were lives of all kinds of animals and all sorts and conditions of men.... There was no regulation of soul in the lives, because the soul must become different of necessity, according to what life is chosen; but all the other things were co-mingled together and mixed with riches and poverty, with disease and health, and some were intermediate among them.[134]

Augustine most probably was acquainted with Plato's poetic description of the transmigration of souls found in the last book of *The Republic*. Regarding Augustine's third and fourth theories that "souls already existed somewhere" and were either "sent by God into the bodies of those who are born" (the third theory), or "descend of their own accord into the bodies of those who are born" (the fourth theory), Augustine

---

134. Plato, *Republic* 10.616E–618D (pp. 418–19).

refuses to speculate. Rather, he cautions the faithful reader to not think that a person should "lose hope of future things because he does not recall his past origins." Further, Augustine argues that the question of the origin of the soul should not distract the Christian believer from accepting that God justly judges the soul of each person and subjects the sinner to punishment for his/her free choice to sin. Says Augustine:

> However, things may be on this score—whether we should omit the problem [of the origin of souls] entirely or defer it now to be considered at another time—it is no hindrance to the present question. It is quite clear that souls suffer punishments for their sins by the most upright and supremely just and unshaken and unchangeable majesty and substance of the Creator. These sins, as we have been discussing for a long time, should be attributed to their own will. Nor should any further cause of sins be looked for.[135]

Writing some twenty-five years later ca. AD 420 in his work *On the Soul and Its Origin*, Augustine reiterates that he has no solution for the questions concerning the soul's origin, stating that "we commit a sin by affecting to be ignorant of nothing among the secret things of God" or by "constructing random theories about unknown things, and taking them for known" or by "producing or defending errors as if they were truth." Augustine admits "my own ignorance on the question whether the souls of men are created afresh in every birth" but steadfastly adds, regarding the belief about souls that "it would be impious to falter in, that they are certainly made by the Divine Creator, though not of his own substance."[136]

Ultimately Augustine argues that it is unimportant to know when or how one began to exist, an event of which we have no memory, so that "concerning my soul I have no certain knowledge how it came into my body; for it was not I who gave it to myself."[137] What is important, says Augustine, is that "I know that I do exist and I do not despair of existing in the future," and most importantly that by using my intellect and free will "I direct my course towards what I am going to be, with the mercy of my Maker as my God."[138]

A summation of Augustine's argument concerning the origin of the soul, how it came into existence, and how it is prone to sin could include

135. Augustine, "On the Free Choice of the Will" 3.22.63.216 (p. 116).
136. Augustine, *On the Soul and Its Origin* 38.24 (p. 371).
137. Augustine, *On the Soul and Its Origin* 25.15 (p. 325).
138. Augustine, "On the Free Choice of the Will" 3.21.61.211 (p. 115).

the following points. According to Augustine God created the soul good, but we do not know when God created the soul or how and when it was united to each person's body or precisely how it contracted original sin. Speculative arguments that claim that it is unjust for God to saddle the soul with the original sin of Adam, so that a preexisting soul would be joined to a body entrenched in concupiscence, leading inexorably to a person sinning, must be rejected because the just God provided man with an intellect and free will to seek divine help in overcoming "the ignorance and trouble" that lead to sin. God in his mercy and justice would not create souls that were doomed to damnation and not allow the soul to know the cause of the damnation in the soul's present human life; rather, the reason and freedom with which he endowed the human person point to his divine will that decrees that man should find ultimate happiness by living according to the moral order God has ordained. Says Augustine:

> Why, then, should we not praise the Creator of the soul with all due religiousness for having supplied the soul with the sort of beginning that by exerting itself and making progress it may reach the fruit of wisdom and justice, and for having furnished the soul was so much dignity that He also put it in its power, if it is willing, to make its way to happiness?[139]

AUGUSTINE ON THE DEATH OF YOUNG CHILDREN, THE MARTYRDOM OF THE HOLY INNOCENTS, AND ALL THOSE WHO DIE FOR CHRIST WITHOUT HAVING BEEN BAPTIZED

Before concluding Book 3 and his entire work *On the Free Choice of the Will*, Augustine provides speculative solutions to two problems that bear upon God's justice in creating human persons. The first problem involves the pain and suffering that may "afflict children who, due to their age, have not committed any sins." Assuming that the souls of young children did not preexist and were not subject to some hypothetical test in which they sinned, the question arises why young children suffer when they have not done anything evil. Augustine proposes that God can bring about good "in correcting adults when they are scourged by the sufferings and death of their young children, who are dear to them," so that the adversity that these adults undergo can incline them to turn away from sin

---

139. Augustine, "On the Free Choice of the Will" 3.23.66.226 (p. 118).

and live rightly. But what of these young children who suffer affliction? Augustine muses that we do not know "what is in store for these young children, whose torments grind down the hardness of their parents, vex their faith and try their compassion"; nor do we know "what compensatory good God has in store for these young children in the hidden depth of His judgments." Augustine notes there is good reason that "the Church commend to us those infants who were killed at the time when Herod was seeking the Lord Jesus Christ to slay Him," which infants "have been received with honor among the martyrs."[140]

The church from its beginning viewed martyrdom for Christ as a sure way to obtain sanctification and salvation. Writing in his *The City of God* about the sack of Rome by barbarians, which occurred in AD 410, Augustine contrasted those Romans who suffered torture for hiding their gold and silver with those Christians who suffered torture for the sake of Christ. Augustine instructs the reader that those who suffered for concealing their earthly possessions "should have learned to love Him Who enriches those who suffer for Him with eternal felicity, rather than gold and silver," for which "it was only worthless to suffer."[141] Regarding those who were martyred for their faith in Christ before being baptized, the consensus of the early church fathers who wrote on this subject was nearly unanimous that these Christian martyrs received a baptism of blood because of their witness to Christ to the point of giving their lives. Cyprian, bishop of Carthage (died AD 258), wrote in a letter that those "who suffer martyrdom before they have received Baptism with water . . . are baptized with the most glorious and greatest Baptism of blood"; and Cyril, bishop of Jerusalem (AD 315–86), taught that "if any man does not receive Baptism, he does not have salvation. The only exception is the martyrs, who, even without water, will receive the kingdom."[142]

Still, the question arises, how can the Holy Innocents who were killed by Herod, who was seeking to kill the infant Jesus, be considered martyrs seeing that these infants could not freely choose to die for Christ? Perhaps an answer can be found in the same divine justice that allows the original sin of Adam to be passed on to his progeny, i.e., to the whole human race. Adam's sin (and all consequent sin) is an infinite offense against the infinite

---

140. Augustine, "On the Free Choice of the Will" 3.23.68.230–231 (p. 119).

141. Augustine, *City of God* (trans Dyson) 1.10 (p. 18).

142. Cyprian, "Letter of Cyprian to Jubaianus, a Bishop in Mauretania," in Jurgens, *Faith of the Early Fathers*, 1:238; Cyril, "Catechetical Lectures," in Jurgens, *Faith of the Early Fathers*, 1:340.

majesty of God, which required rectification. The Holy Innocents, like the unbaptized adult martyrs, witnessed to Jesus Christ, true God and true man, and offered to the Father, knowingly or not, their lives as a meritorious sacrifice, which sacrifice was joined to, and which partook in, the Paschal sacrifice of the Redeemer. Christ's sacrifice was an infinite sacrifice that provided superabundant satisfaction (atonement) for the offense of Adam's original sin and for all mankind's consequent sin. Anyone who suffers and dies witnessing to Christ, including martyred infant witnesses, is joined to Christ's infinitely meritorious sacrifice, and the sufferings of these witnesses helps release the infinite store of redemptive grace that Christ merited for their good and for the good of others.

HOW COULD ADAM SIN?

The second problem that Augustine investigates at the end of Book 3 of *On the Free Choice of the Will* concerns the question of how Adam could fall from grace and God's friendship if God created him wise and virtuous, without sin, without concupiscence, and not subject to suffering and death. By questioning whether "the First Man drew away from God due to foolishness" or whether "he became a fool by drawing away" from God, Augustine finds himself caught within a dilemma that leads him to search for a basic truth regarding the movement of the will from one goal and toward another. Augustine comes to the realization that "the only thing that influences the will to do anything is some impression." What Augustine means by an impression is a perception, a notion, or a concept that draws the mind to consider an object, or aspire to achieve an object, that is derived from higher things or derived from lower things. The will is free because what man accepts or rejects is in his own power so that "there is no power over which impression he is affected by."[143]

But from where do the impressions come? Augustine distinguishes two sources of impressions that designate two different kinds of impressions: the first kind are impressions that "arise from the will of someone trying to persuade," such as the devil or perhaps an associate; the second kind comes to the mind's attention from the bodily senses, or from "the mind itself." The first kind of impression is an exterior influence, which may possibly tempt the will to choose lower goods at the expense of higher goods, whereas the second kind of impression is interior, such

---

143. Augustine, "On the Free Choice of the Will" 3.25.74.255 (p. 124).

as a bodily desire that likewise may tempt the will. However, the more subtle and devious interior influences are those impressions that come from the mind itself. Based on his own analysis of the moral order and man's nature to pursue both higher goods and lower goods, Augustine perceives the dialectical tension between these two goods that is at work in himself and all human persons, especially those with an intellectual bent who are seeking a greater satisfaction within the life of the mind. Augustine tells us:

> In contemplating the highest wisdom—which is surely not the mind, for the highest wisdom is unchangeable—the mind looks upon itself, which is changeable, and in some way enters into its own mind. This happens only in virtue of the difference by which the mind is not what God is, and yet it is something that can please, next to God. However, it is better if it forgets itself before the love of the unchangeable God, or sets itself completely at naught in comparison with Him.[144]

But what could draw the mind away from the highest good and highest wisdom, which is for the human person "the love of the unchangeable God," and lure the mind to reject this love and seek satisfaction in its own changeable existence? This question becomes more problematic when it is asked why Adam turned away from God, given the revelation in Genesis that God made the first man very good and so without sin and without concupiscence. Why would Adam choose to risk his friendship with God and his own happiness in an act of disobedience to the divine command? If it is better that the mind "forget itself before the love of the unchangeable God," what possible motive could divert Adam from loving God first? Augustine finds the answer in the deadliest sin of all, i.e., pride. Augustine tells us:

> If instead [the mind] gets in its own way, so to speak, and it pleases it to imitate God perversely so that it wills to enjoy its own power, it becomes lesser, to precisely the extent that it desires to be greater. And this is: "Pride is the beginning of all sin" [Sir. 10:15; 10:13 RSV]. And "The beginning of pride is when one departs from God" [Sir 10:14; 10:12 RSV].[145]

The sin of pride is most precisely self-induced, or introduced by a devil-induced impression within man to imitate God perversely and enjoy one's

---

144. Augustine, "On the Free Choice of the Will" 3.25.76.261–262 (p. 125).
145. Augustine, "On the Free Choice of the Will" 3.25.76.262–263 (p. 125).

own power without God. While pride is also the sin of Adam and Eve, the first impression arises from the devil's suggestion that when they "eat of it your eyes will be opened, and you will be like God, knowing good and evil" (Gen 3:5). After receiving this first impression from the devil, Adam adopts this satanic suggestion as his own goal, viz., to be like God but without God who created him. Adam's motive for disobeying God had to be pride, but a particular kind of pride identified in 1 John 2:16, which both the King James Version and the Revised Standard, Catholic Edition translate as "the pride of life."

How is this sin defined, and how is this sin distinct from sins motivated by concupiscence? As a sin, pride is an act of will in which one inordinately esteems oneself contrary to the truth. As the first of the seven capital sins or deficient inclinations that are the result of original sin, pride is often admixed with, or motivates, the other six capital sins, viz., envy, anger, lust, avarice, gluttony, and sloth. An example of this admixture could be that when one inordinately esteems oneself, the slightest offense from another person could motivate extreme anger in which one seeks vengeance that is out of proportion to the offense given. When pride helps to motivate the other capital sins, it is fused with concupiscence, where a person's exaggerated sense of self-importance provides a false justification for the satisfaction of his deficient desires, which tend to be insubordinate to a person's free choice to follow right reason and pursue virtue.

As already implied, concupiscence is the inclination to sin that all persons inherit from Adam's original sin. Concupiscence links man's inclination to pride with the deficient, bodily satisfactions toward which the other capital sins prompt (spur, goad) a person to gratify. Adam, however, was created good by God and did not have concupiscence or such urges to sin before his fall. Without the need to satisfy deficient bodily and emotional urges, the only sin that Adam could have committed was one originating in the intellect. Pride of life is basically the urge of the intellect to do one's own will without regard to any authority, including the authority of God. With pride of life a person seeks to replace all authority, and especially God's authority, with his own will so that what results is a kind of self-deification that can be seen as a foundational element in all sin. This was exactly the sin of the devil (he refused to accept God's authority) and the nature of the impression or temptation with which the devil enticed Eve, and through Eve, Adam. Referring to the fruit of the tree of the knowledge of good and evil that God had forbidden Adam to eat, the serpent said to Eve, "You will not die. For God knows that when you eat of it your eyes will be opened, and you will be like God, knowing good and evil." Eve took the fruit of the tree and ate it and gave some of the fruit to Adam, and he ate it. This was the devil's enticement for Adam's freely committing the original sin, viz., "You will be like God."

The original sin brought to all mankind the status of being bereft of God's friendship, having the propensity to sin, and being subject to suffering and death. Augustine completes *On the Free Choice of the Will* by speaking of Christ's promise of salvation:

> To the human race the Devil had offered himself as an example of pride, but the Lord offered Himself as an example of humility, through Whom we are promised eternal life. Consequently, since Christ paid for us with His blood after His indescribable trials and miseries, let us hold fast with great love to our Liberator![146]

For Augustine, "holding fast" to Christ requires acceptance of Christ's grace—a theological concept not clearly explicated in *On the Free Choice of the Will*, but rather only alluded to, implied, or described to a limited extent.

RECONSIDERATIONS

Reconsiderations is Peter King's term for translating the title of Augustine's short, follow-up review of *On the Free Choice of the Will*. *Reconsiderations* was written in 427, over thirty years after the original work was completed. At this time Augustine was concerned with the Pelagian heresy that denied man's need for grace in order to be virtuous and to avoid evil. This follow-up work does not discard Augustine's belief that man's will is free, although it does emphasize in greater detail the need for God's grace to be virtuous and to avoid evil.

His original contention as developed in *On the Free Choice of the Will*, while complex and involving significant qualifications, was rooted in Augustine's own personal experience that the human will is free to choose to pursue good or to pursue evil and helped bring Augustine to reject completely the deterministic religious philosophy of Manichaeism that had once mesmerized him. Augustine explains that those believers "who deny that the origin of evil lies in the free choice of the will" tend

---

146. Augustine, "On the Free Choice of the Will" 3.25.76.264 (p. 125).

to argue that "God as the Creator of all natures ought to be blamed," and consequently "they want to introduce some unchangeable nature of evil that is co-eternal with God in accordance with their irreligious error (for they are Manichaeans)."[147] From a Christian perspective, this blatantly heretical view of the Manichaeans that there are, in effect, two deities, one good and one evil, and that the evil god created and controls the human body, renders the human person with no control over his/her actions and thus renders his will unfree. The professor of history emeritus at Princeton University Peter Brown explained in his seminal work on the life and thought of Augustine that Augustine relied on his own experience and common sense to formulate his position on the freedom of the will. Says Professor Brown:

> There was the burning problem of the apparent permanence of evil in human actions. The problem had placed Augustine in an awkward position. For, previously, he had taken up his stand on the freedom of the will; his criticism of Manichaeism had been a typical philosopher's criticism of determinism generally. It was a matter of common sense that men were responsible for their actions; they could not be held responsible if their wills were not free; therefore, their wills could not be thought of as being determined by some external forces, in this case, by the Manichaean "Power of Darkness."[148]

Professor Brown goes on to explain that Augustine's stance on the freedom of the will in his early work seemed to suggest that Augustine was teaching "in theory at least, the absolute self-determination of the will," so that years later "Pelagius will even quote from Augustine's book 'On Free Will' in support of his own views."[149]

The issue of the freedom of the will, then, for Augustine became his main concern in writing *On the Free Choice of the Will*; and as Pelagianism (and its denial of the need for grace in order to be saved) had not as yet emerged as a distinct heresy, "there was no examination of grace in these books, by which God so predestines the people," so that God himself "even prepares the wills of those among them who are already making use of free choice."[150] Regarding the origin of evil, Augustine cites the argument he already made in the beginning of *On the Free Choice of*

147. Augustine, "Reconsiderations," 1.9 (p. 127).
148. Brown, *Augustine of Hippo*, 141.
149. Brown, *Augustine of Hippo*, 141–42.
150. Brown, *Augustine of Hippo*, 128.

the Will directed against the Manichaeans that "evildoings are redressed by God's justice. . . . It would not be just to redress them unless they came about through the will."[151]

Still, in his *Reconsiderations* Augustine argues that he was not completely silent regarding God's grace, while the Pelagians, though not denying the reality of grace, explicitly asserted the ability of the freedom of the will on its own to do good and avoid evil without interference from any moral weakness or unruly desires affecting human nature. In proffering the gist of the Pelagian view or, for that matter, the essential part of any religion, philosophy, or concept, it is always preferable to cite a primary source germane to what is under consideration. In the case of Pelagius, who presumably was the original source of Pelagian doctrines, there are few of his complete works that are extant. One such work is the *Letter of Pelagius to Demetrias*. Without mentioning original sin, Pelagius in this letter effectively denies that there is any concupiscence that man inherits from the sin of Adam that leads human persons to sin. Pelagius states:

> Certainly we do not so defend the goodness of nature that we would say it is not able to do evil, when we profess that it is capable of good and evil. Rather, we vindicate it against injuries of such a kind that, by its having been corrupted, we would seem to be impelled to the evil; for we can do neither good or evil without willing it, and we have always a freedom to do one of two things, since we are always able to do otherwise.[152]

By claiming that human persons because of their freedom are always able to choose freely either good or evil without any compelling influence from original sin is to ignore a core Christian moral teaching that man needs God's grace to overcome the habitual tendency to sin (called concupiscence) that man inherits from Adam. While human nature is not totally corrupted by original sin, all persons are left in a morally weakened state that results in their sinning at some point or other, in spite of the best efforts of the best of persons to be virtuous. As the pendulum of heresy swung from the deterministic cult of Manichaeism that emphasized man's subjection to evil forces within him, over to a person's free autonomy found in Pelagius's moral theology that emphasized the

---

151. Augustine, "On the Free Choice of the Will" 1.1.1.3 (p. 3); quoted in "Reconsiderations" 3 (p. 128).

152. Pelagius, *Letter of Pelagius to Demetrias*, in Jurgens, *Faith of the Early Fathers*, 2:215.

relative goodness of man's nature, which was subject only to man's free choice, Augustine saw the need later in his life to emphasize man's reliance on God's grace in order to balance the prior emphasis Augustine had placed on the free will.

Without denying what he had written in *On the Free Choice of the Will*, Augustine sought to qualify and balance his discussion of freedom of the will with the need for grace that he emphasizes in his *Reconsiderations*. Augustine speaks of "the new Pelagian heretics—who maintain that the choice of the will is so free that there is no place for God's grace" and that grace is "given in accordance with our deserts" and acts as a help that only facilitates the pursuit of the good, which otherwise can be freely chosen without grace.[153] Augustine took issue with these contentions, first generally in *On the Free Choice of the Will* and more specifically in *Reconsiderations* and in his other anti-Pelagian works. (A note of caution should be entered here—Augustine was not always precise in identifying what Pelagius actually wrote and in what work, or who "the new Pelagian heretics" were and what they exactly wrote in what works. Of what a student of Augustine can be sure is what Augustine thought was the Pelagian heresy and how he refutes his own notion of the heresy.)

In his *Reconsiderations* Augustine does identify Pelagius as the author of the specific work *Nature*, a work that is no longer extant in its entirety but of which Augustine provides fragments by citing various quotations of Pelagius's position on human nature and man's freedom, which Augustine then proceeds to refute in his own work *On Nature and Grace*. Writing in *Reconsiderations*, Augustine provides the crux of his argument with Pelagius, who had quoted Augustine's own work *On the Free Choice of the Will*[154] to support the Pelagian thesis that denied the need for grace to come first in order to avoid sin:

> "Who sins in the case of what one cannot guard against in any way? But there is sin. Hence one can guard against it." Pelagius used this statement of mine in his book [*Nature*]; when I replied to it, I chose the title of my book to be Nature and Grace. Since God's grace was not mentioned in these words of mine (and others like them)—it was not the subject being dealt with at the time—the Pelagians think, or are able to think, that I held their view. But they think this in vain. The will is indeed that by which we sin and that by which we live rightly, which we were dealing

---

153. Augustine, "Reconsiderations" 3 (p. 128).
154. Augustine, "On the Free Choice of the Will" 3.18.50.171 (p. 107).

> with in these statements. Therefore, unless the will itself is set free by God's grace from the servitude in which it was made the slave of sin, and is helped to overcome its vices, mortals cannot live rightly and religiously. And unless this divine kindness by which the will is set free came first, grace would then be given in accordance with deserts, and it would not be grace, which is of course given gratuitously.[155]

For Augustine, God's help—grace—is absolutely necessary for the will to overcome the slavery of sin in which the body is burdened, and in which the mind is subject to the memory intruding itself with the satisfactions gained from one's past sins. Moreover, while human persons can freely beg God for the grace needed to avoid sin and be virtuous, each person needs in the first place the initial impetus of grace to ask God freely for more grace, and then to act freely in accord with this grace. Further, grace is given freely through God's own discretion and is not owed to any person due to his/her possible good works of the past. Still, "God our Savior . . . wills everyone to be saved and to come to knowledge of the truth" (1 Tim 2:4; a passage for which Augustine furnishes only a very narrow interpretation). Only with grace is the will free to choose with a clear understanding of what is good and evil and why choosing the good is in accord with God's will and gratuitously given grace and thus leads to happiness.

Writing in his *On Nature and Grace*, Augustine provides the following quote or paraphrase of Pelagius, who poses the following question: "'And who would be unwilling to be without sin, if it were put in the power of a man? . . . By this very question the knowledge that the thing [i.e., the power to be without sin] is not impossible; because so much as this, many, if not all men, certainly desire.'" In response to Pelagius's propositional question, Augustine poses his own question that in effect rejects Pelagius's implied premise that it has been "put in the power of a man to be without sin" by means of man's own will alone. Augustine thus argues against Pelagius with this question:

> Why on such occasions did he choose only to defend nature, and assert that man was so created as to have it in his power not to sin if he wished not to sin; and, from the fact that he was so created, [not] definitely say that the power was owing to God's grace which enabled him to avoid sin, if he was unwilling to commit it; and yet refuse to say anything concerning the fact

155. Augustine, "Reconsiderations" 3–4 (pp. 129–30).

that even nature itself is either, because disordered, healed by God's grace through our Lord Jesus Christ or else assisted by it, because in itself it is so insufficient?[156]

While *On Nature and Grace* is polemical in tone, this short anti-Pelagian work provides necessary premises for reconciling man's free will—through which all evil acts are committed—with the need for divine grace. Given the disorderly effects of original sin on human nature, in order for man not to sin and avoid vice, grace is first needed to avoid evil and vice, and, by implication, grace is continuously needed to choose freely what is good so as to develop virtue.

Augustine sums up the core of his *Reconsiderations* argument toward the end of this work by telling the reader that "of our own accord we were able to fall, namely by free choice, but not also to rise up." He goes on to state that "this misery of our just damnation includes ignorance and trouble, which every human being suffers from the first moment of his birth," so that as a consequence "no one is set free from this evil except by God's grace." Augustine accuses the Pelagians of being unwilling to accept "for this misery to stem from a just damnation, since they deny Original Sin"; and he finally repeats his argument that "even if ignorance and trouble were primordial features of the nature of human beings, God still ought to be praised rather than blamed."[157]

A CONSIDERATION OF THE SUBTLE BUT CRITICAL DIFFERENCE BETWEEN AUGUSTINE'S UNDERSTANDING OF FREE WILL AND GRACE IN *ON THE FREE CHOICE OF THE WILL* AND *RECONSIDERATIONS*

The argument regarding ignorance and trouble is found in Book 3 of *On the Free Choice of the Will*. Here, Augustine argues that even "if ignorance of the truth and trouble in doing right is natural to human beings," God is still to be praised because God provided human beings with that "from which they begin to rise towards the happiness of wisdom and peace," and God is obviously not to be blamed for this gift because "no one rightly condemns this happiness for its natural beginning." At the time of man's creation he was given a natural capacity to rise toward the happiness of wisdom and peace, but "if someone is unwilling to make progress or is

---

156. Augustine, *Treatise on Nature and Grace*, 75.
157. Augustine, "Reconsiderations" 6 (pp. 132–33).

willing to backslide from his progress, he will rightly and deservedly pay the penalties." More specifically, Augustine argues that the "Creator of the soul is praised on all sides for creating in man's soul the capacity for the highest good from its beginnings" and *then* "assisting our progress; perfecting and satisfying those who make progress" while, on the other hand, "ordaining the most just damnation for the sinner—that is, for someone refusing to lift himself up to perfection from its beginnings or now relapsing from some progress—according to his deserts."[158]

It seems that in this earlier anti-Manichaean work, *On the Free Choice of the Will*, God's damnation is for those who first reject from its natural beginning their God-created capacity for the highest good for which all human persons yearn and who then, subsequently, reject God's continuous assistance—grace—for achieving this highest good. This is a distinction in this earlier work, *On the Free Choice of the Will*, to the position he put forward in the later work, *Reconsiderations* (quoted above), that "unless this divine kindness by which the will is set free came first, grace would then be given in accordance with deserts, and it would not be grace, which is of course given gratuitously."[159] However, in *On the Free Choice of the Will*, Augustine is seemingly telling us that a person must freely and willingly make progress toward the goal of achieving the happiness of wisdom and peace, and then God will assist, perfect, and satisfy our progress with the gift of grace. This suggests that unless we freely choose without grace to "rise towards the happiness of wisdom and peace" relying solely upon our own free will, God will not be "assisting our progress; perfecting and satisfying those who make progress," and this assistance obviously refers to divine grace.

As Augustine moved toward his anti-Pelagian writings, he emphasized repeatedly the need for God's grace to come first in order for a person to avoid evil and do anything good. Without first receiving grace and by relying solely on his free will, all man can do is sin. Says Augustine in *Reconsiderations*:

> For of our own we were able to fall, namely by free choice, but not also to rise up. And this misery of our just damnation includes ignorance and trouble, which every human being suffers from the moment of his birth. No one is set free from this evil except by God's grace.[160]

158. Augustine, "On the Free Choice of the Will" 3.22.64.220; 3.22.6.221 (p. 117).
159. Augustine, "Reconsiderations" 4 (p. 130.)
160. Augustine, "Reconsiderations" 6 (p. 132).

Without God's grace, a human person cannot begin to choose the good and avoid the evil. But in this position that Augustine espouses in *Reconsiderations*, and throughout all of his anti-Pelagian works written much later in his life, Augustine argues that grace is needed first to avoid concupiscence and sin and to do good. Without grace, man is not able to take the first step in choosing the highest good or any good. Grace is always needed as God's gratuitous gift in order to accomplish good and avoid evil. This position is apparently not held in *On the Free Choice of the Will*. While grace is not outright denied in this earlier work, there Augustine suggests that grace is initially not necessary to choose freely to "rise toward the happiness of wisdom and peace."

In *Reconsiderations* Augustine establishes two distinct meanings of freedom: first, there is freedom of choice to reject what is good and to choose evil, which choice is rooted in humanity's subjection to concupiscence which, in turn, is rooted in original sin that carries with it deficiencies of ignorance and trouble. According to Augustine, the choice of evil is the only freedom of choice man can solely exercise on his own without the help of grace. However, only with the help of grace can man exercise freedom of choice to choose good and avoid evil. Regarding this first meaning of freedom the quote cited above is directly applicable: "No one is set free from this evil except by God's grace." The second meaning of freedom is the freedom to seek perfection, not only to avoid sin, but also to excel in virtue, which freedom, to some extent, frees man from the urges of sin that enslave the person. By this freedom that is "the good use of free choice [which] is virtue," a human person cannot exercise solely on his/her own but can only attain through the gift of divine grace gratuitously given by God. Augustine argues:

> Free choice of the will is found among the intermediate goods for the reason that we can use it badly, although it is such that we cannot live rightly without it. Now the good use of free choice is virtue, which has its place among the great goods which no one can use badly. And since all goods—great, intermediate, and small—come from God, as noted, it follows that the good use of free will, which is virtue and is counted among the great goods, also comes from God.[161]

---

161. Augustine, "Reconsiderations" 6 (p. 132).

Chapter Four

An Analysis of Three of Augustine's Anti-Pelagian Works

On Grace and Free Choice, On Reprimand and Grace, and *On the Gift of Perseverance,* with Contrasting Views of Other Theologians

AUGUSTINE'S *ON GRACE AND FREE CHOICE*

Grace Sets Us Free from Evil Deserts but Does Not Destroy Human Freedom

WRITTEN BETWEEN 426 AND 427 and addressed to a monastic community, Augustine supplies at the very beginning of *On Grace and Free Choice* why this book and others with a similar theme written by him during the time period of 412 up until 429 (the year before his death) are referred to as anti-Pelagian works. These anti-Pelagian works counter the views of those

> who preach and defend human free choice in such a way that they dare to deny and try to get rid of the grace of God—the grace by which we are called to Him and are set free from our

evil desserts, and through which we acquire good deserts by which we might attain eternal life.[1]

Augustine is making clear here at the outset of this book that no one can be set free from evil deserts and attain the good desert of eternal life without God's grace.

At the same time Augustine warns against those "who defend the grace of God in such a way that they deny human free choice, or who hold that free choice is denied when grace is defended."[2] Augustine affirms free choice by relying upon multiple quotes from Scripture that reveal divine precepts that are to be obeyed and quotes that admonish those who sin. Three examples are "Be unwilling to neglect the grace that is in you" (1 Tim 4:14); "each person is tempted when he is drawn away and enticed by his own lust. When lust has conceived, it brings forth sin; and sin, when it is accomplished, brings forth death" (Jas 1:15); and the negative precept: "Be sober, just, and unwilling to sin" (1 Cor 15:34).[3] Augustine argues that being "unwilling" to do or not do something "is sufficient proof of free choice." On the one hand, a person has himself to blame when he willingly violates God's command. On the other hand, a person who refuses to disobey God can hope for a reward from God for his being unwilling to violate God's commands. Augustine states that "to be willing and to be unwilling are proper to the will."[4]

Augustine asks why else God would reveal any moral commands unless such commands could be freely obeyed and so that no excuse could be given by the evildoer who might claim ignorance of God's law. Augustine tells us:

> Now God has revealed to us through His own Scripture that human beings have free choice of the will. I shall remind you how He revealed this, not with my human words but rather with His divine eloquence. First of all, the divine precepts would themselves be pointless for human beings unless we had free choice of the will, by which we might reach the promised rewards through carrying them out. For the precepts were given to human beings in order that they not have an excuse on the grounds of ignorance, as the Lord says of the Jews in the gospel:

---

1. Augustine, "On Grace and Free Choice" 1.1 (p. 141).
2. Augustine, "On Grace and Free Choice" 1.1 (p. 141).
3. All scriptural quotations are translated directly by Peter King from Augustine's text.
4. Augustine, "On Grace and Free Choice" 4.5 (p. 146).

> "Had I not come and spoken to them, they would have no sin; but now they have no excuse for their sin" [John 15:22]. Of what sin is He speaking if not the great one He foreknew would be there when he said these things, that is, the sin in which they were going to put Him to death?[5]

What Augustine concludes is that God's revelation would not bid that all his commands must be obeyed unless there were free choice for a person to "take his stand in God's law" by submitting to God's teaching. The fundamental question arises: If man has recourse to his own free will, what need has he of grace in living a good life and avoiding sin? This is essentially the question raised by the Pelagians. Referring to the Pelagian heresy, Augustine cites Jer 17:5: "Accursed is the man who has his hope in man, and makes strong the flesh of his arm, and whose heart abandons the Lord." Making strong the flesh of his arm is interpreted by Augustine to mean "the power of acting" where a person believes that the inadequate power of one's flesh can be sufficiently strengthened by himself alone to act well without God's help, i.e., while "abandoning the Lord."

Pelagianism Denies the Effects of Original Sin and Discounts the Need for Grace

Referring further to Pelagianism, Augustine remarks that ongoing arguments against the heresy were not sufficient to prevent its being spread, so that "it was necessary in the end for it to come before the episcopal councils."[6] The two provincial councils of Carthage and Milevis, both held in 416, condemned the principal teachings of Pelagianism, and these condemnations were eventually upheld by papal statements during Augustine's lifetime. However, the most articulate conciliar condemnation of Pelagianism was made a century after Augustine's death at the Second Council of Orange in 529 (which was approved by Pope Boniface II in 531). In its canons on original sin, the council decreed:

> If anyone says that it was not the whole man, that is, both body and soul, that was "changed for the worse" by the offense of Adam's sin, but believes that the freedom of the soul remained untouched and that only the body was made subject to corruption,

---

5. Augustine, "On Grace and Free Choice" 2.2 (p. 142).
6. Augustine, "On Grace and Free Choice" 4.6 (p. 147).

he is deceived by the error of Pelagius and contradicts the words of Scripture....

If anyone asserts that Adam's sin was injurious only to Adam and not to his descendants, or if he declares that it was only the death of the body which is punishment for sin, and not [also through] the sin, the death of the soul, that passed from one man to all the human race, he attributes an injustice to God and contradicts the words of the Apostle: "Through one man sin entered into the world and through sin death, and thus death has passed into all men because all have sinned," Romans 5:12.[7]

Since the early first millennium, Christian teaching has maintained that original sin weakened human nature morally in that each person is born subject to concupiscence, which is an insubordination of human desires against the dictates of right reason and against one's conscience. Another way of saying this is that man is prone to sin and that man's freedom is compromised so that human beings became subject to ignorance and trouble and the divine punishment of death of the body and the spiritual death of the soul. Further, this condition originated with Adam, who personally committed the original sin and passed it on to all his descendants, who inherited the punishment for original sin as well as the moral weakness that it causes.

In his *Commentaries on the Thirteen Epistles of Paul*, which is one of his few extant books, Pelagius provides some evidence of his heretical views but not in a way that could be cited as conclusive proof of what he really believed or stated that was in conflict with orthodox Christian teaching. In this work Pelagius intersperses verses of Paul's letters with his own commentary. Pelagius's text repeats Paul's letter to the Romans, in which 5:19 states: "for as by the disobedience of one sinning man, many were made sinners, so also by the obedience of one, many shall be made just." Immediately following this verse is Pelagius's commentary stating: "Just as many sinned by the *example* of Adam's disobedience, so also many are justified by the obedience of Christ."[8] Other comments by Pelagius regarding various verses in Paul's letters could be interpreted as denying that Adam's sin, or that punishment for the original sin, was passed on to mankind. Assuming this to be Pelagius's position then, Adam's sin merely passed on bad example to mankind. However, it is perhaps better to base orthodox condemnations of Pelagianism on what has

---

7. *Church Teaches*, "Original Justice and Original Sin," 157.
8. Pelagius, *Commentaries*, "Letter to the Romans," 73 (emphasis added).

been historically attributed to be the teachings of Pelagians as these are cited and described in Augustine's (and others') anti-Pelagian writings.

With original sin, man's free will is limited in its power to obey God's law because human nature is prone to sin, but free will is still operative and culpable for violations of the moral law. According to Augustine, what the Pelagians failed to admit is the absolute need for God's grace to empower the person to freely choose to obey the moral law. Augustine in *On Grace and Free Choice* continues to quote Scripture to buttress his argument, citing Jas 1:14: "each person is tempted when he is drawn away and enticed by his own lust"; and Rom 12:21: "Be unwilling to be overcome by evil." Augustine immediately adds: "what use to him [a person enticed by evil] is this, unless with the succor of grace it comes to pass?" Augustine also cites Paul in 1 Cor 15:56, which states: "The sting of death is sin; and the power of sin is the Law," and Augustine explains that "unless grace helps, the Law will be nothing but the power of sin. Lust is increased and strengthened by the prohibition of the Law, unless the spirit of grace helps us."[9] For Augustine, Paul's revelation that "the power of sin is the Law" means that without God's grace no one can overcome the power of lust to sin, so that the person is left acknowledging in resignation his inability to keep the commandments, his own guilt as a sinner who violates the law, and his only real desert to be the wrath of God.

God's Grace Needed to Follow Moral Law

At this point, the unbeliever might object: How can the law even be known in the first place without faith in God's revelation? The answer lies in the natural law to which Paul makes reference when he tells us that the Gentiles, who do not have the law (through revelation accepted in faith), nonetheless have the law written on their hearts; see Rom 2:14–15. As mentioned above, Augustine in his *Reply to Faustus the Manichaean* speaks of three laws: first is the law of the Hebrews, which Paul calls the law of sin and death; second is that of the Gentiles, which Paul calls the law of nature (which is the natural moral law written on everyone's heart); and third is the law of the Spirit of life in Christ Jesus, which is the life of grace. Augustine further emphasizes here in *On Grace and Free Choice* the absolute need for the grace of Christ by repeating 1 Cor 15:56 and by adding verse 57 followed by his own commentary: "'But thanks be to God

---

9. Augustine, "On Grace and Free Choice" 4.8 (p. 148).

who gives us victory through our Lord Jesus Christ.' Therefore, even the 'victory' in which sin is overcome is nothing but God's gift, helping our free choice in the struggle."[10]

Whereas God's grace must come first and is absolutely necessary in avoiding sin and doing good works, a person must freely choose to work with this grace in order to receive the "victory" given by God through our Lord Jesus Christ. But how do we initially obtain the gift of God's grace, especially in overcoming the temptation to sin? In answering this question, Augustine insists (with the backing of Scripture once again) that the human will must depend on and work with God's grace in resisting temptation and coming to Christ. On the one hand, while praying implies reliance on God's help, the human will must choose to turn to God and pray as Christ directs in Matt 26:41: "Be watchful that you not enter into temptation." Augustine acknowledges that the Lord's directive seems only to address the free choice of the will. But, on the other hand, Augustine tells us, when Christ "added 'and pray' He showed that God provides help that we not enter into temptation." And this reliance on God's help is reinforced by what Christ said to Peter: "'I have prayed for you, Peter, that your faith may not fail' [Luke 22:32]. Human beings are therefore assisted by grace, so that their wills are not bidden to no purpose."[11]

Pelagians argue, says Augustine, that when one prays to God the person is freely taking an initiative to seek God and thereby deserves credit from God, which he rewards by giving grace. Augustine cites a favorite passage of Pelagians, 1 Chr 28:9, which states in part: "if you seek Him, you shall find Him." Augustine tells us that according to the Pelagians:

> Our deserts consist in the fact that we are seeking Him. . . . The Pelagians . . . postulate human deserts in the words "if you seek Him" and hold that grace is given in accordance with these deserts in the words "you shall find Him." They labor as hard as they can to show that God's grace is given in accordance with our deserts, that is to show that grace is not grace. For if it is rendered to people in accordance with their deserts, "the reward is not paid as a matter of grace, but of debt" [Rom 4:4], as the Apostle Paul says quite clearly.[12]

---

10. Augustine, "On Grace and Free Choice" 4.8 (pp. 148-49).
11. Augustine, "On Grace and Free Choice" 4.9 (p. 149).
12. Augustine, "On Grace and Free Choice" 5.11 (pp. 150-51).

Contrary to the Pelagians, Augustine insists grace is not given by God as a reward for our works but is given gratuitously, purely as God's gift. Augustine also refers to certain Pelagians who could be called semi-Pelagians in that they concede the possibility that God does not give grace as a reward for our good works but insist that God will give grace for one's goodwill, which includes the goodwill to believe. These semi-Pelagians are quoted by Augustine (without Augustine giving any source for the citation) as claiming that "the goodwill of the person praying comes first, and this is preceded by the will to believe, so that the grace of God Who hears our prayers follows in accordance with these deserts."[13] Augustine argues that even the act of praying requires one to first receive and respond to this gratuitous gift of grace that comes first as the gift of faith that prompts one to pray. God's gift of grace is always prompting us when we pray or perform a good work, and God's gift of grace is especially productive when one turns away from evil acts and turns toward conversion. What is essential to repeat is that grace must come first in order for a person to actually have faith, convert, pray, and do good works. Says Augustine: "The spirit of grace brings it about that we have faith, so that through our faith we may achieve by prayer the ability to do what we are bidden to do."[14]

To support his position that God's grace is not given as something deserved for good works but is first and foremost God's gift to us sinners, Augustine references Paul's persecution of the church referred to in 1 Cor 15:9–10 in which Paul admits, "I am not fit to be called an apostle, because I persecuted the Church of God." Paul earned only evil deserts for the evil acts he committed persecuting Christians, but for these evil acts God gave Paul the grace of conversion and then the grace to become the Lord's "Vessel of Election" to bear Christ's "name before the nations, and kings, and the children of Israel" (Acts 9:15). But if grace is given gratuitously by God so that a persecutor like Paul can turn away from evil works and do good works for attaining salvation, where does free choice enter into the doing of these good works? It might seem that good works are entirely God's work performed by a human person solely through God's grace moving the person without free choice having anything to do with the good work. It also seems that what Augustine wrote in his *Reconsiderations* would always be the case, viz., "of our own accord we were

---

13. Augustine, "On Grace and Free Choice" 14.27 (p. 163).
14. Augustine, "On Grace and Free Choice" 14.28 (p. 164).

able to fall, namely by free choice, but not also to rise up."[15] This statement might be interpreted to mean that free choice solely on its own has no role to play in doing good, avoiding evil, and attaining salvation but, rather, free choice by itself can only choose to do evil. What Augustine most probably means is that free choice must be provided the necessary assistance of grace in order to rise above sin, do good, and be deserving of good deserts.

Teachings of Luther and Pelagians Are Diametrically Opposed

This possible harmonious relationship of divine intervention, i.e., supernatural grace, working together with the free choice of a human person is denied by the Protestant reformer Martin Luther. Writing in his *The Bondage of the Will*, Luther cites Paul's letter to the Romans and interprets it to mean that free choice can do nothing but choose evil and work against grace. Says Luther:

> This is how Paul, writing to the Romans, enters into an argument against free choice and for the grace of God: "The wrath of God is revealed from heaven against all ungodliness and wickedness of men who in wickedness hold back the truth of God" [Rom 1:18]. Do you hear in this the general verdict on all men, that they are under the wrath of God? What else does this mean but they are deserving of wrath and punishment? He gives as the reason for the wrath, the fact that they do nothing but what deserves wrath and punishment, because they are all ungodly and wicked, and in wickedness hold back the truth. Where now is the power of free choice to attempt anything good? . . . And that which deserves wrath and is ungodly, strives and prevails against grace, not for grace.[16]

Considering the transgression of Adam and man's fallen nature that we all inherit, and without mentioning the free will's working with grace, it may be understandable why Luther insists that man's free choice has no ability to do anything but sin and oppose grace. Writing further, Luther claims: "Original sin itself, therefore, leaves free choice with no capacity to do anything but sin and be damned."[17]

---

15. Augustine, "Reconsiderations" 6 (p. 132).
16. Luther, *Bondage of the Will*, 178.
17. Luther, *Bondage of the Will*, 203.

Luther's argument is diametrically in opposition to that of the Pelagians, while Augustine rejects both extremes. On the one hand, the Pelagians argue that man can merit God's grace by having a good will, having faith in God, and praying for his help so that "the grace of God Who hears our prayers follows in accordance with these deserts."[18] For the Pelagians, through one's free choice one can do good works, observe the commandments, believe, and pray, and these free will acts of the person are performed first without the benefit of grace and actually merit God's grace. Pelagians argue that, to begin with, a person can freely choose to obey God's law and thereby be justified. Augustine, however, cites Gal 5:4: "You who are made just in the Law have fallen from grace." Augustine offers the following comment in regard to Paul's verse: "However, the Law is not grace, for the simple reason that in order for the Law to come to pass, the Law itself cannot be of assistance, whereas grace can." Augustine attacks the Pelagians for having "dared to make the claim that grace is the nature in which we were created such that we have a rational mind" and are "made in God's image." But, says Augustine, continuing the attack, "this is not the grace which the apostle commends through faith in Jesus Christ."[19] In rejecting original sin, the Pelagians deny that man inherits a fallen nature and is in need of redemption and believe that man comes into this world already graced (or at least free from sin), so he is already empowered to freely choose to do good, believe, and avoid evil without receiving additional grace.

On the other hand, for Luther, there is no free choice to work with grace in doing good works or in believing and praying, because the only good we can do is completely caused by God's grace, and all our free choice can do is violate God's law and sin. A response to Luther's argument might be found in Augustine's interpretation of Paul's 1 Cor 15:10, which interpretation affirms the role of free choice in cooperation with grace. This verse immediately follows Paul's admittance that he is not fit to be called an apostle because of his persecution of the church: "But by the grace of God I am what I am, and his grace in me was not fruitless, but I labored more abundantly than all of them; not I, however, but the grace of God which was with me" (1 Cor 15:10). Augustine interprets Paul to mean:

---

18. Augustine, "On Grace and Free Choice" 4.27 (p. 163).
19. Augustine, "On Grace and Free Choice" 13.25 (p. 162).

> That is: I was not alone, but God's grace was with me. Accordingly, *it was neither the grace of God alone, nor the apostle himself alone, but the grace of God with him*. However, it was the grace of God alone that the apostle be called from heaven and converted by so great and efficacious a calling, for his deserts were great but evil.[20]

Augustine is emphasizing here that free will can and must work with grace in order for a person to do good works. However, it is God's grace that is always first given gratuitously, and then this grace must act on the person, enabling him to accept the grace he has received, in order for the person to freely choose to act by means of grace and in accordance with grace.

God's Grace Empowers a Person's Free Choice to Choose Rightly

In the case of Paul, whose deserts were evil before his conversion, God gratuitously supplied the grace of conversion, so that Paul then could freely act in accord with God's will. Augustine concludes that despite any person's evil acts: "clearly, once grace has been given, our deserts begin to be good, though by means of it. For if grace were to withdraw itself, human beings would fall, no longer raised up but cast down by free choice."[21] Here, Augustine alludes to God exercising his will to withdraw or to deny grace to a person with the result that the person's free will becomes impotent in his attempt to achieve good deserts. Or, God can will to provide a person with grace whose past bad actions result in bad deserts. But, what of the person who rejects God's grace and refuses to work with grace? Augustine speaks of those who have a "'heart of stone' [which] signifies precisely a will that is inflexible and completely hardened against God." Augustine also speaks of those who have evil deserts but to whom God gives grace to take away their "heart of stone" and warns us to "not think that human beings themselves do nothing in this case through free choice" but, rather, to do as "the Psalmist says: 'Be unwilling to harden your heart' [Ps 94:8; 95:7–8 RSV]."[22]

The subtle complexities of the relationship between God's grace given gratuitously and man having free choice bring Augustine to a series of questions that are not easily answered. Augustine first cites Ezekiel

---

20. Augustine, "On Grace and Free Choice" 5.12 (p. 151) (emphasis added).
21. Augustine, "On Grace and Free Choice" 6.13 (p. 152).
22. Augustine, "On Grace and Free Choice" 14.29; 15.31 (pp. 165–66).

regarding those who harden their hearts but to whom God exhorts and then promises to give grace: "He who says here 'Make for yourselves a new heart and a new spirit' also says: 'A new heart also will I give you, and a new spirit will I put within you' [Ezek 36:26]." Augustine then asks: "How then does He Who says 'Make yourselves' also say 'I will give you'? Why does He bid it, if He is going to give it? Why does He give it, if a man is going to do it?"[23] At the beginning of *On Grace and Free Choice*, Augustine already argued that God bids us keep his commandments, which would be pointless for God to do unless we had free choice of the will. But free choice of the will does not by itself ensure that what we do will is good, so we need God's grace to have a good will and do what God bids. In answering Augustine's questions, in order to make ourselves a new heart and a new spirit, we need God's grace to achieve these goals. Says Augustine, explaining the sometimes perplexing conflict between free choice to do God's bidding and God's grace facilitating or prompting our doing it:

> The reason must be that He gives what He bids when he helps the one He bids to do it. The will is always free in us, but it is not always good. For it is either (a) free from justice, when it is the servant of sin, and then it is evil; or (b) free from sin, when it is the servant of justice, and then it is good. But God's grace is always good. Through grace it happens that a human being who previously had an evil will has a good will. Through grace it also happens that this good will, which is now begun to exist, increases, and becomes so great that it can fulfill the divine commandment, which it shall will to do, since it shall will firmly and completely.... Willing is useful when we have the ability; having the ability is useful when we will. For what good is it if we will what we cannot do, or are unwilling to do what we can.[24]

A summary of what Augustine is saying might be that God has given us a free will and expects us to use it to achieve what he bids us to do. But our wills and minds are finite and our human nature is fallen, and knowing these truths makes it clear to us that we must continuously rely on God's help to accomplish the good and avoid the evil toward which our natures have a definite inclination. In short, God helps us, and without his help we cannot do the good work that he bids us to do. However, we must

---

23. Augustine, "On Grace and Free Choice" 15.31 (p. 166).
24. Augustine, "On Grace and Free Choice" 15.31 (pp. 166–67).

freely choose to accept and work with God's help (grace) to do God's bidding even as our fallen nature bids us to seek gratification.

Augustine makes clear that God's grace is absolutely needed to have a good will, but the question also arises: Does Augustine make it explicit that grace is always needed first before we can begin to will to do good works in accordance with divine commandments so that one can achieve salvation? We have already seen Augustine's reference to Paul's conversion in which Paul received the grace of God, not through his own good deserts because his actual deserts were evil, but, rather, through God's gratuitous gift of grace being first bestowed on Paul without Paul's merit. Augustine comments additionally on Paul's reference to his being judged by God and to Paul's reception of the crown of justice:

> "There remains for me the crown of justice, which the Lord, the just Judge, shall award me at that last day" [2 Tim 4:8]. To whom would the just Judge award a crown if the merciful Father had not given him grace? How would this be a "crown of justice" unless grace which makes the irreligious just, had come first? How would the crown be awarded as something due, unless grace were first given gratuitously?[25]

Once again, God's grace is not a denial of a person's free choice but, rather, an affirmation that God acts within a person to do good works, which can be freely chosen by the person, who then must freely accept and work with the grace received. This would be the case even for a person who does not realize it is God's grace working within him that enables him to do good works. When a person accepts the revealed truth of God's grace working within himself/herself, then one realizes it is not one's innate goodness that enables one to perform good works but God's grace given to one. There is no basis for pride in oneself. Thus, it is the person receiving God's grace who can freely cooperate with that grace in order to do good works. Says Augustine:

> Now one should not think that free choice has been taken away because the apostle said: "God is the one Who works in you both willing and doing works in conformity with goodwill" [Phil 2:13]. If this were so, he would not have said immediately before that: "Work out your own salvation with fear and trembling" [Phil 2:12]. When he bids them to work, this is addressed to their free choice—but then "with fear and trembling" so that they not become filled with pride over their good works,

25. Augustine, "On Grace and Free Choice" 6.14 (p. 153).

attributing their working well to themselves, as if good works were their own.[26]

What is one's own good work is the act of freely cooperating with God's grace to do good works while accepting with faith that grace is first given by God gratuitously and that it is this grace that directs and empowers one to do any good works.

Salvation Can Result from Faith Working Through Love

While we are saved by grace, Paul tells us that we must humbly work out this salvation "with fear and trembling." Cooperation with God's grace, beginning with the grace of faith, is essential in achieving this salvation that God works in a person through the redemptive grace of Christ. Without this grace one is facing damnation. So, there is no other way to achieve justification in the first instance without the redemptive grace of Christ. Obeying the moral law, understood here not as the disciplinary old law (which includes circumcision) but the moral law written on everyone's heart and brought to perfection by Christ as the new law of love, is a necessary part of the process of salvation. Yet the grace of Christ's redemptive sacrifice must be received in faith and accepted first in order to practice Christian love and be saved. Augustine, referring to Paul, tells us that:

> Grace through faith in Jesus Christ belongs exclusively to those who have this faith: "For not all have faith" [2 Thess 3:2]....
> Christ died so that (a) the Law be fulfilled through Him, Who declared "I am come not to destroy the Law but to fulfill it" [Matt 5:17]; and (b) the nature that was lost through Adam would be recovered through Him, Who said that He came "to seek and to save what had been lost" [Luke 19:10; Matt 18:11].[27]

That grace is given first by God as the gift of faith that saves us is made even more explicit by Augustine, who cites Paul first and then provides exposition of Paul's teachings regarding faith. Paul tells us in Eph 2:8–9 that "by grace you have been saved through faith; and this is not from yourselves but is a gift of God." Paul is telling us that faith must be received first as a gift of God in order for anyone to believe and be saved,

---

26. Augustine, "On Grace and Free Choice" 9.21 (p. 158).
27. Augustine, "On Grace and Free Choice" 13.25 (p. 162).

and that this gift is given freely, without cost, solely out of God's mercy. Augustine points out that the Pelagians claim that they have received the gift of grace because they freely chose to believe "as though attributing faith to themselves and grace to God." Augustine points out that when Paul says that "we are saved through faith" immediately Paul "adds 'and this is not from yourselves but is the gift of God.' Again, to prevent [the Pelagians] from claiming to have deserved such a gift by their works, he goes on to add: 'It is not from works, lest anyone be filled with pride.'"[28]

But, argues Augustine additionally, while no one deserves the grace of faith given as a gift which saves, this does not render good works unnecessary for salvation. When Paul states in Rom 3:28 that: "We hold that a person is made just through faith without the works of the Law," this is not to be interpreted to mean that Paul is maintaining:

> that faith is enough for a person, even if he lives an evil life and does not have good works. By no means does the Vessel of Election [i.e., Paul; see Acts 9:15] think this! After he had said in a certain passage, "In Jesus Christ neither circumcision or its absence means anything" he straightaway added: "but faith which works through love" [Gal 5:6]. This is the faith that separates those faithful to God from unclean demons. For even they, as the Apostle James says, "believe and tremble" [Jas 2:19], but they do not do their works well. Therefore, they do not have the faith by which the person lives, that is, the faith "which works through love" so that God renders to him eternal life in accordance with his works.[29]

Augustine's discussion of the relationship between faith and good works that is found in Paul's letters is an extension of Augustine's discussion of the relationship between grace and free choice also found generally in Paul's letters. Faith itself is a grace given gratuitously by God for our salvation, as stated in the letter to the Ephesians, 2:8–9: "By grace have you been saved through faith; and this is not from yourselves but is the gift of God: it is not from works, lest anyone be filled with pride." Augustine considers Paul's apparent limitation of what is necessary for salvation to there only being the need for faith and there being no need for good works in order to attain salvation by noting that Paul saw "*that people certainly could think he said this as though good works were not necessary for believers but faith alone would be sufficient for them*" (emphasis

---

28. Augustine, "On Grace and Free Choice" 7.17 (p. 155).
29. Augustine, "On Grace and Free Choice" 7.18 (pp. 155–56).

added). Augustine's resolution of the problem "is for us to understand that our good works, for which eternal life is rendered, themselves belong to God's grace."[30] This is why no one can have pride and boast that one performs good works alone through one's free choice that saves him/her, because it is really God's grace that empowers a person to perform good works. Augustine notes that Paul substantiated this point that God enables man to perform good works by immediately adding (after revealing in Eph 2:8–9 that we have been saved by grace through faith) Eph 2:10, which states: "For we are His workmanship, created in Jesus Christ in good works, which God has made ready that we may walk in them." Doing good works and living a good life is a grace with which God empowers a person—which empowerment the person must freely choose to accept or not.

Luther Rejects Good Works as Necessary for Salvation

Augustine's understanding that "our good works for which eternal life is rendered, themselves belong to God's grace" is an interpretation of Paul's letters that was rejected by Martin Luther. Luther wrote *The Freedom of a Christian* in 1520 as one of three seminal works that distinguished his theology from that of Catholicism and established the rudiments of what became the first perduring Protestant major denomination, Lutheranism. In this work Luther narrowly defines the meaning of faith in the Word of God to explicitly exclude good works. Luther explains:

> The Word is the gospel of God concerning his Son, who was made flesh, suffered, rose from the dead, and was glorified through the Spirit who sanctifies. To preach Christ means to feed the soul, make it righteous, set it free, and save it, provided it believes the preaching. *Faith alone is the saving and efficacious use of the word of God*, according to Romans 10:9: "If you confess with your lips that Jesus is Lord and believe in your heart that God raised him from the dead, you will be saved."
> ... Again, in Romans 1:17, "*He who through faith is righteous shall live.*" The Word of God cannot be received and cherished by any works whatever but only by faith. Therefore, it is clear that, as the soul needs only the Word of God for its life and righteousness, so it is justified by faith alone and not any works; for if it could be

---

30. Augustine, "On Grace and Free Choice" 8.20 (p. 156).

justified by anything else, it would not need the Word, and consequently would not need faith.[31]

Augustine acknowledges that Paul saw that people could think, based on what Paul taught in several of his letters, that good works are not necessary for salvation but that "faith alone would be sufficient for them." But, as cited above, Augustine also acknowledges what was quickly added after Eph 2:8-9 in Eph 2:10: *"For we are His workmanship, created in Jesus Christ in good works, which God has made ready that we may walk in them."* Obviously, this passage is saying that God provides us with grace to do good works. However, this grace does not render good works unnecessary for a life of righteousness and for being justified, which is what Luther argues. This acknowledgment of necessity for good works is made even more explicit in Rom 2:5-7 where Paul states that it is *"the just judgment of God, who will repay everyone according to his works: eternal life to those who seek glory, honor, and immortality through perseverance in good works."*

When Luther uses terminology that is exclusive, such as found in the expressions "the Word of God cannot be received and cherished by any works whatever"; "the soul needs only the Word of God"; and the soul "is justified by faith alone and not by any works whatever," there results on the part of Luther an omission of the full meaning of what Paul is revealing. Paul is telling us that, while we are saved by faith that is received from God as a gift, which, along with all God's grace, is given gratuitously and not as a reward for our good works, we must still choose to have "perseverance in good works" so that God "will repay everyone according to his works."

When it comes to interpreting written Scripture there is always a need to find references to verses, if possible, within other biblical books that closely relate to the passage in question. There are several examples from Paul's own letters that are related to many of his teachings regarding justification or salvation through faith and not works. However, what Paul reveals in one passage is often expanded upon or qualified by another passage. On the surface, there are seemingly conflicts in what Paul sometimes says. We have already seen Augustine's reference to some apparent conflicts in Paul's letters such as being "saved through faith, and this is not from you . . . it is not from works" (Eph 2:8), which receives clarification in Gal 5:6, which states: "For in Christ Jesus, neither circumcision

---

31. Luther, *Freedom of a Christian*, 280 (emphasis added).

nor uncircumcision counts for anything, but only faith working through love." Augustine also cites Eph 2:10: "For we are His workmanship, created in Christ Jesus in good works which God has made ready that we may walk in them." What Augustine demonstrates here in his own commentary on Paul is, while faith is necessary for salvation, there is also a need to use faith to do works of love. Augustine goes on to cite Phil 1:29: "For it is given to you on behalf of Christ, not only to believe in Him but also to suffer for His sake." Whatever one does for the sake of Christ, including suffering, must necessarily include handing on the gospel to others and practicing the gospel through word and example. Augustine notes that not only faith is given as a gift of grace, but everything morally good that God bids us to do must first be given as a gift of grace. We must freely accept the gift of grace that empowers us to accomplish the good God bids us to do. Augustine confirms this in a theological statement, which was cited above and repeated here, that contends that the "spirit of grace brings it about that we have faith, so that through faith we may achieve by prayer the ability to do what we are bidden to do."[32]

Resolving Apparent Contradictions in Paul's Letters

Apart from Augustine's more scholarly and scripturally based arguments, which are intended to reconcile the apparent discrepancies in Paul's letters concerning salvation through faith apart from works, there are always those who will juxtapose various verses that are in apparent conflict, especially when these verses are taken out of context. Scriptural scholars routinely warn neophytes about the absurdities that result from "proof-texting," i.e., citing one specific verse in order to draw a universal principle, in this case, of Christian teaching. There are always those who will cite a verse like Gal 2:15–16: "We ourselves who are Jews . . . know that a man is not justified by works of the law but through faith in Jesus Christ, even we have believed in Christ Jesus, in order to be justified by faith in Christ and not by the works of the law because by works of the law shall no one be justified." Or, there are those who will cite a verse such as Rom 3:28: "For we hold that a man is justified by faith apart from works of law" and contrast it with Rom 2:6: "For he will render to each man according to his works: to those who by patience in well-doing seek for glory and honor and immortality, he will give eternal life; but for those who are

---

32. Augustine, "On Grace and Free Choice" 14.28 (p. 164).

factious and do not obey the truth, but obey wickedness, there will be wrath and fury." What appear to be obvious contradictions in what Paul is revealing can lead some to conclude that such verses are irreconcilable.

Perhaps what could assist the believer in resolving possible contradictions found in Paul's letters regarding faith and good works could be discovered in an unlikely source, viz., the dialectical method employed by the absolute idealist Georg Hegel. For Hegel, all of reality consists of the absolute Idea, which establishes a rational unity of all that exists. The absolute Idea is conceived in the absolute Spirit or Mind, which, for Hegel, actually exists in the philosophic mind of man. This is Hegel's critical mistake—refusing to accept a transcendent, immutable absolute Spirit as God whose divine plan for man and all of creation has not been revealed in its entirety and includes certain mystery unknown to rational man. However, what is valuable in Hegel's philosophy is that reason conceives physical creation to be a unified idea, which is a structured, ordered reality that includes certain perceived realities that initially appear to be contradictory or contrary. An example of such perceived contrariness is the nature of light rays that presented a conundrum. Scientists in the eighteenth and nineteenth centuries asserted that light rays consist of waves of light; but in the early twentieth century Einstein showed that light must consist of photons or particles. Scientific consensus has since concluded that light must consist of a duality of both waves and particles. Such apparent inconsistencies that can be observed in nature by scientists require a dialectical process of thought to explain. Says the twentieth-century Princeton professor of Hegel's philosophy W. T. Stace: "reason . . . is that stage of the development of mind which rises to the principle of the identity of opposites." Reason is to be distinguished in Hegel's philosophy from the lower development of mind, which is the understanding that

> regards opposites as mutually exclusive and absolutely cut off from each other. . . . Understanding meets every question with an inflexible "either—or." The truth is either A or not-A, either being or not-being. A thing either is, or is not. Reason breaks up this hard and fast schematism of the understanding, sees that A and not-A are identical in their very difference, that the truth does not lie, as understanding supposes, either wholly in A, or wholly not-A, but rather in the synthesis of the two.[33]

---

33. Stace, *Philosophy of Hegel*, 101.

What Hegel is saying is that, for philosophy, truth must incorporate all reality, and all reality must be incorporated or brought together into a rational unity that explains all that exists. This is not to say that the understanding (unconditionally distinguishing A from not A) is not valuable or suitable for realizing social, technological, and scientific advances in man's practical pursuits. Without the clear distinctions of the understanding, laws (both civil and scientific) cannot be utilized for their intended purposes. Social communication and discourse would break down without the categories of the understanding, and civilized society could not be maintained. However, without the synthetic implications found in reason, the higher comprehension made possible by philosophical/rational knowledge would be lacking the unified order of all that exists as one reality—which reality, for the Christian, has its origin in the transcendent, immutable, and omnipotent God who is the creator of all reality outside of himself. Theological truth, which for the believer has precedence over philosophical truth, finds its premises rooted in God's revelation, which God, in his inscrutable omniscience, has made known to man for the sake of man's salvation. However, divine revelation uses human language to express notions that are seemingly limited by man's understanding to be mutually exclusive and irreconcilable.

Biblical exegesis must look to include and reconcile that which appears to be at odds. What is A, in this case "faith," must demonstrably include what is not-A, i.e., "good works," so that what may result from synthetic reasoning is a unification of both revealed truths into a whole that preserves their respective essential meaning and incorporates them into a more complete revealed truth—i.e., faith that works through love. This synthetic unification of faith and good works does not mean that faith ceases to exist as an act of acceptance of the truth that God reveals; nor does it mean that good works cease to exist as morally good acts that are meritorious for divine reward. What it means is that you do have neither a mere simple identity of faith and good works nor a simple preservation of the differences between the two. What it means is that faith and good works cease to exist as separate entities in complete opposition. While their differences are preserved, faith and good works now exist in a new unity that combines their differences. Faith now includes the acceptance of the new law of love revealed by Christ, which means that faith now also includes the doing of good works so that faith working through love is needed for attaining salvation.

When it comes to distinctions of revealed theological concepts such as faith and good works, the understanding and its clear distinctions remain necessary in comprehending what man needs to know for the sake of his salvation. However, what God reveals in written Scripture is not confined to the limitations of practical human understanding. When Paul speaks of "justification by faith apart from works of the law," he also indicates acceptance of, belief in, and assent to all that Christ revealed in his gospel. It is Paul who utilizes a synthetic concept when he states in Gal 5:6: "for in Jesus Christ neither circumcision nor uncircumcision is of any of avail, *but faith working through love*" (emphasis added). In Christ's gospel, faith includes more than simple assent to what Christ teaches; it also includes acting in accord with what Christ bids us to do, such as found in Luke 6:35: "Love your enemies, and do good, and lend, expecting nothing in return." This is not to say that the assent of faith is not essential. The Christian must accept what Christ says in Mark 16:16: "He who believes and is baptized will be saved; but he who does not believe will be condemned." What Christ says here must be synthesized, i.e., combined with, and formed into, a unified whole with what Christ says in Matt 25:34–36:

> Then the King will say to those at his right hand, "Come, O blessed of my Father, inherit the kingdom prepared for you from the foundation of the world; for I was hungry and you gave me food, I was thirsty and you gave me drink, I was a stranger and you welcomed me, I was naked and you clothed me, I was sick and you visited me, I was in prison and you came to me."

In short, faith understood in its whole and complete sense as intended by Christ includes good works as necessary for salvation. And as Augustine further explains, it is the gift of grace that provides us with the ability to have faith and do the good works included in faith. This is what Christ teaches and bids us do. As previously quoted, Augustine confirms this: "the spirit of grace brings it about that we have faith, so that through faith we may achieve by prayer the ability to do what we are bidden to do."[34]

---

34. Augustine, "On Grace and Free Choice" 14.28 (p. 164).

Pelagians Deny the Necessity of Grace to Practice Christian Love; Hegelians Claim a Person Can Be Autonomous Through Rational, Philosophic Thought

It is the gift of grace that enables one to accept the faith God has revealed through Christ, and it is the gift of grace that empowers us to practice what Christ has bidden us to do, viz., live his gospel of love. This is precisely what the Pelagians refuse to accept, i.e., that love is given as a gift of grace without which we cannot live Christ's gospel of love. Augustine tells us that Pelagians believe that charity comes from their own willful choice and not as a gift of grace:

> The Darkness in the Pelagian writings says, "We have love from ourselves." If the Pelagians had genuine love—that is, Christian love—they would also know where it came from! The apostle knew when he said: "Now we have received not the spirit of the world, but the spirit which is from God, that we might know which things have been given to us by God" [1 Cor 8:1]. John says: "God is love" [1 John 4:16].
>
> The Pelagians also claim that they even have God Himself not from God but from themselves. And while they admit that our knowledge of the Law is from God, they hold that charity is from ourselves.[35]

The Pelagian "claim that they even have God Himself not from God but from themselves" could be that of presumptuous pride similar to the Hegelian idea that man's self-conscious reason in itself can contain the "thoughts of God" whenever man conceives the philosophy of absolute idealism. Both systems of thought are rooted in the notion that man is autonomous either in his free will (as claim the Pelagians) or man is autonomous in his rational, philosophical mind (as claim the Hegelians); both deny man's need for the divine gifts that actually bring about man's completion as the being whom the Creator intended. Of course, the Pelagians do not deny God as the omnipotent creator who provides the opportunity for man's ultimate salvation, whereas the Hegelians refuse to accept any transcendent omnipotent deity but will only accept the spirit of reason immanent within man as the ultimate conceiver of reality as an idea. The true Christian, on the other hand, has hope in receiving both faith and charity as divine gifts and understands that charity is the fulfillment of faith in what is hoped for in Jesus Christ; see Heb 11:1.

---

35. Augustine, "On Grace and Free Choice" 19.40 (p. 175).

Persons do not create faith, hope, and love through their own free choice; rather, faith, hope, and love are God's gratuitous gifts to us, which lift human persons from their fallen state to divine life as disciples of Christ. A person's free choice is to accept these gifts of grace so as to do the good works prompted by them.

Augustine ends *On Grace and Free Choice* with a complex inquiry based on divine revelation concerning the power of God's grace to direct both a person with a good will or a person with a bad will to perform actions God ordains without taking away a person's free choice. Augustine asserts that he has "argued sufficiently against those who vehemently attack the grace of God through which the human will is not taken away" and yet goes on to further assert that:

> If Scripture is inspected carefully it shows not only good human wills are in God's power—that is, wills which He makes good from evil, and, once made good by Him, He directs to good acts and to eternal life—but also [human wills] which maintain their worldly [sinful] condition are in God's power, in such a way that He makes them inclined as He wills when He wills: either to rewards offered to some people, or to penalties inflicted on others, as He judges in His judgment which is completely hidden but undoubtedly completely just.[36]

Augustine Says God Inclines or Does Not Incline Persons to Do Good; Calvin Claims God Preordains Some to Eternal Life and Others to Damnation

It is important to distinguish what Augustine is saying above from what Calvin argues (as previously cited) regarding man's predestination. Calvin wrote:

> By predestination we mean the eternal decree of God, by which He determined with Himself whatever He wished to happen with regard to every man ... some are preordained to eternal life, others to eternal damnation.[37]

Like Luther, Calvin is arguing that man has no free choice to make in regard to his salvation or damnation. Augustine never argued for this

---

36. Augustine, "On Grace and Free Choice" 20.41 (p. 176).
37. Calvin, *Institutes* 3.21.5 (p. 206).

position in *On Grace and Free Choice*. What Augustine does say is that all persons "are in God's power, in such a way that He makes them *inclined* as He wills."[38] Inclined means having a tendency toward, or a disposition to do, something; it does not mean being determined by the eternal decree of God.

Now it can be legitimately argued that by inclining persons to act in a certain way, God exercises a certain commanding influence over them. Augustine cites God's words from Josh 7:12: "The children of Israel could not stand before the face of their enemies," and Augustine provides the following commentary: "Why did they not stand through free choice but rather flee when their will was shaken by fear, if it was not because God has dominance even over human wills and, when angered, turns those He wills to dread?"[39] It might be argued that if God did not give the children of Israel the grace of courage to stand and fight, then it would be tantamount to God's willing a decree that Israel be defeated. Or, another argument could be made that God's grace came to the children of Israel in the form of fear and dread so as to prompt both their repentance for disobeying God's covenant and also a return to obedience. A question arises regarding the nature of the grace that God gives. Is God's grace always given efficaciously so that the recipient is empowered to produce the effect God intended? Later, theologians argued that God's grace can also be given sufficiently (see 2 Cor 12:9) so that the person empowered receives enough grace so as to accomplish an act God intends, but perhaps with great difficulty. Such subtle and complex questions concerning grace are never fully resolved by Augustine.

Regarding the example Augustine cites from Josh 7:12, it would seem that God withheld the grace of courage from the children of Israel, which resulted in their susceptibility to dread. Yet, God's withholding grace does not make God responsible for the evil that might result. Augustine cites still another example from Exodus in which Pharaoh refused God's demand made through Moses to "let my people go that they may serve me," because God affected Pharaoh's will by having "hardened the heart of Pharaoh," so that Pharaoh "did not listen to them; as the Lord had spoken to Moses" (Exod 9:12). Explaining this example presents a greater difficulty in that God is revealed to have actively hardened the heart of Pharaoh; this directly results in Pharaoh's act of evil, which was

---

38. Augustine, "On Grace and Free Choice" 20.41 (p. 176) (emphasis added).
39. Augustine, "On Grace and Free Choice" 20.41 (p. 176).

to deliberately reject God's command and to keep God's people enslaved. It would seem then that God is directly responsible for Pharaoh's evil act. But, such a conclusion is antithetical to the Christian understanding of God; God is perfect in his goodness and all his attributes and has no deficiency—deficiency being the essence of evil—so that God cannot will evil action in the wills of human beings. Augustine asserts:

> The Almighty accomplishes in human hearts even the movement of their will, to accomplish through them what He wills to accomplish through them—He Who does not know at all how to will anything Unjust.[40]

Perhaps the best explanation of this quandary is that God withdraws his grace as he wills so that a person's own vice (in this case Pharaoh's vice) dominates his heart and actions.

What Does It Mean That God Inclines Some Hearts to Do Good and Hardens the Hearts of Others So That They Do Evil?

Yet Augustine's assertion above does not adequately explain how God accomplishes the movement of a person's free will to do evil, such as Pharaoh's will, whose heart God hardened. Augustine does go on to provide a more reasonable explanation of how God works to accomplish his will to do good by inclining the wills of human persons. In his *On Free Choice of the Will* Augustine acknowledges that God has foreknowledge of how all persons have used and will use their gift of free will. He explicitly states: "God, although He does not force anyone into sinning, nevertheless foresees those who are going to sin by their own will."[41] Now, Augustine tells us that "God works in human hearts to incline their wills to whatever He wills,"[42] so that when persons freely respond to God's grace and do good, God's will is accomplished through those persons; but when persons freely turn away from God and refuse God's grace they will perform "evil due to their deserts." Augustine further explains that God "is always just" and that there is "no iniquity in God," so that when it is found in Scripture "that people are led astray by God, or that their hearts are dulled or hardened, have no doubt that their evil deserts came first, so that they

---

40. Augustine, "On Grace and Free Choice" 21.42 (p. 179).
41. Augustine, "On the Free Choice of the Will" 3.5.12.42 (p. 81).
42. Augustine, "On Grace and Free Choice" 21.43 (p. 180).

suffered these things justly."⁴³ This can be interpreted to mean that when people turn away from God they are rejecting God's grace. Their deserts for this evil are to lose God's grace because of the evil they previously committed, and it is in God's discretion to refuse further grace so that their "hearts are hardened" and they continue in their sins. Whereas God can and has provided merciful grace for those whose deserts are evil, nevertheless, God in his perfect justice can remove his mercy at any time and thereby allow obstinacy to continue in the hearts of sinners.

God may also work to move those who originally choose evil to freely turn their hearts toward doing good. So Augustine further speculates:

> Now if God is able, either through angels (good or evil) or in some other way, to work even in the hearts of evil people in accordance with their deserts—and He did not produce their evilness, but either it was originally drawn from Adam or it was increased by their own will—what surprise is it if He works good in the hearts of His elect through the Holy Spirit, He Who worked it that their hearts became good from evil?⁴⁴

Yet, Augustine persistently affirms in *Grace and Free Choice* man's free will "in the one whom He permits to be led astray or to be hardened" and, so too, no one should "take free choice away from Pharaoh just because in many passages God says 'I have hardened in Pharaoh or I have hardened the heart of Pharaoh.'" Augustine will argue that it "does not follow that Pharaoh himself did not harden his own heart." Augustine concludes that Pharaoh chose his own obstinacy and that "consequently, God hardened [the heart of Pharaoh] by his just judgment, and Pharaoh himself did so by free choice."⁴⁵

There can be those who could argue that Augustine fails to resolve the dilemma of the omnipotent God who moves the hearts of mortal men to choose one way or another and, at the same time, man retains his free choice over against his Creator's insurmountable power. A fuller answer is provided by Thomas Aquinas, who asks "Whether the Will of God Imposes Necessity on the Things Willed?" An affirmative objection to what will be Thomas's conditional reply to this question is the following citation taken by Thomas from Augustine's *The Enchiridion on Faith, Hope, and Love*: "No one is saved, except whom God willed to be saved.

---

43. Augustine, "On Grace and Free Choice" 21.43 (p. 181).
44. Augustine, "On Grace and Free Choice" 21.43 (p. 181).
45. Augustine, "On Grace and Free Choice" 23.45 (p. 183).

He must therefore be asked to will it; for if He wills it, it must necessarily be." In reply to this quotation from Augustine stated as an objection to Thomas's qualified position, the Angelic Doctor states: "By the words of Augustine we must understand a necessity in things willed by God that is not absolute, but conditional. For the conditional statement that if God wills the thing it must necessarily be, is necessarily true." Thomas's reply implies that there are two aspects to God's will. On the one hand, God's will is absolutely determined and unconditional, so that what he actively wills will be an absolute necessity. On the other hand, God's will is conditional, so that God can passively allow a rational creature, such as a human person, to have the power to freely choose to bring about a result that God allows to happen. God does not will for evil to happen, but he allows human persons (or fallen angelic powers) to choose to do evil. Thomas completes his response in a third reply: "Things effected by the divine will have that kind of necessity that God wills them to have, either absolute or conditional. Not all things, therefore, are absolute necessities."[46]

With his *On Grace and Free Choice*, Augustine investigates the heart of the problem regarding God's revelation of his own omnipotence and omniscience and of man's free will that must rely on God's grace to do what is good. And although his resolution may not be fully adequate, Augustine influenced and still influences much of Christian theology in regard to the mystery of how God exercises his providential will over all creation without willing anything evil while still allowing man to choose freely to do good or to choose to do evil and be enslaved by sin. Without God's grace man's free will falls into sin; only with God's grace can man choose freely to do good. Thus, man's true and full freedom lies in his free choice to work with God's grace, which must be given first so as to do God's will in accomplishing good. God's grace is always given gratuitously as God's gift and is not received as an earned desert. Once grace has first been given to a person who then freely chooses to work with this grace, that person's deserts begin to be good, but only by means of grace. Even those who have evil deserts may receive God's grace, just as Paul received grace that would lead to his conversion though his deserts were evil. God's gift of the grace of faith that works through love may bring a person to eternal life when that gift is accepted and made productive. The power to do good works for which eternal life may be rendered by God is

---

46. Thomas Aquinas, *Summa Theologica* Ia, q. 19, art. 8, resp. to obj. 1 and 3.

itself a gift of grace, which a person has freely accepted in faith and with which he has cooperated.

ON REPRIMAND AND GRACE

On Reprimand and Grace is found in the same Peter King edition that has been used in this work: *On the Free Choice of the Will, On Grace and Free Choice, and Other Writings*. Of the books found in this volume, *On Grace and Free Choice, On Reprimand and Grace, Reconsiderations*, and *On the Gift of Perseverance* are among the most theologically developed and comprehensive of Augustine's anti-Pelagian writings in that they deal with the complex issues involving the reconciliation of man's free will with the determinate will of God in his predestination of man through grace. Like *On Grace and Free Choice, On Reprimand and Grace* was written between 426 and 427 and addressed to the same monastic community at Hadrumetum in what is now Tunisia in North Africa. ("Reprimand" has been rendered by other translators as "rebuke" or "admonition" or "correction.") A controversy had arisen at the monastery after one of its monks retrieved a letter written by Augustine from the library of Evodius the bishop of the nearby city of Uzlis. Augustine's letters were numbered chronologically in the seventeenth century by the Benedictine monks of the Abbey of St. Maur in France.

Augustine Corrects Monks Who Refuse Responsibility for Their Wrongdoing

It was Letter 194, written by Augustine in 418 and addressed to the priest Sixtus (who became Pope Sixtus III in 432), that had been retrieved from the library of Evodius and was brought back to the monastery at Hadrumetum by a monk. This letter refuted the errors of the Pelagians, especially their rejection of grace as being God's gratuitous gift without any merits on the part of the recipient. Pelagians also rejected the belief that it is entirely God's choice to give his grace to ensure a person's justification and salvation. Peter Brown tells us that "Letter 194 to Sixtus had been a manifesto of unconditional surrender" and that Augustine's correspondence left "no doubt as to the implications of the defeat of Pelagius," because "it was God alone who determined the destinies of men, and these destinies could only be seen as an expression of His Wisdom."

Professor Brown also tells us that the monks began to "argue that, if their wills depended upon God, the abbot should refrain from rebuking them, and should content himself with praying to God for their amendment."[47] *On Reprimand and Grace* was written as a response to the monks at Hadrumetum who had become disposed to dismiss the authority of their abbot and their rule on account of their assumed deficiency of God's grace and the incapacity of their wills to do anything about their moral shortcomings and lack of discipline.

Augustine wastes no time in *On Reprimand and Grace* in telling the reader that "the Lord Himself not only has shown us what evil to turn away from and what good to do . . . but also assists us to turn away from evil and to do the good, which nobody can do without the spirit of grace."[48] Yet, while Augustine begins this work by emphasizing the essential need for grace, he also emphasizes man's free choice for doing both evil and good. He makes clear the distinction that when one freely chooses to do evil that person "is free from justice and enslaved to sin," to which he adds "in doing good no one can be free unless he has been set free by Him Who said: 'If the Son sets you free, then you shall truly be free' [John 8:36]."[49] For Augustine, no one could be truly free from the enslavement of sin without grace, so that free choice in choosing good is always dependent upon grace.

The problem that Augustine will have to resolve in *On Reprimand and Grace* is how man can have free choice if man is dependent on God to give him the grace to do the good, because, without this grace, man's free choice is only a choice to do evil. Would not man's choices then be entirely dependent on God's choice to give a person grace to choose to do the good and avoid the evil, without which grace man is not truly free? Based on this reasoning, the monks at Hadrumetum called on their abbot and those in authority under him to refrain from reprimanding the monks so as to correct their wrongdoings and weaknesses. If God alone gives the grace necessary to do good as a gratuitous gift to those he chooses, then those who do not receive God's grace and who morally fail to do the good and avoid vice are not to be rebuked by those in authority, so that each monk could respond, "is it my fault that I do not have what I have not received from God? If He does not give it, there is no other source at all from which such a great gift might be had." Augustine sums

---

47. Brown, *Augustine of Hippo*, 401–2.
48. Augustine, "On Reprimand and Grace" 1.2 (p. 185).
49. Augustine, "On Reprimand and Grace" 1.2 (p. 186).

up the argument of the monks: "'Therefore,' they say, 'let our superiors merely prescribe what we ought to do, and pray on our behalf that we do it; but let them not reprimand or censor us if we do not do it.'"[50]

Augustine's answer to this argument is that, according to revelation, all three actions must be done—prescribing, reprimanding, and praying. Says Augustine:

> The apostles, the leaders of the churches, did them all. They prescribed what deeds should be done; they offered reprimands if they were not done; they prayed that they be done. The apostle prescribes when he says, "Let all your deeds be done with charity" [1 Cor 16:14]. He reprimands when he says: "It is altogether a failing already that you bring lawsuits against one another. Why do you not rather suffer the wrong?" [1 Cor 6:7–9].
> Let us listen to him praying too: "May the Lord make you increase and abound in charity towards one another and towards all" [1 Thess 3:12].[51]

Although Augustine does not explicitly say this, it would seem that reprimands can be an exterior type of grace that God intends to be administered by a human being to bring another person in sin to reformation. Augustine tells us that a reprimand "is beneficial only when it makes someone repent his sins." However, one should not conclude that the person reprimanded freely and immediately chooses on his own to repent of his sins but rather that person must understand that it is only the Lord "Who gives this [repentance]" and it is only the Lord "Who had regard for the Apostle Peter and made him weep for his denial."[52] Augustine emphasizes that what a person freely chooses on his own without God's grace is evil. What is also indicated by Augustine is that a person can freely refuse to accept God's grace by freely choosing to do evil even when the person has received divine grace to do good. Augustine speaks of the possibility of a person "having been born again and made just" and yet that same person "falls back into an evil life by his own will" and, Augustine acknowledges, that "he has lost the grace of God, which he had received, by his own free choice of evil."[53] Augustine reiterates that a person can neither earn nor attain grace on his own solely by his own action. Rather, God freely gives grace gratuitously to whom, when, and

---

50. Augustine, "On Reprimand and Grace" 4.6 (p. 188).
51. Augustine, "On Reprimand and Grace" 3.5–4.6 (pp. 187–88).
52. Augustine, "On Reprimand and Grace" 5.7 (p. 189).
53. Augustine, "On Reprimand and Grace" 6.9 (p. 192).

for what purpose God wills, as Rom 11:5–6 verifies: "At the present time there is a remnant, chosen by grace. But if it is by grace, it is no longer on the basis of works; otherwise grace would no longer be grace." Man cannot freely choose to merit grace so as to do good and be free from evil. Augustine makes this abundantly clear by stating: "The human will does not attain grace through its freedom, but rather attains its freedom through grace."[54] Here, the freedom to which Augustine refers is the freedom through grace, which freedom is attained when grace separates a person from the enslavement to evil and directs a person's free choice to acts of goodness.

The Power and Nature of Efficacious Grace Viewed by Banez and Molina

While reprimands are good and ought to be given to those who morally need them by those who are directed by God to be moral advocates, Augustine qualifies this exhortation by insisting "that God is able (a) to correct whomever He wills, even when no human being offers a reprimand, and (b) to bring him to the healthful regret that is repentance through the completely hidden and *efficacious* power of His medicine."[55] It is the supernatural nature of God's "efficacious power" that Augustine leaves conceptually undeveloped. Theologians since Augustine conceived of a distinction between efficacious grace and sufficient grace, which has been a source of much controversy as to the precise meaning of each and as to how God works his will within man without destroying man's freedom to choose. It is always a significant help to find adequate definitions that simplify understanding of the meaning of complex ideas without substantially sacrificing the content of these ideas. The twentieth-century Jesuit scholar, author, and professor of theology John A. Hardon provides a concise definition of both types of grace in his *Modern Catholic Dictionary*. In his entry under "Efficacious Grace," Father Hardon defines this grace as:

> The actual grace to which free consent is given by the will so that the grace produces its divinely intended effect. In the controversy between the Dominicans [led by Domingo Banez (1528–1604)] and the Jesuits [led by Luis De Molina (1525–1600)] there was

---

54. Augustine, "On Reprimand and Grace" 8.17 (p. 200).
55. Augustine, "On Reprimand and Grace" 5.8 (p. 190) (emphasis added).

no agreement on what precisely causes actual grace to become efficacious. In the Banezian theory, the efficacy of such grace depends on the character of the grace itself; in the Molinist theory it depends on the fact that it is given under circumstances that God foresees to be congruous with the dispositions of the person receiving the grace. In every Catholic theory, however, it is agreed that efficacious grace does not necessitate the will or destroy human freedom.[56]

Efficacious grace, then, in Catholic teaching makes it certain that the recipient freely chooses and actually performs a good action that God intends the person to perform. But it is certainly a legitimate inquiry to ask how precisely a person can retain free choice of the will while being directly moved by God's efficacious grace to produce a divinely intended effect. Augustine's answer to this apparent dilemma is based on his elementary premises that distinguish the freedom of Adam from the freedom of those descendants of Adam who receive efficacious grace. Adam was created with the ability not to sin because his human nature was not yet fallen and did not suffer from concupiscence. So, too, Adam was created with the ability not to die and the ability not to abandon the good. Augustine tells us that Adam had a certain type of grace that kept him from evil provided Adam freely chose to retain and work with this divine assistance. On the one hand, if Adam freely chose, he could (and did) abandon this divine assistance of grace. On the other hand, the Second Adam, Jesus Christ, was a divine Person whose human nature was so graced that it could not will to be or to do evil. Says Augustine regarding the union of divine nature and the human nature in the incarnation of Jesus Christ in contrast to Adam's graced nature before his fall:

> Nor was it to be feared that human nature, taken up in this indescribable way by God the Word into the unity of His person, would sin through free choice of will.... God took Him up in such a way that He would never be evil....
>
> The First Man did not have this grace by which he would never will to be evil. But he definitely had grace (a) in which, if he had willed to continue, he would never be evil; (b) without which he could not have been good, even with free choice; but (c) which he could have abandoned through free choice. Therefore, God did not want Adam, whom He left to his free choice, to be without His grace, seeing that free choice is sufficient for

---

56. Hardon, *Modern Catholic Dictionary*, 180.

evil, but hardly for good, unless it is assisted by the omnipotent Good One.[57]

But Adam did freely abandon the divine assistance of grace by committing the original sin and its infinite offense against the infinite Being—God. Perhaps motivated by the intellectual sin of pride, Adam became subject to concupiscence, death, and the abandonment of the good. All of Adam's descendants are under the penalty of original sin, which also subjects them to concupiscence, death, and the abandonment of the good. The infinite offense against God that marks all of mankind since Adam needed to be atoned for by a divine Person who alone could make reparation for this infinite offense against God—which sin is. And that divine Person had to become a man who was without sin in order to vicariously take the place of sinful human beings so as to redeem them from the debt owed to God resulting from sin. Augustine tells us that "the Son of Man born of the Holy Spirit and the Virgin Mary" was "conjoined, in the unity of a person, human being to God, flesh to Word." Augustine further explains that it was *not* "to be feared that human nature, taken up in this indescribable way by God the Word into the unity of His Person, would sin through free choice of the will." As a result of the redemptive sacrifice, "through this Mediator, God has shown that He makes those whom He redeemed through His blood to be made good, even after, out of evil."[58]

Only Christ merited the grace through his redemptive sacrifice that could make man and his works good before God. Merit, which is a reward for good works performed, cannot strictly be earned by man before God; man's free will actions only deserve a reward before God when these actions proceed from divine grace merited by Christ. Augustine confirms this need for grace (received first before any human action) in order for man's actions to become and to deserve good: "Yet clearly, once grace has been given, our deserts begin to be good, though only by means of it. For if grace were to withdraw itself, human beings would fall, no longer raised up but cast down by free choice."[59]

There is a paradox regarding man's freedom resulting from the redemptive grace of Christ. Adam, who did not receive the redemptive grace of Christ, was created by God with the ability not to sin. Those

---

57. Augustine, "On Reprimand and Grace" 11.30–11.31 (pp. 211–12).
58. Augustine, "On Reprimand and Grace" 11.30 (p. 211).
59. Augustine, "On Grace and Free Choice" 6.13 (p. 152).

baptized into Christ's grace and who remain in it are still only able, at best, to not sin. It is the elect who have received the efficacious grace of final perseverance who will have eternal life and who will not be able to sin seriously so as to abandon the good. Augustine testifies to this truth by comparing the type of freedom enjoyed by Adam with the final freedom enjoyed by those who receive God's gift of final perseverance:

> The first freedom of the will was therefore to be able not to sin; the final freedom will be much greater: not to be able to sin. The first immortality was to be able not to die; the final immortality will be much greater: not to be able to die. The first power of perseverance was to be able not to abandon the good; the final happiness of perseverance will be not to be able to abandon the good. The final goods will be better and more powerful.[60]

Yet, while human persons in their human condition here on earth are still subject to concupiscence, there are those saints among us whom God has elected to receive the efficacious grace of final perseverance so that, while tempted to sin, they will no longer sin seriously in a way that is unto death. Augustine refers to 1 John 5:16–17, which reveals: "Ask, and God will give him life for those whose sin is not mortal. There is sin which is mortal; I do not say that one is to pray for that. All wrongdoing is sin, but there is sin which is not mortal." The saintly elect here on earth who may receive the efficacious grace of final perseverance will not sin mortally and abandon the faith that works through love. Augustine tells us that the saintly elect, which includes future martyrs for the faith, are "no more the slaves of 'the sin that is unto death,'" and as a result "they had been set free by God's grace through the Second Adam, and by this liberation they have free choice, through which they may serve God, not through which they may be captured by the Devil."[61]

How can this be that the saintly recipients who have received this efficacious grace of final perseverance retain free choice while still having a fallen nature and yet they also persist in doing good and in resisting serious evil because of this grace? The short answer can be found in Phil 2:13 as rendered in the Peter King edition: "God is the one Who works in you both willing and doing works in conformity with goodwill." This verse from a letter of Paul contains elements both of Domingo Banez's and Luis De Molina's views of efficacious grace. On the one hand, it is God

---

60. Augustine, "On Reprimand and Grace" 12.33 (p. 214).
61. Augustine, "On Reprimand and Grace" 12.35 (p. 216).

who works the willing in doing good works; it is in the character of the grace itself (as Banez maintained) so that this grace strengthens the wills of the recipients. They are victorious in their "struggle against the urgings of sins" with the result that the urging to do good works that the grace provides becomes the dominant motive for the free choice of the will to choose righteously. On the other hand, the doing of the good works is in conformity with the goodwill's predispositions to freely choose to do good because the will is oriented by grace in any given situation (as Molina maintained).

In both views of efficacious grace, the person freely chooses to do good works that God intended for the person to accomplish. It would seem that Banez's view of efficacious grace is closer to Augustine's view of efficacious grace presented as the particular grace or assistance of final perseverance. In both their views, it is God with his efficacious grace who dominates the person who chooses to do good acts. The professor of theology and dean of the graduate school at Christendom College Robert J. Matava tells us that, in Banez's thought (as presented by his younger Dominican contemporary Diego Alvarez [1550–1631]), "the dependence of the human person on God in being entails the human person's dependence on God in acting, and this dependence on God in acting entails that God predetermines the will." As a Dominican, Banez follows Thomas Aquinas in viewing God as the necessary first cause of all things and the ultimate source of all goodness; and it is God who imparts to man a role as a participating cause of his actions through his free choice. Professor Matava goes on to explain Banez's view of what is especially applicable to persons to whom God gives efficacious grace, thus determining their good act:

> For Banez, human persons cannot determine themselves autonomously from God's causation of their acts of choice, for to determine oneself just is to choose, and to choose is an act. It is precisely this self-determination which God causes when he causes the act of choice. On Banez's view then, when God causes the act of choice, God's action includes the determination as such which makes the act of free choice to be the specific choice it is.[62]

This commentary on Banez's understanding of how God causes man to choose to act justly is similar to Augustine's view cited above

---

62. Matava, *Divine Causality and Human Free Choice*, 125.

regarding the saintly elect and martyrs that "had been set free by God's grace through the Second Adam, and by this liberation they have free choice, through which they may serve God, not through which they may be captured by the Devil." Speaking of those saints who are predestined and received the efficacious grace of final perseverance, Augustine states that they could "not persevere without this gift, but also they do indeed persevere through this gift." He also quotes John 15:5: "Without me you can do nothing," in reference to the saints and further refers to John 15:16: "You have not elected me, but I have elected you and appointed you to go forth and bear fruit, and that your fruit remain." Augustine adds the following commentary to these quotes from John's Gospel: "In these words, He showed them that He had given them not only justice, but perseverance in it as well." The martyred saints freely "stood fast in their faith, even though the world—I do not say 'terrified' them, but rather savagely attacked them," and even though they "did not see the future of goods that they were going to receive." Augustine asks concerning this steadfast courage of martyrs: "where does this come from, if not by God's gift?"[63] Augustine further adds a citation from Paul's letter to the Rom 14:4 in reference to the predestined who is born again that "'God is able to make him stand fast.'" Augustine provides the following interpretation: "Thus God gives perseverance. God is able to make those who are standing to stand fast, so that they stand fast with the utmost perseverance, or to make those who have fallen stand upright again."[64]

Through his efficacious intervening gift, i.e., his efficacious grace, God produces his divinely intended effect without destroying human freedom. The person who receives this efficacious grace freely chooses to perform righteous acts, be they acts leading to final perseverance or an efficacious grace intended by God for the person to produce a solitary good act. Because of this efficacious grace the satisfaction of doing a good act becomes the dominant motive of why the person freely acts as he does without fail. Without God's efficacious grace, however, the sinful urgings of fallen human nature could corrupt a person's motives so that an evil act would be committed rather than a righteous act. Augustine gives the following description of a specific efficacious grace—final perseverance:

> Even as regards perseverance in the good, God did not want His saints to glory in their own powers but rather in Him. God not

---

63. Augustine, "On Reprimand and Grace" 12.34–12.35 (pp. 214–15).
64. Augustine, "On Reprimand and Grace" 12.37 (p. 217).

only gives them assistance of the sort He gave the First Man, without which they cannot persevere even if they so will, but He also works in them the willing. As a result, since they will not persevere unless they are able to and will to persevere; the possibility of persevering, and the will to do so, is given to them by the bestowal of divine grace. Their will is set afire by the Holy Spirit to such an extent that they can do so precisely because they willed to, and they will to do so precisely because God works it that they so will.[65]

It has already been suggested that Banez's view of efficacious grace is in close agreement with that of Augustine's view (at least as it is presented in *On Reprimand and Grace*). God works in the human person the actual willing that chooses to achieve the good that God intends for the person to choose in accord with his divine will. We have already cited in Professor Hardon's definition of efficacious grace Luis de Molina's theory of how God works his will in a person so that his grace produces its divinely intended effect—efficacious grace that "is given under the circumstances that God foresees to be congruous with the dispositions of the person receiving the grace." While God foreknows what a person will do with or without grace, his foreknowledge does not force a person to do the act the person performs. Augustine reconfirms this truth (as he first argued earlier in *On the Free Choice of the Will*) stating: "Although God foreknew that Adam was going to do unjustly, His foreknowledge did not force him to do it."[66]

But how precisely can God bring about his divine will in a person without directly causing the person's will to lose its freedom of choice? In Molina's view, it is important to emphasize a person's freedom to accept or reject God's gift of grace while emphasizing God's power through efficacious grace to enlighten a person's mind and nature to move the dispositions of the person indirectly through extrinsic circumstances, so that the person will know and choose in accordance with God's will. Alfred J. Freddoso, who was the director of undergraduate studies in philosophy and professor of Thomistic studies at the University of Notre Dame, provides a concise summary of Molina's view of efficacious grace:

> On Molina's view . . . God gratuitously wills for human beings not only a supernatural end, namely, the everlasting beatific vision of God Himself, but also the supernatural means by

---

65. Augustine, "On Reprimand and Grace" 12.38 (p. 218).
66. Augustine, "On Reprimand and Grace" 12.37 (p. 217).

which we are to attain that end within the order of salvation contingently established by God. More specifically, through the life, death, and resurrection of Jesus Christ human beings are gratuitously furnished with supernatural aids and graces that empower us and dispose us to act righteously and thus to merit eternal life within the framework of the order of salvation freely ordained by God. So, on the one hand, the fundamentally gratuitous nature of salvation is preserved, along with the doctrine that it is only by God's special supernatural assistance that any of us is empowered to merit salvation or is even so much as moved toward exercising that power; whereas, on the other hand, the emphasis on merit is meant to highlight the fact that God does not force salvation on us, but leaves us free instead to refuse His gracious offer and to condemn ourselves by our own sins. One crucial difference between Molina and his Banezian opponents centers about the question of whether God's assistance, when efficacious, is, as the Banezians claim, intrinsically or essentially efficacious or whether it is not instead efficacious only contingently or by "extrinsic denomination," to use the relevant Scholastic term.[67]

According to Freddoso's explanation of Molina's view, it would seem that God by his grace can use external factors regarding a person's life to motivate efficaciously a person's free choice to complete meritorious actions in accord with God's will. But so far, we are dealing for the most part only with efficacious grace in the view of some of the last works of Augustine and in the view of Banez; this grace actually produces the divinely intended effect that God wills to result from the person's actions. What needs to be investigated is grace that may precede efficacious grace, viz., sufficient grace, which is that actual grace that does not guarantee that the person will complete the good action that God intends the recipient to perform.

Sufficient Grace and Free Will

Sufficient grace is, as the name suggests, an actual grace given by God with power to produce a good action by the recipient on condition that he persistently consents to, and works with, God's power that the person receives.

---

67. De Molina, *On Divine Foreknowledge*, Disputation 47, 87n6.

Because man can refuse or reject working with God's sufficient grace at any time in the present, it might never become efficacious in a future act, i.e., it would never eventually produce the result that God intended—the timely performance of a good act. The 1967 version of the *New Catholic Encyclopedia* tells us under the entry "Grace, Sufficient":

> A division of internal actual grace, sufficient grace is used in two senses: (1) grace that gives sufficient ability to perform a salutary act, prescinding from the result (grace efficacious with the efficacy of power)—grace is always sufficient in this sense or it would not be grace; (2) purely sufficient grace, which does not obtain a good free act, but gives sufficient power to produce one—grace inefficacious in the production of a good, free act.[68]

In the first sense of sufficient grace (given in this definition), this grace is conferred on the recipient with the power in itself for the recipient to perform a single good act now impending. In the second sense of sufficient grace, while that grace given is in itself sufficient for a person to perform the good act, the grace is rendered inefficacious because of the person's free choice to resist the grace that God provides.

For Banez and his followers, there is a rejection of the idea that grace is only efficacious if the recipient works with or cooperates with the grace. Rather, it seems that Banez and his followers contend that an actual grace shows itself to be innately efficacious when it moves the person to perform the good act that God intended. If the grace fails to move the person to perform the good act, it is merely sufficient and inefficacious. For Molina and his followers, sufficient grace is not efficacious or inefficacious in itself but rather is rendered efficacious or inefficacious by the free choice of the recipient to cooperate with it. This is made clear by Molina himself, who states:

> The assistance of grace is not efficacious or inefficacious by its very nature, but rather that it is being efficacious or inefficacious depends on whether or not the faculty of choice that is moved and stirred by it wills to consent to and cooperate with it—as the Council of Trent clearly taught.[69]

Professor Freddoso comments on Molina's Disputation 53:

---

68. *New Catholic Encyclopedia*, 682.
69. De Molina, *On Divine Foreknowledge*, Disputation 53.7 (p. 203).

> Predictably, Banezians contend that cooperating grace is intrinsically efficacious when good acts ensue and intrinsically inefficacious or merely sufficient when evil acts ensue. Molina counters that although actual grace is a supernatural influence on us that inclines and incites us to act well, it is not in itself efficacious or inefficacious, but is instead efficacious or inefficacious only because of our free cooperation with it or the freely chosen lack thereof.[70]

As presented by Professor Freddoso, Molina's view is that sufficient grace becomes efficacious grace through the free choice of the recipient. This makes Molina's view as truly substantiating of human freedom in regard to acceptance or rejection of God's grace. This is not to attribute to Molina a rejection of Augustine's premise that actual grace is completely a gratuitous gift of God given by God for his intended purpose to empower the recipient to perform a salutary act. Rather, Molina's conception presents a qualification of the view that God is the sole performer of the act who works his will through the recipient so as to produce a good result. Molina contends, rather, that the recipient of sufficient grace must freely cooperate with this grace so as to perform the good act God intends him to perform, and thus the recipient is active in cooperating with sufficient grace that thereby may become efficacious grace.

Professor Freddoso strongly contends that Molina does not diminish or minimize God's omnipotence as the creator and ultimate cause of all that exists. The professor states:

> As Molina sees it, God is the paradigmatic indeterministic cause, an all-powerful being capable of freely impeding any and every deterministic natural tendency in the created world. He is the first or primary cause and His causal activity is absolutely pervasive. He created the original constituents of the universe ex nihilo, and no creature can exist or possess causal power through any interval of time unless God conserves it and its powers in being at every instant in that interval. What's more, no creaturely or secondary cause is able to exercise its causal power unless God also acts contemporaneously to bring about its effect.

But God is the source of all things good and is never the cause of evil effects. How does God act contemporaneously with a rational creature,

---

70. De Molina, *On Divine Foreknowledge*, 37.

who is a secondary cause such as a human person who performs an evil act? Freddoso further explains that while:

> All creatures have genuine causal power too . . . in order for them to exercise this power God must also act to produce the relevant effect. When He thus cooperates with secondary causes, He acts as a general or universal cause of the effect, and His causal contribution is called His general concurrence or concourse (concursus generalis) . . . the particular nature of the effect is traceable *not to God's causal contribution*, necessary though it is in order for any effect to be produced at all, but rather to the natures and causal contributions of the relevant secondary causes, which act as particular causes of the effect.[71]

As previously noted, God has an active, determined will and a passive, conditional will. Made in his image and likeness, human beings have an intellect and free will with which a person can choose to exercise human causal power so as to produce a specific effect. A person can choose to do either good or evil, and God actively wills to enable and preserve contemporaneously human causal power; yet, God passively or conditionally wills that a person be allowed to exercise this causal power freely. At the same time, God can provide a person with grace that can become efficacious for the person who accepts it. Professor Matava provides an explanation of Molina's view of this relation between God's omnipotence and human freedom:

> Because freedom entails the ability to do otherwise in the presence of all antecedent conditions, God's causality, for Molina, cannot determine creaturely free choices. Molina therefore maintains that of two people receiving the same grace, it is possible that one be converted and the other not. Molina even maintains it is possible that a person who receives less grace than another may be saved by freely consenting to it, while the one receiving greater grace may be lost by rejecting it. Thus, on Molina's account, the efficacy of actual grace depends on the consent of human free choice.[72]

Molina published his *Concordia* in 1588, some twenty years after the Ecumenical Council of Trent issued its Decree on Justification, which stated, in part, that "they who by sins were alienated from God may be disposed through His quickening and assisting grace to convert

71. De Molina, *On Divine Foreknowledge*, 16–17 (emphasis added).
72. Matava, *Divine Causality and Human Free Choice*, 106.

themselves to their own justification by freely assenting to and cooperating with that said grace."[73] As a good Jesuit, Molina sought to stay in favorable standing with the Catholic Church as well as with his order. Within Molina's lifetime, Pope Pius V decided in regard to the controversy between Banez and Molina that neither side was to censure the other or proffer harsh attacks against the other. To this day, the teaching authority of the church has not doctrinally resolved the conflicting views of these two theologians, even as various theologians and schools of thought have weighed in on this controversy. Among Jesuits such as Robert Bellarmine and Francis Suarez, who were both contemporaries of Molina, there developed a system of congruism which emphasized the harmonious agreement of God's grace with the inclinations and the peculiar circumstances surrounding a person. This congruence of grace helps enable the person to freely consent to sufficient grace, which free consent God foresees so that this sufficient grace may be transformed into efficacious grace that actually produces its divinely intended effect.

God Can Bring About His Preordained Will Without Destroying a Person's Free Will

The distinction between sufficient and efficacious grace provides a focal point for investigating how God can bring about his preordained will of having a person perform good acts without destroying free choice of the person's will. Augustine will insist in *On Reprimand and Grace* that it is God's grace that not only enables one to do any good acts but provides a person with the will to do these good acts throughout one's life, even to the endpoint of that person receiving the gift of final perseverance. In his *On Reprimand and Grace* Augustine makes reference several times to Phil 2:13, which was cited previously and which states: "God is the one Who works in you both willing and doing works in conformity with good will." Augustine makes the argument that both the ability to persevere and the will to attain final perseverance cannot be achieved by persons unless it "is given to them by the bestowal of divine grace." Because of man's fallen nature, the will of each person "would give way in its weakness among so many great temptations." Unless a person receives God's grace, a person "would not will in such a way that [he] would be able to persevere." For Augustine, man's will is "unhealthy and feeble" and is

---

73. *Dogmatic Canons and Degrees*, "Decree on Justification," 26.

in need of "divine grace," which grace alone can strengthen the human will because "it moves unchangeably and insurmountably."[74] Grace that is "unchangeable and insurmountable" must be efficacious, and efficacious grace brings about the effect that God wills it to produce, as Banez contended. Still, the question remains, how can such efficacious grace allow for the will to freely choose to accept this grace without divine control of the human will?

Perhaps a partial answer can be found in 2 Cor 12:7-10, which is the passage that Augustine himself cites for the sake of emphasizing the need for humility in the face of one's own weaknesses while boasting only of the power of Christ's grace. Just prior to this passage, Paul speaks of a man he knew in Christ who was undergoing mystical experiences of "Paradise." Paul goes on to state that he himself wishes to refrain from boasting of any supernatural disclosures, but in order to prevent himself "from being too elated by the abundance of revelations, a thorn was given me in the flesh, a messenger of Satan to harass me." This experience must have been extremely distressful for Paul, because Paul adds: "Three times I besought the Lord about this that it should leave me." What is most insightful of this passage is the Lord's response to Paul: "My grace is sufficient for you, for my power is made perfect in weakness." It should be evident to the reader that the Lord is not speaking only to Paul. Most translations of Paul's Greek use the word "sufficient" to modify "grace," and what Christ is seemingly revealing to Paul and to all believers is that every human person, when he/she is a recipient of God's gratuitous help, must often struggle with sufficient grace in spite of adversities and weaknesses in order for the power of God's grace to be "made perfect." This perfection seems to imply the transition of sufficient grace into efficacious grace, which requires a person's free will cooperation in the struggle to overcome adversities. But to what adversities does the phrase "a thorn was given to me in the flesh" refer? In chapter 12 verse 9, Paul himself speaks of his own "weaknesses, insults, hardships, persecutions, and calamities," any and all of which suggest the types of difficulties that could make working with God's sufficient grace all the more demanding in order to complete effectively a worthy task.

Discouragement can enter into any person's life when he/she has a responsibility to meet but finds himself/herself encountering frustrating and even painful obstacles. These difficulties can tempt a person to

---

74. See Augustine, "On Reprimand and Grace" 12.38 (p. 218).

neglect the responsibility at hand and even possibly court the satisfactions of vice. In such instances, it would seem that sufficient grace requires a great deal of willpower in freely cooperating with this grace in the Molinian sense. Moreover, prayer to God is needed for more assistance in order to meet this responsibility and to resign oneself to bearing with an ongoing difficulty. This would not be a situation that prompted boasting of one's accomplishments; rather, it would be a situation in which one would seek to beg God for help. But this is not to deny that God can give a person efficacious grace understood in the Banezian sense of an interior grace where God empowers the person to work through the accomplishment of the task at hand. This would be an acceptance of Phil 2:13, that it is God who works within the person both the willing and the doing of good works in conformity with a good will. It would seem then that, both Banez's understanding of efficacious grace as an intrinsic power in itself given by God for the person to accomplish good acts as well as Molina's understanding of sufficient grace disposing a person to exercise his free consent in order for the grace to become efficacious, these two views may be reconciled. While both views are contrasting and, when viewed in isolation seemingly conflicting, they are not necessarily contradictory.

Both views contain truths that uphold the absolute power of God and God's endowing a person with free will to be used to do God's will in the performance of good acts. A reconciling of both views could perhaps be the positing of two types of efficacious grace. Banez's view of efficacious grace emphasizes the truth of God's omnipotence, which certainly would include the power of God's determinate will to empower man to carry out a good act without fail. Molina's view of efficacious grace emphasizes both God's determinate and conditional will, which disposes the human person to accomplish good acts while exercising a person's free volition that God sustains. For Molina, the person must freely choose to assent to, and cooperate with, sufficient grace; this sufficient grace disposes a person to a good act but which grace only becomes efficacious when the person actually carries out God's will.

Do Banez's and Augustine's Definitions of Efficacious Grace Claim That God Works the Willing of Perseverance, and Does This Deny Free Will?

However, an apparently irresolvable difficulty arises with the strict definition of efficacious grace in the Banezian sense, i.e., grace that depends upon the innate character of the grace in itself to infallibly produce the effect that God intends and for which God gratuitously gave the grace. This irresolvable difficulty arises when this definition of efficacious grace is applied to Augustine's concept of the grace of perseverance. Because Banez argues that efficacious grace is intrinsically efficacious and because the grace of perseverance is itself efficacious, then seemingly the necessary conclusion to be drawn is that God provides this grace of perseverance *only* to those he wishes to save. This seems to be the view that Augustine finally adopted in his last two anti-Pelagian books. As previously quoted, Augustine tells us regarding perseverance that this divine assistance is needed for salvation:

> Without which they cannot persevere even if they so will, but He also works in them the willing. As a result, since they will not persevere unless they are able to and will to persevere, the possibility of persevering, and the will to do so, is given to them by the bestowal of divine grace.[75]

If the gift of perseverance is given to some human persons by God as a bestowal of divine grace, then those to whom God does not bestow this grace are not able to persevere and will not ultimately be saved. Based on these premises, the logical conclusion is that only God determines whom he wills to save and whom he does not will to save. A person's free choice to work with grace, or cooperate with grace, would *not* enter into the final decision of that person's own salvation. In *On Reprimand and Grace*, Augustine makes this argument and substantiates this argument repeatedly. For Augustine, man is inherently sinful by the human nature he inherits, and sin "deserves a just penalty." Reprimands, when not beneficial for bringing this sinful person to repentance, are nonetheless just penalties for the sinner. A person's free choice seemingly can do nothing to bring about forgiveness of sins or prevent God's decision to forgive a person's sins. Says Augustine:

---

75. Augustine, "On Reprimand and Grace" 12.38 (p. 218).

> No human choice resists Him when He wills salvation. For being willing or being unwilling is in the power of the one who is willing or unwilling in such a way that it does not get in the way of the divine will, nor surpass His power. He does what He wills even when it comes to those who do what He does not will.[76]

In this major anti-Pelagian work written during the last few years of his life, Augustine so emphasizes the omnipotence of God in an attempt to eradicate the lingering Pelagian heresy that he seemingly rejects man's free choice to cooperate with God's grace. Augustine further writes that there can be "no doubt that human wills cannot resist the will of God" and that even when one tries to incur God's favor, no one can "prevent Him from doing what He wills even in the case of human wills themselves."[77]

It may be conceded that God can provide an efficacious grace that makes a person do God's will in spite of his/her own will initially choosing to do otherwise. Was it not the case that Paul en route to Damascus was determined to go there to arrest, persecute, and perhaps even kill Christians? But Paul was struck down blind on the road and heard a voice saying to him, "Saul, Saul, why do you persecute me?" Saul had to be led into a house in Damascus without sight and encountered by Ananias, a disciple sent by Jesus Christ, who laid hands on Saul, with the result that scales fell from his eyes and he regained his sight. Saul was then baptized by Ananias and went on to try to convince Jews in Damascus that Jesus was the Christ. The grace Saul received effectively changed him from being an avid persecutor of Christ to an enthusiastic evangelist.

Augustine has said that "God can do what He wills even when it comes to those who do what He does not will" and even change the will of persons to do his will. More often than not, God provides the needed grace for persons to do the right thing; and God also "works in them the willing" to do the right thing while leaving intact that person's ability to freely choose. How can this be the case? The answer can be found in Augustine's exposition on the conflict between the two wills found in Book 8 of his *Confessions* (discussed in chapter 1 of this work). The human person on earth is in a constant state of conflict between the higher faculties and the lower faculties. As Augustine puts it: "When eternity attracts the higher faculties and the pleasure of some temporal good holds the lower, it is one same soul that wills both, but not either with its whole will; and

---

76. Augustine, "On Reprimand and Grace" 14.43 (p. 222).
77. Augustine, "On Reprimand and Grace" 14.45 (p. 223).

it is therefore torn both ways and deeply troubled while truth shows the one way as better but habit keeps it to the other."[78] The higher faculties of the human person are the intellect and will. Augustine argues in *On Reprimand and Grace* that God can provide the willing, and this willing can move the human person to do what God has empowered the person to do with his grace. In this way, directly with grace God seemingly ends the conflict of the two wills within the person. However, in most instances, God leaves intact the free will of the soul to ultimately end the conflict between the person's two wills, and the person is left to either choose what God has directed that person's intellect and divinely given will to do, or to defy God and choose the person's own fallen human will to satisfy his own gratifications.

No one can be a believing Christian and at the same time deny God's omnipotent power to do what he wills and to save whom he wills to save. But neither is it a Christian belief that God can contradict his own absolute attributes, including those of justice and righteousness. Psalm 11:7 states clearly: "For the Lord is righteous, he loves righteous deeds; the upright shall behold his face." And in Acts 10:34 Peter addresses the household of Cornelius, the Roman centurion, stating: "truly I perceive that God shows no partiality, but in every nation anyone who fears him and does what is right is acceptable to him." Yet, in *On Reprimand and Grace* Augustine opts to interpret Scripture in a narrow sense when it comes to the question of whom God wills to save. Referring to 1 Tim 2:4, which states that "God wills all people to be saved," Augustine writes that this verse "was said in such a way that all the predestined are understood, since every kind of a human being is among them."[79] Yet, the very next verse (1 Tim 2:5) says: "For there is one God and there is one mediator between God and men, the man Christ Jesus, who gave himself as a ransom for all." It would seem that if the author of 1 Timothy meant to refer only to the predestined, he would have used that word instead of "all" and "all people." Similarly, 2 Pet 3:9 tells us that "the Lord . . . is forbearing toward you, not wishing that any should perish, but that all should reach repentance." In Matt 25:31–42 Christ makes it clear that the righteous who feed the hungry, give drink to the thirsty, clothe the naked, and welcome strangers will enter into eternal life because "truly, I say to you, as you did it to one of the least of my brethren, you did it to

---

78. Augustine, *Confessions* 8.10.24 (p. 157).
79. Augustine, "On Reprimand and Grace" 14.44 (p. 223).

me." Such scriptural verses indicate God's willingness to extend the grace of Christ to all persons to perform righteous deeds. Previously, Augustine himself had admitted that "divine precepts would themselves be pointless for human beings unless we had free choice of the will, by which we might reach the promised rewards through carrying them out."[80]

In *On Reprimand and Grace* Augustine Apparently Limits Predestination to God Alone Without the Consent of a Person's Free Choice

Once again, perhaps Augustine's overzealous condemnation of Pelagianism in *On Reprimand and Grace* led him too far astray from the acceptance of God creating man with a free will and the ability to beg for God's grace (admitting that this ability is itself a grace) and to act in accord with God's grace. But when it comes to interpreting Rom 8:29–30, Augustine is intent to interpret God's predestination of all persons (with only some being glorified) in a strict deterministic sense. Paul states the following in this passage from his letter to the Romans:

> For those whom He foreknew beforehand He also predestined to conform to the image of His Son, that He might be the firstborn among many brethren. Moreover, those whom He has predestined He also called [namely in accordance with His plan], and those whom He called He also made just, and those whom He made just He also glorified.

It must be acknowledged that Christian doctrine, both Catholic and Protestant, recognizes predestination as an article of faith. And it is also generally accepted by Christians that it is in God's power to predestine those he chooses to receive grace. The divergence of belief arises regarding the type of grace that leads to salvation and glorification and on whether God deliberately refuses to give salvific grace to some while he gives it to others. Does God refuse even sufficient grace to all persons, so that each person can freely choose to cooperate with that grace? Or is it the case that God has already predetermined because of his foreknowledge of how each person would use grace that some would be denied the opportunity to freely agree to persevere or refuse to cooperate with the grace they need to be saved? Augustine's answer to these questions in *On Reprimand and Grace* seems to combine all of the acts that God

---

80. Augustine, "On Grace and Free Choice" 2.2 (p. 142).

performs, viz., foreknowing, predestining, calling, justifying, and glorifying, into one single divine decree that has already taken place from all eternity. Says Augustine:

> All these things have already been done: "foreknew," "predestined," "called," "made just"—these things were already foreknown and predestined, and many people were already called and made just. . . .
>
> The apostle used past-tense verbs with regard to events still to come, as though God had already done the things He already arranged from eternity to take place. . . . Therefore, perseverance in the good up to the end is given by Him. It is given only to those who will not perish, since those who do not persevere will perish.[81]

There is a plausible interpretation of what Augustine is saying that reflects God's infinite attribute of omniscience. God does not know things as does man, who has a finite human mind, a human mind that thinks in time. God exists and knows things all at once without a past or a future in an ever-present now and without resorting to the limitations of human reason that employs analysis, synthesis, induction, and deduction. God does not think discursively so that one topic and line of reasoning follows another. However, man rationally speculates with human limitations, so there is usually a progression of thought based on primary premises that can logically demonstrate a conclusion. God's omniscience includes his foreknowledge of all changeable beings and events. For the human intellect, speculating on God's knowledge regarding man, man's free will choices, and man's final destination, there must be a primary premise in what Paul reveals in Rom 8:29–30 that precedes all the other actions God takes. That primary premise is God's foreknowledge in which God knows how man will freely use graces—specifically sufficient graces—or not use them. In human reason, God's foreknowledge would temporally precede God's predestination, but with God's omniscience there is no temporal succession of thought, as God knows all things in an ever-present now. Still, God's foreknowledge is logically prior to his predestination of man in that God predestines according to his divine judgment of perfect justice, which is informed by his foreknowledge of the free will choices and actions of all human persons. John A. Hardon, SJ, defines "predestination," in part, as follows:

---

81. Augustine, "On Reprimand and Grace" 9.23 (p. 205).

> In the strictest sense it is God's eternal decision to assume certain rational creatures into heavenly glory. Predestination implies an act of the divine intellect and of the divine will. The first is foreknowledge, the second is predestination....
> The main difficulty in the doctrine of predestination is whether God's eternal decision has been taken with or without consideration of human freedom.[82]

Even as God knows all things all at once, God's foreknowledge of how man will freely use the graces he receives is seemingly the most probable basis for God's providing the efficacious grace of final perseverance to some and not to others. What only God knows in his infinite wisdom and omniscience is his complete plan of salvation for men. God made us in the state of journeying in time through life; we struggle to make free will choices to search for God, seek his assistance, and hopefully find an eternal destiny in union with God. Man's free will, enlightened by a rational intellect, is an essential means to realize these goals through the turmoil and difficulties of life. God's gift of hope is an essential requirement to keep searching for God and an eternal destiny with him. Without free choice to seek God's help (induced by God's grace itself), and without working with this help, man's hope is lost in this world. Understanding God's predestination of persons with a consideration for man's human freedom rests seemingly on God's willingness to extend his help (grace) to a greater degree to some, and less perhaps to others, based on his foreknowledge of how individual persons would freely cooperate with his grace. However, in *On Reprimand and Grace*, Augustine lacks a resolution of the difficulty that arises between accepting both God's active omnipotent will and God's passive allowance of man's freedom to cooperate with divine grace. Thus, in this book Augustine ultimately chooses to accept God's determinate will (i.e., conclusively determined will) seemingly to the exclusion of God's conditional will and of man's freedom to cooperate with grace, so as to assign to God alone the complete determination of man's salvation or damnation.

ON THE GIFT OF PERSEVERANCE

On Grace and Free Choice and *On Reprimand and Grace* were both written between 426 and 427, with the former written first, and are

---

82. Hardon, *Modern Catholic Dictionary*, 434.

approximately of equal length. *On the Gift of Perseverance* was written between 428 and 429 on the eve of the besieging of Hippo by the Vandals, approximately a year before Augustine's death. *On the Gift of Perseverance* is less than one-half the length of these two earlier anti-Pelagian books. What is different in all three of these books is how Augustine treats free choice. In *On Grace and Free Choice* Augustine defends free choice of the will as a truth that "God has revealed to us through his own Scripture" and adds that "the divine precepts would themselves be pointless for human beings unless we had free choice of the will, by which we might reach the promised rewards through carrying them out."[83] *On Reprimand and Grace* has a determinate view of God's will, evidenced by such quotes as "He wills when He wills even in the case of human wills themselves."[84] But Augustine also adds:

> You should also be reprimanded for the very reason that you are not willing to be reprimanded! You are not willing to have your faults pointed out to you. You are not willing for them to be struck down, or to experience a useful pain that leads you to find a physician.[85]

This quote implies that reprimands act as a type of grace where the one who reprimands makes explicit a person's fault, which causes useful pain prompting the person to choose to seek more grace from God so as to be healed. In *On the Gift of Perseverance*, however, the emphasis is on God's selective conferring of grace, where "anyone who is set free should take delight in grace; anyone who is not set free should recognize what is owed," so that Augustine can conclude:

> In as much as one looks both to justice and to grace, it can rightly be said to the guilty one who is damned and of the guilty one who is set free: "Take what is yours and go your way!" . . . "to this one I will to give" what he is not owed. "Am I not permitted to do as I will? Or are you envious because I am generous?" [Matt 20:14–15].[86]

What Augustine continues here in *On the Gift of Perseverance* is essentially the same argument emphasizing the omnipotence of God's will with which he concluded *On Reprimand and Grace*, which stated: "To

83. Augustine, "On Grace and Free Choice" 2.2 (p. 142).
84. Augustine, "On Reprimand and Grace" 14.45 (p. 223).
85. Augustine, "On Reprimand and Grace" 5.7 (p. 189).
86. Augustine, "On the Gift of Perseverance" 8.16–8.17 (pp. 229–30).

the extent that it is up to us, we who are not capable of singling out the predestined from those not predestined." Regarding our moral responsibilities, "a severe reprimand should be administered to all medicinally in order that they not perish or not ruin others." But ultimately, "it is up to God, however, to make the reprimand useful 'for those He foreknew . . . [He] also predestined.'"[87] Augustine speaks of predestination in a way to suggest that it is God alone who determines those who will be saved without regard to a person's free choice to cooperate with grace because God has already determined "those people who have been predestined for the kingdom of God, whose number is settled so that no one is added to them or taken from them."[88] So too, in *On the Gift of Perseverance*, Augustine will reemphasize his argument previously made that the free will on its own can do nothing but sin and adds that it is only God who makes the person do good and avoid evil without reference to a person needing to freely choose to work with God's grace. Says Augustine: "The one who falls, falls by his own will. The one who stands, stands by the will of God . . . he does not make himself stand fast, but rather God does."[89] It also seems to be the case that Augustine is saying in both these books that God does not will to save all but only those predestined by him and set free from their guilt.

Yet, in *On Reprimand and Grace*, Augustine does provide certain moral directives to Christians, such as to preach the gospel to those without faith so as "not to exclude anyone or single anyone out, but instead to will that all those to whom we preach this peace be saved." No one knows who is "going to be saved," and so we are "to will that all to whom we preach this peace be saved." Augustine cites 1 Tim 2:4 that tells us that "God wills all people to be saved," which can be "understood as follows: He makes us will this by making us call it out" that we have been given "'the Spirit of adoption of children, in which we call out Abba Father!' [Rom 8:15]."[90] However, in *On the Gift of Perseverance*, the emphasis is not on moral directives but on providing explanations of God's ways toward fallen humanity. From a human perspective, certain persons might seem to be moral and religious, but God will give the gift of perseverance to one and not to the other, which defies the human understanding of

---

87. Augustine, "On Reprimand and Grace" 16.49 (pp. 226–27).
88. Augustine, "On Reprimand and Grace" 13.39 (p. 219).
89. Augustine, "On the Gift of Perseverance" 8.19 (p. 231).
90. Augustine, "On Reprimand and Grace" 15.46–15.47 (pp. 225–26).

justice. Augustine's answer will only be: "Who can know God's intent? Who can scrutinize what is inscrutable?"[91]

Augustine's View of Baptism and Penance and How the Meaning of These Sacraments and Their Necessity Developed Over Time

Perhaps the best explanation of how God gratuitously gives grace for the salvation of human persons is found in Augustine's explanation of baptism. Augustine tells us that "it is not in human power but rather in God's power for human beings to have 'the power to become the children of God' [John 1:12]."[92] This "power to become the children of God" is explained in Christian doctrine as the sacred power of the sacrament of baptism, which Augustine defends as the necessary means to absolve the guilt of original sin. While the Pelagians deny that there is any original sin, or penalties from original sin inherited by mankind from Adam, Augustine upholds the necessity of this sacrament for salvation:

> The Catholic Church defends it against the Pelagians. It asserts that there is original sin, and the guilt belonging to it, contracted by birth, must be dissolved by rebirth.... On this score we may destroy the error of the Pelagians; why do they think it should be doubted that God also delivers young children, to whom He gives His grace through the sacrament of baptism, "from the power of darkness and transfers them to the kingdom of the son of God's charity" [Col 1:13]?[93]

But what of young children or even adults who die without baptism? What explanation can be given for those who suffer damnation by God because they did not receive baptism, which removes the guilt of original sin? Augustine rejects any explanation that justifies the divine judgment of damnation for those who die without baptism on the grounds that God had foreknowledge of all those who would refuse to have faith in and follow the gospel of Christ (had the gospel been preached to them) and so allowed them to die without baptism. Augustine argues emphatically that "it is false that the dead are judged according to the deeds they would have done had the gospel reached them while alive." And because this is false, Augustine will further argue that "there is no reason to say of

91. Augustine, "On the Gift of Perseverance" 12.27 (p. 240).
92. Augustine, "On the Gift of Perseverance" 8.20 (p. 231).
93. Augustine, "On the Gift of Perseverance" 11.27 (p. 239).

infants who perish (because they die without Baptism) that they perished deservedly, on the grounds that God foreknew that if they had lived and the gospel had been preached to them, they would have heard it without believing it." Augustine argues that it is not on the basis of God's foreknowledge of sins persons would have committed had those persons lived that God judges a person as deserving damnation. Rather, those who die without baptism "are held in bondage by Original Sin alone, and for this alone they depart into damnation."[94]

Augustine does not mention any other means of being freed from the bondage of original sin except through sacramental baptism with water and word. Other church fathers also mention a baptism of blood attained through martyrdom[95] for being a witness to Jesus Christ. Cyprian, bishop of Carthage, who was martyred for the faith in 258, wrote in a letter (ca. 254–56) to Jabaianus, a bishop in Mauretania, that "[catechumens who suffer martyrdom before they have received baptism with water] are not deprived of the Sacrament of Baptism. Rather they are baptized with the most glorious and greatest Baptism of blood, concerning which the Lord said that He had another Baptism with which He Himself was to be baptized." And Cyril of Jerusalem (ca. 315–86) wrote in his *Catechetical Lectures* that the only means of salvation is through baptism and that "the only exception is the martyrs, who even without water, will receive the kingdom. . . . For the Savior calls martyrdom a Baptism saying: 'Can you drink the cup which I drink, and be baptized with the Baptism with which I am to be baptized?'"[96]

There has also been in the church in modern times an understanding of a baptism of desire, which holds that the remission of original sin and the attainment of unity with God can be found through a desire and searching for God and a love for God and Jesus Christ, which establishes a desire for baptism. In the twentieth century, the Second Vatican Council of the Catholic Church decreed what is effectively a general and extended baptism of desire, stating: "those who, through no fault of their own, do not know the Gospel of Christ or his Church, but who nevertheless seek God with a sincere heart, and moved by grace, try in their actions to do his will as they know it through the dictates of their conscience—these

---

94. Augustine, "On the Gift of Perseverance" 9.23 (pp. 234–35).

95. Cyprian, "Letter of Cyprian to Jubaianus, a Bishop in Mauertania," in Jurgens, *Faith of the Early Fathers*, 1:238.

96. Cyril, "Catechetical Lectures," in Jurgens, *Faith of the Early Fathers*, 1:349.

too may achieve eternal salvation."[97] While Augustine never went beyond the teaching that sacramental baptism is necessary for a person's salvation, it can be historically verified that there has been a development of Christian doctrine that includes belief in salvation through a baptism of desire for God. Nevertheless, it is understandable, especially in the early church, that lacking this development of doctrine Augustine would tend to teach the necessity of sacramental baptism, which unites one to Jesus Christ, God the Son made man, and to his Father through the Holy Spirit. What is more problematic, perhaps, is Augustine's argument for why God allows only some persons to be baptized and acquire a necessary foundation for salvation but not others.

God Sets Only Some Free from Sin; God's Ways Are Inscrutable

Obviously, the problem regarding the remission of personal sin committed after baptism and throughout one's life also gives rise to the question of why God allows some to find forgiveness but not others. Augustine argues:

> Nor is anyone, young or old, set free from the everlasting death that is the completely just repayment for sin, except by Him Who died for the remission of our sins, both original and personal, without having any original or personal sin of His own.

But why does he set free these rather than those?

> Again and again we reply . . . : "Who are human beings to answer back to God?" [Rom 9:20]. "His judgments are inscrutable and His ways past finding out!" [Rom 11:33].[98]

God's ways are indubitably inscrutable, and some of his ways remain shrouded in mystery and are past finding out. But we do know from divine revelation regarding the forgiveness of personal sin that Christ instituted sacraments, among which is the sacrament of penance, which Christ established on Easter Sunday evening, as recorded in John 20:19–23. Then Christ appeared to the disciples who were gathered in fear behind locked doors and "breathed on them and said to them, 'Receive the Holy Spirit. If you forgive the sins of any, they are forgiven; if

---

97. *Dogmatic Constitution on the Church, Lumen Gentium*, in Flannery, *Vatican Council II*, 367.

98. Augustine, "On the Gift of Perseverance" 12.30 (p. 241).

you retain the sins of any, they are retained.'" Those who avail themselves of the sacrament of penance in faith and sincere contrition will have their personal sins (committed after baptism) forgiven. Still, it can be argued that God's grace is first needed in order to have faith and contrition, and as Augustine has argued repeatedly here and elsewhere, "God's grace is not given according to our deserts."[99] Nonetheless, the person who pursues God's grace and avails himself/herself of penance, even out of fear of damnation, can receive forgiveness of sin, which forgiveness becomes increasingly vital for those nearing the end of their lives and who hope for salvation. About this sacrament, Augustine tells us:

> Times of penance are rightly established by those who govern the Church in which sins themselves are forgiven. Indeed, outside the Church they are not forgiven, for it is the Church that has received the Holy Spirit as her own as a pledge without which no sins are forgiven in such a way that those to whom they are forgiven receive eternal life.[100]

Augustine acknowledges that through the Holy Spirit the sacrament of penance provides the forgiveness of sin needed for eternal life, which undoubtably is intertwined with the gift of perseverance. Augustine does not distinguish in detail between sacramental grace received in baptism and penance for the forgiveness of sins and those actual graces that preserve a person from falling into serious sin during life and at the end of life. Yet, it seems that for the believer who accepts in faith Christ's sacraments, an increase in the theological virtues of faith, hope, and charity results from the worthy reception of a sacrament; and when the sacrament of penance is received with sincere contrition, there results a forgiveness of all personal sin, even serious sins. Augustine's great teacher and mentor, Ambrose, wrote in his two books on penance that "what was impossible was made possible by God, who gave us so great a grace . . . for sins to be forgiven through penance"; this authoritative grace was given by Christ "to His Apostles, and by His Apostles it has been transmitted to the offices of priests." Ambrose asserts even more clearly than Augustine that through "the preaching of the Lord . . . we have been commanded to restore the grace of the heavenly Sacrament to those guilty even of the

---

99. Augustine, "On the Gift of Perseverance" 12.31 (p. 242).
100. Augustine, *Enchiridion on Faith, Hope, and Love*, 89.

most grave crime, if, with their whole heart by an open confession of their sin, they do penance."[101]

While God gratuitously gives the gift of perseverance as he ordains, it would seem indisputable that those who avail themselves of the sacrament of penance for the forgiveness of their sins are best disposed to receive and accept God's final gift of grace. There exists, in fact, a symbiotic relationship between sacramental graces that are distinctive for each of the seven sacraments and those actual graces that God gratuitously confers on a person. On the one hand, the sacramental graces that are conferred on the recipient provide a specific sanctifying effect that corresponds to the respective purpose of each of the sacraments. Baptism, for example, cleanses a person from all sin, both original and personal sin, so that the person is spiritually reborn, united to Christ, made a child of the Father, and filled with the Holy Spirit. In commissioning the apostles, Christ tells them: "Go into all the world and preach the gospel to the whole creation. He who believes and is baptized will be saved" (Mark 16:15–16). The sacrament of penance absolves the sins committed after baptism that are confessed by the sincere penitent to the priest who acts in the Person of Christ. On the other hand, actual graces are God's temporary interventions in a person's life that enlighten the mind and strengthen the will, so that the person performs actions that may lead to salvation.

In order to attain heaven, one has to be free of deadly sins (also called mortal sins), which, when committed after baptism, require (when the sacrament of penance is not available) a sincere act of perfect contrition, which is sorrow out of perfect love for God. For most, there is a need for the sacrament of penance to attain forgiveness of serious sin because sorrow for sin is most often motivated by fear of God's just punishment, but forgiveness of sin, especially serious sin, requires love of God motivating the sorrow for offending God. Fear of God's just punishment for one's serious sins requires the sacrament of penance in order for these sins to be forgiven, because only with this sacrament does the Holy Spirit transform a person's sorrow out of fear into sorrow out of love of God. And as quoted above, Christ told his apostles: "If you forgive the sins of any, they are forgiven" (John 20:23).

In reference to the Eucharist, Christ made it clear that "truly, truly, I say to you, unless you eat the flesh of the Son of man and drink his blood

---

101. Ambrose, "Penance," in Jurgens, *Faith of the Early Fathers*, 2:161.

you have no life in you; he who eats my flesh and drinks my blood has eternal life, and I will raise him up at the last day" (John 6:53–54). For all three of these sacraments (baptism, penance, and the Eucharist) that Christ instituted, there is reference to their respective salvific effect. The Council of Trent coined the expression *ex opere, operato*, which literally means "from the work performed," to describe how the sacraments actually and without fail confer the salvific grace that they signify, provided the recipient is properly prepared and disposed to receive the sacrament. Regarding the proper disposition with which to receive the Eucharist, Paul tells us: "Whoever . . . eats the bread or drinks the cup of the Lord in an unworthy manner will be guilty of profaning the body and blood of the Lord. Let a man examine himself, and so eat of the bread and drink of the cup. For anyone who eats and drinks without discerning the body eats and drinks judgment upon himself" (1 Cor 11:27–29).

In order to freely choose to receive any of the sacraments, a person must first have the actual grace that moves the person to avail himself/herself of a particular sacrament. Regarding the sacrament of penance, actual grace can move a penitent to experience guilt and fear of God's punishment, so that the person seeks reconciliation through this sacrament. Further, actual grace can move one to acquire perfect sorrow out of perfect love of God, which is necessary for the forgiveness of serious sins committed after baptism when the sacrament of penance is not available. Sacramental grace coming from the Holy Spirit can only be attained through the sacrament of penance, which works *ex opere operato* for the forgiveness of sins.

Toward the end of *On the Gift of Perseverance*, Augustine provides the following quote regarding all seeking and choosing that can lift a person up to God:

> For "our heart and our thoughts are not in our power." Accordingly, the same person who said this, Ambrose, also says:
>
>> Who is happy as one who always ascends in his heart? But without divine assistance who can make it happen? Surely there is no way. And indeed the same book of Scripture says earlier: "happy is the one whose help is from You, Lord; he ascends in his heart" [Ps 83:6].[102]

Augustine has argued repeatedly that free will on its own without access to God's grace is only free to sin and not to do good works. Our heart,

---

102. Augustine, "On the Gift of Perseverance" 13.33 (p. 244).

and all our thoughts, require God's grace to will the good and to conceive the good, which also requires one to cooperate with this grace so as to do God's will by ascending in one's heart and persevering in God's love, especially at the final moments of human life on earth.

Bibliography

Anselm. *Proslogium*. In *St. Anselm's Basic Writings*, translated by S. N. Deane, 47–80. 2nd ed. Chicago: Open Court, 1996.

Aristotle. *Metaphysics*. In *The Basic Works of Aristotle*, edited by Richard McKeon, 682–926. Translated by W. D. Ross. New York: Random House, 1968.

Augustine. *Against the Academicians and the Teacher*. Translated by Peter King. Indianapolis: Hackett, 1998.

———. *The City of God Against the Pagans*. Translated by Henry Bettenson. London: Penguin, 1984.

———. *The City of God Against the Pagans*. Edited and translated by R. W. Dyson. Cambridge: Cambridge University Press, 2018.

———. *Confessions*. 2nd ed. Translated by Frank J. Sheed. Indianapolis: Hackett, 2006.

———. *Enchiridion on Faith, Hope, and Charity*. In *On Christian Belief*, edited by Boniface Ramsey, 265–343. Translated by Bruce Harbert. Part 1, vol. 8 of *The Works of St. Augustine*. Hyde Park, NY: New City Press, 2005.

———. *Essential Letters—The Works of St. Augustine*. Selected and introduced by Przemyslaw Nehring, translation and notes by Roland Teke. Hyde Park, NY: New City Press, 2021.

———. *Faith and the Creed*. In *On Christian Belief*, translated by Michael G. Cambell, 151–74. Part 1, vol. 8 of *The Works of St. Augustine*. Hyde Park, NY: New City Press, 2005.

———. *On Christian Teaching*. Translated by R. P. H. Green. New York: Oxford University Press, 1997.

———. *On Free Choice of the Will*. Translated by Anna S. Benjamin and L. H. Hackstaff. Indianapolis: Bobbs-Merrill, 1977.

———. "On the Free Choice of the Will." In *Augustine: On the Free Choice of the Will, On Grace and Free Choice, and Other Writings*, edited and translated by Peter King, 3–126. New York: Cambridge University Press, 2010.

———. *On Genesis: A Refutation of the Manichees*. Introductions, translations, and notes by Edmund Hill. Hyde Park, NY: New City Press, 2023.

———. "On the Gift of Perseverance." In *Augustine: On the Free Choice of the Will, On Grace and Free Choice, and Other Writings*, edited and translated by Peter King, 229–45. New York: Cambridge University Press, 2010.

———. "On Grace and Free Choice." In *Augustine: On the Free Choice of the Will, On Grace and Free Choice, and Other Writings*, edited and translated by Peter King, 141–84. New York: Cambridge University Press, 2010.

———. "On Reprimand and Grace." In *Augustine: On the Free Choice of the Will, On Grace and Free Choice, and Other Writings*, edited and translated by Peter King, 185–227. New York: Cambridge University Press, 2010.

———. *On the Soul and Its Origin*. Translated by Peter Holmes and Robert Ernest Wallis. In *St. Augustine's Anti-Pelagian Works. Nicene and Post-Nicene Fathers* 5, 315–71. Peabody, MA: Hendrickson, 1995.

———. "Reconsiderations." In *Augustine: On the Free Choice of the Will, On Grace and Free Choice, and Other Writings*, edited and translated by Peter King, 127–33. New York: Cambridge University Press, 2010.

———. *Reply to Faustus the Manichean*. In *Nicene and Post-Nicene Fathers* 4, edited by Philip Schaff, 155–345. Peabody, MA: Hendrickson, 1995.

———. "Sermon 43." In *Catechism of the Catholic Church*, 43. 2nd ed. Translated by United States Catholic Conference. Washington, DC: United States Catholic Conference, 1994.

———. *A Treatise on Nature and Grace*. Translated by Peter Holmes et al. Savage, MN: Lighthouse, 2018.

———. *The Trinity [De Trinitate]*. Introduction, translation, and notes by Edmund Hill. 2nd ed. Hyde Park, NY: New City Press, 2022.

Barrett, Lincoln. *The Universe and Dr. Einstein*. New York: Bantam, 1968.

Blackburn, Simon. "Behaviorism." In *The Oxford Dictionary of Philosophy*, 50–51. 3rd ed. Oxford: Oxford University Press, 2016.

Brown, Peter. *Augustine of Hippo: A Biography*. Berkeley: University of California Press, 2000.

Calvin, John. *Institutes of the Christian Religion*. Translated by Henry Beveridge. Grand Rapids, MI: Eerdmans, 2001.

Catechism of the Catholic Church. 2nd ed. Libreria Editrice Vaticana, 1997.

The Church Teaches: Documents of the Church in English Translation. Translated by Jesuits at St. Mary's College. Repr., Charlotte, NC: TAN, 1973.

Cicero. *First Book of On Duty*. In *Selected Works of Cicero*, translated by Isabel K. Raubitschek and Anthony E. Raubitschek, 320–85. Roslyn, NY: Walter J. Black, 1948.

Copleston, Frederick. *A History of Philosophy*. Vol. 3, *Ockam to Suarez*. Mahwah, NJ: Paulist, 1953.

Darwin, Charles. *The Origin of the Species by Means of Natural Selection or the Preservation of Favored Races in the Struggle for Life*. 6th ed. In *Readings in Western Civilization*, edited by George H. Knoles and Rixford K. Snyder, 2:692–97. 3rd ed. New York: J. B. Lippincott, 1960.

De Molina, Luis. *On Divine Foreknowledge*. Part 4 of *Concordia*, translated with an introduction and notes by Alfred J. Freddoso. Ithaca, NY: Cornell University Press, 1988.

Descartes, René. *Discourse on Method and Meditations on First Philosophy*. Translated by Donald A. Cress. 4th ed. Indianapolis: Hackett, 1998.

Dogmatic Canons and Degrees: Authorized Translations of the Dogmatic Decrees of the Council of Trent. Rockford, IL: Tan Books, 1977.

Dostoyevsky, Fyodor. *The Brothers Karamazov*. Translated by Andrew R. MacAndrew. New York: Bantam Dell, 2003.

Hardon, John A. *Modern Catholic Dictionary*. Bardstown, KY: Eternal Life, 2001.

Hegel, G. W. F. *Natural Law and Political Science in Outline; Elements of the Philosophy of Right*. Translated by T. M. Knox as *Hegel's Philosophy of Right*. New York: Oxford University Press, 1976.

———. *Phenomenology of Mind*. Translated by J. B. Baillie. New York: Harper and Row, 1967.

Hulsman John, ed. *The Rule of Our Warfare: John Henry Newman and the True Christian Life*. New York: Scepter, 2003.

Flannery, Austin, ed. *Vatican Council II: The Conciliar and Post-Conciliar Documents*. Vol 1. Rev. ed. Northport, NY: Costello, 1996.

John Paul II. *Evangelium Vitae*. In *The Encyclicals of John Paul II*, edited with introductions by J. Michael Miller, 792–894. Huntington, IN: C.S.B.R.'s Sunday Visitor Publishing Division, 1996.

Jurgens, William A., trans. *The Faith of the Early Fathers*. 2 vols. Collegeville, MN: Liturgical Press, 1970.

Kant, Immanuel. *Critique of Practical Reason*. Translated by Mary Gregor. Rev. ed. New York: Cambridge University Press, 2015.

———. *Critique of Pure Reason*. Translated, edited, and introduction by Marcus Wrigelt. New York: Penguin Classics, 2007.

Lucretius. *On the Nature of the Universe*. Translated by R. E. Latham. Hammondsworth, UK: Penguin, 1986.

Luther, Martin. *The Bondage of the Will*. In *Martin Luther's Basic Theological Writings*, edited by Timothy F. Lull, 173–226. Minneapolis: Fortress, 1989.

———. *The Freedom of the Christian*. Translated by W. A. Lambert, revised by Harold J. Grimm. 2nd rev. ed. Philadelphia: Fortress, 1970.

Matava, R. J. *Divine Causality and Human Free Choice: Domingo Banez, Physical Pre-Motion and the Controversy* De Auxilis. Leiden: Brill, 2016.

New Catholic Encyclopedia. "Grace, Sufficient." In vol. 6:682. New York: McGraw-Hill, 1967.

Otto, Rudolph. *The Idea of the Holy*. Translated by John W. Harvey. London: Oxford University Press, 1923.

Pelagius. *Commentaries on the Thirteen Epistles of Paul with the* Libellus fidei. Introduced and translated by Thomas P. Scheck. Mahwah, NJ: Newman, 2022.

Plato. *The Republic*. In *Great Dialogues of Plato*, translated by W. H. D. Rouse, 125–422. Edited by Eric Warmington and Philip Rouse. New York: New American Library, 1956.

Plotinus. *The Enneads*. Edited by Lloyd P. Gerson. Cambridge: Cambridge University Press, 2018.

Przywara, Erich, ed. *The Heart of Newman: A Synthesis*. San Francisco: Ignatius, 1997.

Sartre, Jean-Paul. *Being and Nothingness: An Essay in Phenomenological Ontology*. Translated by Sarah Richmond. New York: Washington Square Press, 2018.

Scheler, Max. *Formalism in Ethics and Non-Formal Ethics of Values: A New Attempt Toward the Foundation of an Ethical Personalism*. Translated by Manford S. Frings and Roger L. Funk. Evanston, IL: Northwestern University Press, 1973.

Skinner, B. F. *Beyond Freedom and Dignity*. Indianapolis: Hackett, 2002.

Stace, W. T. *The Philosophy of Hegel: A Systematic Exposition*. Toronto: Dover, 1955.

Thomas Aquinas. *Summa Theologica*. Translated by Fathers of the English Dominican Province. 5 vols. Allen, TX: Thomas Moore, 1981.

Wallace, William. *The Elements of Philosophy: A Compendium for Philosophers and Theologians*. Eugene, OR: Wipf & Stock, 2011.

Subject Index

Academicians, 5–6
aporia, 31
alogical acts of consciousness, 86–87

bad faith (self deception), 46–49
behaviorism, 116–20, 122–23
baptism and penance, 175–77, 239–44

'commanding dictate,' 99
'cogito, ergo sum,' 127
concupiscence, 54
conflict between the two wills, 41–42
    need for God's grace to overcome this conflict, 43

Darwinism
    natural selection, 146
    survival of the fittest, 146–47

emanation, 17
evolution, 146
evil, 3-4, 7, 16–17, 106–7, 181–82,
'evil genius,' 126

faith alone justifies, 203
faith and good works (faith working through love), 206
faith is a gift of grace, 207
fideism, 161
For-itself/In-itself, 48–49
free will, 10, 103–4, 112–13, 119–21, 123, 144–45, 149, 151–53, 156–58, 164–66, 182, 185–87
    God's foreknowledge and man's free will, 155–59, 223

free will and grace, 167–68, 182–87, 190, 192–95, 197–200, 208–9, 210–214

God
    as an unmoved mover and final cause, 10–13
    as an incorruptible first cause, 11
    as cause of restlessness in man, 12
    creator, 11–13
    God's heavenly city, 83–84
    God's omnipotence never in conflict with God's essential, immutable essence, 163–64
    'infinite substance,' 102–3
    ontological argument for God's existence, 52–53, 103
    perfectly simple and still a Trinity of three Persons in one God, 21–23
    supreme and perfect good, 10–11
    the need for reason to be supplemented by divine authority, 21-22, 76–80
    grace, 182–87, 192–95
    efficacious power (grace), 217–24
    sufficient grace, 224–30

hypostasis, 15–19

identity-in-difference, 75–77
identity-in difference related to God and creation, 78–79
impressions, 177–79
'internal sense' (common sense), 132–36

law
- eternal law, 103, 109–12
- three revealed laws: law of Hebrews, law of nature (or of Gentiles), law of the Spirit of life, 35
- moral law written on man's heart (natural law), 34, 100, 110
- temporal law understood through practical reason alone but ultimately based on eternal law, 110

logos, 18
lust, 42–43, 112, 114–15

Manichaeism, 2–7, 100
modalists, 9
man
- made in God's image, 32–33
- has rational understanding, good inclinations and a will with which to choose, 35
- has fallen human nature, 37

matter and form, 141–45
moral order, 33–35, 161–62
'mysterium tremendum,' 91–93

natural inclinations, 33, 35–37
naturalism, 144–46, 148
nominalism, 160, 162, 164
number, 137–44
numinous experience, 89–91

'Ockham's Razor,' 126

Pelagianism, 103–4, 190–96
perseverance, 236–42
phenomena/noumena, 66–67
phenomenology, 85
pride, 178–80
providence, 13–14
predestination:
- Calvin's position, 159, 209
- Augustine's later position, 209–11

Plato's view of the transmigration of souls, 173

reprimand, 237–38

Sabellians, 29
sin, 37–40, 191–93

'thinking thing,' 127
Trinity
- divine processions, 28, 31–32
- homoousios (same substance), 22
- Plotinian three hypostases, 15, 17
- Porphyry's concept, 19–20
- Augustine's Catholic understanding, 20–28
- Hegel's concept, 79–82

universal doubt (systematic doubt), 125–26

wisdom, 137–42

www.ingramcontent.com/pod-product-compliance
Lightning Source LLC
Chambersburg PA
CBHW050846230426
43667CB00012B/2164